T0336603

HANDBOOK FOR SUPPLY CHAIN RISK MANAGEMENT

Case Studies, Effective Practices and Emerging Trends

Edited by

Omera Khan, Ph.D.
George A. Zsidisin, Ph.D., C.P.M.

Copyright © 2012 by J. Ross Publishing

ISBN-13: 978-1-60427-038-9

Printed and bound in the U.S.A. Printed on acid-free paper.

10 9 8 7 6 5 4 3 2 1

Library of Congress Cataloging-in-Publication Data

Handbook for supply chain risk management: case studies, effective practices, and emerging trends/edited By Omera Khan, George A. Zsidisin.
    p. cm.
Includes bibliographical references and index.
ISBN 978-1-60427-038-9 (hardcover: alk. paper)
1. Business logistics—Case studies. 2. Risk management—Case studies. 3. Delivery of goods—Management—Case studies. 4. Globalization. I. Khan, Omera, 1976. II. Zsidisin, George A.
    HD38.5.H352 2011
    658.7—dc23
                    2011037064

Phone: (954) 727-9333
Fax: (561) 892-0700
Web: www.jrosspub.com

DEDICATION

To Shaan, Khadija, Hassan, and Hadin

Omera Khan

To my mother Anna Zsidisin, aunt Marie Debiec, and sister Emily Steinhagen, for love and support throughout the years.

To my boys, Nick, Lucas, and Blaise for helping me feel like a kid again.

George A. Zsidisin

TABLE OF CONTENTS

ACKNOWLEDGEMENTS

This is the third book published by the International Supply Chain Risk Management Network (ISCRIM). We would like to thank the members and associates affiliated with the group and their universities that have sponsored ISCRIM annual meetings during the past 10 years. The idea for this book emerged at one of the many stimulating discussions held at an ISCRIM meeting, and the authors would like to acknowledge the valuable time and commitment that members dedicated to this book project.

We would like to acknowledge the contributing authors for their chapters that have made this book possible and thank them for their time and patience in editing and reediting their chapters. The process may have been tedious at times, but it resulted in a collection of distinct and interesting cases.

Additionally, we thank the organizations and numerous individuals who participated in the audits and studies, and made the cases possible. Their insights and generosity of time allowed the authors of the cases to collate and synthesize the data that forms the genesis of the book.

We also thank J. Ross Publishing for their interest and commitment to work with us on this book, in particular publisher Drew Gierman for his continued support and guidance. In addition, we are thankful for the feedback of Professor Bob Ritchie from Lancashire Business School on the draft manuscript, and particularly his guidance and unwavering support towards the end of the project.

Finally, we appreciate the patience of our families and friends for their support and continuous encouragement during the writing of this book.

Omera Khan
George A. Zsidisin

ABOUT THE EDITORS

Dr. Omera Khan is a Senior Lecturer in Logistics and Supply Chain Management at the University of Hull, where she has developed programs on logistics and supply chain management and teaches a number of other postgraduate and undergraduate courses. Omera has gained international recognition for her research and has conducted several research projects on the topics of supply chain risk management, the impact of product design on the supply chain and the risks of global sourcing, which have been commissioned by government agencies, research councils and companies. She is a Visiting Professor at SP Jain Business School in Dubai and Singapore, where she has developed and taught courses on supply chain risk management and resilience, agile supply chains, supply chain frameworks, and performance based logistics. Omera is also a Visiting Professor at the University of Boras in Sweden where she is coordinating research on demand chain management and leading the development of a center on demand chain risk management in textiles. She is a research affiliate at MIT where she is collaborating on international research projects in the area of product design and risk management.

George A. Zsidisin is an Associate Professor in the Department of Management, Bowling Green State University. He has published over 40 articles in academic and practitioner journals, coedited *Supply Chain Risk: A Handbook of Assessment, Management, and Performance* (Springer), and has given numerous presentations to companies, groups, and conferences throughout North America and Europe. Professor Zsidisin is currently the coeditor of the *Journal of Purchasing & Supply Management*, and serves on the editorial boards of several academic journals.

CONTRIBUTORS

Özgür Arslan was born in Istanbul, Turkey. He has earned a BA in Economics at Istanbul University, an MA in Capital Market and Stock Exchange at Marmara University, and an Executive MBA at Sabancı University. After several years of experience in the telecommunications industry, he is currently working in the energy sector. His research experience lies in the areas of project management, project procurement management, supply chain management, and supply chain risk management. He is a member of the Project Management Institute and Istanbul Project Management Association.

Bjorn E. Asbjornslett is Professor in Marine Systems Design at the Norwegian University of Science and Technology, NTNU, where his research and teaching is focused on maritime transport system design, with a special focus on risk-based approaches to HSE, security, vulnerability, and sustainability of maritime logistics. Dr. Asbjornslett has professional experience working as a cost engineer in the Norwegian oil and gas industry, as supply chain manager in the FMCG industry, researcher in the European Institute of Advanced Project and Contract Management, and as senior researcher in MARINTEK, the Norwegian Marine Technology Research Institute

Constantin Blome is Assistant Professor for Sourcing in Emerging Markets. He holds a PhD from Technical University Berlin/Germany sponsored by the German National Merit Foundation. Before joining EBS, he had his own consultancy, worked as senior consultant for the Supply Management Group, Switzerland, and has been research fellow at the Indian Institute of Management in Bangalore, India. Furthermore, he is teaching at several universities in Europe and training executives. His research has been published in the *Journal of Supply Chain Management* and *Journal of Purchasing & Supply Management*. The focus of his research is risk management, performance measurement, and sustainability in procurement and supply chains.

Simon A. Burtonshaw-Gunn is a business school academic, management author, and practicing business consultant with significant experience in both the public and private sectors covering a range of organizations and industries. He covered in excess of 400,000 miles undertaking assignments in Asia, North Africa, the Middle East, the Far East, and Eastern Europe. To support this experience, he holds two Masters degrees and a PhD in strategic management topics, with Fellowships at four professional bodies, including the Chartered Management Institute where he has been a Goodwill Ambassador since 2009.

Natalie M. Dengler is Adjunct Professor in the Hagan School of Business of Iona College and a consultant in business continuity. She served as Vice President at JPMorgan Chase where she managed the Infrastructure and Technology business continuity coordinator team for security and risk management. She had oversight responsibility for the business resiliency program and has coordinated response globally for actual disasters. She received her MBA in Operations Research and Qualitative Analysis from St. Johns University and holds certificates in Construction Management from New York University and International Management from Fairleigh Dickinson University. She is a Fellow in the Business Continuity Institute (FBCI).

Paul Dittmann is Director of Corporate Partnerships at the University of Tennessee. Prior to joining the university, he held Fortune 150 positions, such as Vice President, Logistics for North America, Vice President Global Logistics Systems, and most recently served as Vice President of Supply Chain Strategy, Projects, and Systems for the Whirlpool Corporation. At the university, Dr. Dittmann manages special projects for companies, including supply chain audits. In addition, he has consulted for more than 50 corporations. He recently coauthored a book, *The New Supply Chain Agenda*. He is also a member of the University of Missouri Industrial Engineering Hall of Fame.

Reham A. Eltantawy is Assistant Professor in the Department of Marketing and Logistics at the University of North Florida, Coggin College of Business. She holds a PhD from Florida State University. Dr. Eltantawy has been published in prominent supply chain management journals, including *Industrial Marketing Management, International Journal of Production and Operations Management, International Journal of Physical Distribution & Logistics Management, Journal of Business and Industrial Marketing, Journal of Business Logistics,* and *Journal of Supply Chain Management.* She was the winner of the Outstanding Paper Award at the Emerald Literati Network Awards for Excellence (2009) and the Academy of Marketing Association Interorganizational Track Best Paper Award (2007).

Kurt J. Engemann is the Director of the Center for Business Continuity and Risk Management, and a Professor of Information Systems in the Hagan School of Business at Iona College. He has consulted professionally in the area of risk modeling for major organizations and has been instrumental in the development of comprehensive business continuity management programs. He is Editor-in-Chief of the *International Journal of Business Continuity and Risk Management* and the *International Journal of Technology, Policy and Management.* He has a PhD in Operations Research from New York University and is a Certified Business Continuity Professional.

Barbara Gaudenzi has been an Assistant Professor in Logistics and Risk Management at the University of Verona (Italy) since January 2005. Dr. Gaudenzi earned a PhD in *Dottrine economico-aziendali e governo dell'impresa* at the University Parthenope, Naples (Italy). She is coordinator of the postgraduate course in Risk Management at the Faculty of Economics, University of Verona. She is a member of international networks and organizations, such as The International Supply Chain Risk Management (ISCRIM), the Academic Working Group of the United Nations Environment Programme Finance Initiative, and Council of Supply Chain Management Professionals.

Larry C. Giunipero is Professor of Supply Chain Management at Florida State University. Dr. Giunipero's primary research, teaching, and consulting interests are in the area of supply management. He holds a PhD from Michigan State University. He has published over 60 articles in various academic journals such as *Decision Sciences, Sloan Management Review, Industrial Marketing Management, Journal of Supply Chain Management, The International Journal of Logistics Management,* and *The International Journal of Physical Distribution and Logistics Management.* He has performed consulting and training projects for over 30 corporations; his primary research interests are in supply management.

Volker M. Groetsch is a PhD student at the EBS Business School in Wiesbaden. His research interests are in risk management, governance, and accounting problems in the field of supply chain management. Until 2006, he studied international business administration at the EBS Business School, the Universidad Adolfo Ibáñez (Chile), and the Koç Graduate School of Business (Turkey). Before enrolling in graduate studies, Groetsch attended post-graduate language and business training in Beijing, funded by the German Academic Exchange Service. He also trains executives as an assistant instructor.

Çağrı Haksöz is Assistant Professor of Operations Management at Sabancı University, İstanbul, Turkey. His research focuses on risk management in global supply chains, design and management of options in supply chain contracts, and empirical studies in supply chain management. Before joining Sabancı University, Haksöz taught at New York University, Stern School of Business, Cass Business School, City University of London, and New York University—London. He actively teaches and advises executives worldwide. He holds a PhD and MPhil in Operations Management from New York University, Stern School of Business, and BSc in Industrial Engineering from Bilkent University, Turkey.

Omar Keith Helferich is a Marketing and Supply Chain/Logistics faculty member at Central Michigan University. He has published numerous articles on security, sustainability, logistics, and supply chain management, coauthored two logistics textbooks, and conducted over 175 industry and academic presentations covering the topics of logistics and supply chain management, security, and sustainability. Dr. Helferich coauthored a Council of Supply Chain Management Professionals white paper, investigating supply chain security and disaster management, and a chapter on supply chain security in *The Handbook of Global Supply Chain Management* (Sage) and *Managing Risk and Security* (Haupt).

Michael Henke received a PhD in Business Administration from the Technical University of Munich, Germany. Prior to joining EBS as a Senior Professor, Dr. Henke worked as Senior Consultant with the Supply Management Group in St. Gallen, Switzerland. In his current role, Michael Henke is responsible for teaching and research in the areas of financial and management accounting, supply management, supply risk management, supply performance management, supply controlling, and other areas. Additionally, he is leading and developing research projects in the field of financial supply chain management in cooperation with well-known international enterprises. His research findings can be found in numerous journal articles and books. At the Supply Chain Management Institute, he is overall responsible for activities within purchasing and supply management.

Olivier Lavastre is Associate Professor in Management Science at Grenoble University. He teaches industrial management, operations management, and information systems in supply chain management. He is a researcher at the Centre for Studies and Applied Research in Management. His work focuses on buyer-seller relationship management, supply chain risk management, and interorganizational innovative practices in supply chain management.

Wojciech Machowiak, a Doctor of Technical Sciences, is Senior Lecturer and researcher in the Poznan School of Logistics, Poland, where he teaches at the undergraduate, graduate, and postgraduate levels. Dr. Machowiak worked for more than twenty years as a manager in various businesses, including as chief organizer and executive director of the first express delivery system in Poland. Author of numerous book chapters and articles on enterprise risk management and supply chain risk management, his main fields of interest are interrelations between risk management and critical situations, and capabilities of supply chain risk management as an instrument of strategic management. He is a member of ISCRIM and the Polish Risk Management Association.

Ila Manuj is Assistant Professor of Logistics at the Department of Marketing and Logistics, University of North Texas. Her research interests are in the areas of risk and complexity management in global supply chains. She has published papers in *Journal of Business Logistics* and *International Journal of Physical Distribution and Logistics Management*. Dr. Manuj has coauthored several book chapters and presented at national and international conferences. She worked with CARE (India), a not-for-profit social development organization, before pursuing her doctorate degree.

Holmes E. Miller is Professor of Business at Muhlenberg College. He has a PhD in Management Science from Northwestern University. Dr. Miller was instrumental in establishing the risk and disaster management program globally for Chase Manhattan Bank. He developed and conducts the seminar in Disaster Management at Muhlenberg College and teaches courses in the areas of operations management, management science, electronic commerce, and information systems. His research interests include risk management, disaster planning, and decision analysis. Prior to coming to Muhlenberg, he taught at Rensselaer Polytechnic Institute and consulted for Fortune 500 companies.

Odd Torstein Morkve is Principal Consultant at Det Norske Veritas (DNV). Mr. Morkve holds an MSc in Naval Architecture and an MSc in Logistics and SCM from

Cranfield University, UK. Mr. Morkve's main responsibility in DNV is to develop tools and services for evaluation and optimization of maritime logistics systems with regard to costs, greenhouse gas emissions, and energy consumption. He has wide-ranging experience in running advanced R&D and commercial projects in these areas. Prior to joining DNV, Mr. Morkve was research manager in charge of the value chain optimization group at MARINTEK, Department of Logistics and Strategy.

Arben Mullai is a Master Mariner, M.Sc. in Shipping Management and PhD in Engineering Logistics, Lund University, Sweden. He has twelve years of seagoing and shipping management experience. He has studied and worked at the Department of Engineering Logistics, including the position of Lecturer as well as logistics consultant. Mr. Mullai has participated in five EU projects concerning safe and reliable transport chains, maritime risks, sourcing, and procurement. His main research areas are logistics, supply chain management, transport, sourcing, environment, risk modeling, analysis, and management. He has produced 27 scientific articles, conference papers, book chapters, research project reports, and working papers.

Josef Oehmen is Research Scientist in the Department of Mechanical Engineering at the Massachusetts Institute of Technology (MIT). His main research interest is application-oriented risk management in the value chain. Previously, he was the Director for Supply Chain Management at the ETH Center for Enterprise Sciences at ETH Zurich, where he also wrote a PhD thesis on supply chain risk management. Dr. Oehmen received a Master's Degree in Mechanical Engineering from the Technical University of Munich, and an MBA from the Collége des Ingènieurs in Paris. He is a member of the supervisory board of Climate InterChange, a company developing and implementing projects for the reduction of carbon emissions.

Ulf Paulsson is Associate Professor in the School of Economics and Management, Lund University, Sweden. He holds a Licentiate in Business Administration with a thesis on product development in forwarding agents, and a PhD in Engineering with a thesis on management of disruption risks in supply chains. He is one of the initial members of the ISCRIM network and editor of its newsletter since inception in 2002.

Malik G. Salameh undertakes a wide range of international strategic consultancy assignments for a FTSE 100 defence prime contracting organization. He read *Aeronautical Engineering* for his first degree, before completing an MSc in Business and Operations Management, followed by a PhD in Management. He is an active member of a number of professional bodies, including the Royal Aeronautical Society, Chartered Institute of Marketing, Chartered Management Institute, and Chartered Institute of Personnel and Development. He has been selected as postdoctoral examiner for Warwick University Business School.

Michael E. Smith is Associate Professor of Global Management and Strategy at Western Carolina University, where he teaches strategy and supply chain management at the graduate and undergraduate levels. Dr. Smith spent more than 15 years in executive management prior to completing his PhD. His research has been published and presented in numerous national and international venues. In addition to membership in the Institute for Supply Management and service as Chair of the Institute's Indirect/ MRO Sourcing Group, Dr. Smith is a member of the International Supply Chain Risk Management Network.

Christopher Tang is Edward Carter Professor of Business Administration at the UCLA Anderson School. Dr. Tang has extensive teaching, research, and consulting experience in the areas of supply chain management and retailing. In addition to winning various teaching awards, he has published four books and more than 80 research articles in a number of leading international academic journals. Moreover, he has taught in various executive programs, served on 15 editorial boards, and advised clients throughout the United States, European Union, and Asia. Dr. Tang received his BSc (First class honors) from King's College, University of London, and MA (M.Phil.) and PhD from Yale University.

Cliff Thomas, MBCP, CISA is a Partner at Atlas Preparedness Group, located in Fort Collins, CO. Cliff has more than 20 years of preparedness experience, including positions in industry, government, military service, and academia. Cliff has managed large corporate preparedness programs and consulted for numerous organizations, providing services in the areas of business continuity and crisis management. He has led entrepreneurial endeavours, including the development of preparedness-related online training, software, videos, and GIS risk analysis tools.

Jerry D. VanVactor, DHA, FAHRMM is an active duty medical service corps officer in the United States Army, where he is a health care logistics manager. He has been in the U.S. military since 1989 and involved in a variety of supply chain management roles since 1994. Dr. VanVactor's education includes Doctor of Health Administration, Masters in Healthcare Management, and BS in Health Science with an undergraduate minor in Procurement and Acquisitions Management. He is a Certified Materials and Resource Professional and Fellow of the Association for Healthcare Resource and Materials Management.

M. Douglas "Doug" Voss is Assistant Professor of Marketing and Supply Chain Management at The University of Central Arkansas, and Director of the University of Central Arkansas Center for Cooperative Logistics Education, Advancement, and Research (CLEAR). Dr. Voss received a PhD in logistics and marketing from Michigan State University, and M.S. and B.S. in Transportation and Logistics Management from the University of Arkansas. Before beginning his position at The University of Central Arkansas, Doug was a postdoctoral research associate at Michigan State University, and worked in the truckload motor carrier industry.

ABOUT THE INTERNATIONAL SUPPLY CHAIN RISK MANAGEMENT NETWORK

The International Supply Chain Risk Management (ISCRIM) network is a team of researchers and practitioners engaged in analyzing, developing, and disseminating evidence and practices related to the effective and efficient management of supply chains and their associated risks. The international network was founded in 2001 by a small group of active researchers from the UK, U.S., and Sweden. The original purpose of the ISCRIM network was to speed up and improve the quality of research, enhance the pace of dissemination, and widen the scope and volume of activity relating to supply chain risk management. The principle means of achieving these goals has been through sharing and leveraging joint knowledge, experience, skills, and resources within the network.

Today, the primary objectives of ISCRIM are to facilitate the rapid advancement of knowledge and understanding of supply chain risk management. The objectives are put into practice through proactive engagement and collaboration among key practitioners and researchers in this evolving field, providing a core of expertise, information, and knowledge that can be accessed by interested practitioners, researchers, and policy makers engaged in supply chain management. Of importance are the risks associated with increasingly complex, global supply chain configurations and the greater risk exposure.

The ISCRIM team has grown and developed since its inception, and represents a large core of experienced international practitioners, researchers, writers, and publishers within this discipline and related areas. ISCRIM members are from 20 countries with diverse representation from leading world-class institutions. The international recognition of this group and its members has been reflected by journal editors and research publishers, which resulted in the production of three major international handbooks over the last six years, and recently the translation of one of the handbooks into Chinese.

FUTURE DEVELOPMENTS

Forecasting future developments in the supply chain risk management field is a risky business, given the rapid evolution of the field, partnering activities with associated fields, and the preparedness of researchers to exchange information and collaborate with each other. Suggestions for future development drawn from the authors, the cases, and the wider ISCRIM membership have been distilled into the following opportunities and challenges:

1. Developing new frameworks to capture the increasing complexity, dynamism and the continuous evolution of the multidisciplinary perspectives of todays supply chains.
2. Applying supply chain risk management practices in small- and medium-sized enterprises.
3. Conducting comparative studies within and across sectors and geographic contexts to isolate and evaluate common risk drivers and contingency factors.
4. Deriving performance metrics and measurement tools for assessing the impact of risk and the effectiveness of SCRM practices. These metrics should incorporate both financial and nonfinancial effects.
5. Understanding the parameters necessary for creating more robust supply chain relationships (e.g. confidence in partners, trust).
6. Recognizing the importance of developing the skills of individuals to competently manage supply chain risks through undergraduate, postgraduate and professional development programs.
7. Continuing the expansion of research studies in the field and sub-fields of supply chain risk management.
8. Creating and applying acceptable standards of performance, both within the public and private sectors, in the area of supply chain security.
9. Developing robust analytical tools and frameworks to support decision makers that face increasing patterns of novel risk situations.

ISCRIM, in collaboration with Zurich Global Insurance, has established a website (www.iscrim.org) for providing research. A list of ISCRIM members and their institutions is available on the website.

Web
Added
Value™

Free value-added materials available from
the Download Resource Center at www.jrosspub.com

At J. Ross Publishing we are committed to providing today's professional with practical, hands-on tools that enhance the learning experience and give readers an opportunity to apply what they have learned. That is why we offer free ancillary materials available for download on this book and all participating Web Added Value™ publications. These online resources may include interactive versions of material that appears in the book or supplemental templates, worksheets, models, plans, case studies, proposals, spreadsheets and assessment tools, among other things. Whenever you see the WAV™ symbol in any of our publications, it means bonus materials accompany the book and are available from the Web Added Value Download Resource Center at www.jrosspub.com.

Downloads for *Handbook for Supply Chain Risk Management: Case Studies, Effective Practices and Emerging Trends* consist of instructional materials for professors teaching supply chain risk management.

INTRODUCTION

The study of risk and the practice of risk management are not new. *Risk* is an ever-present aspect of personal and organizational life, reflected in the future outcomes associated with investment decisions, human resources, new products and services, and the management of supply chains. Although originating fairly recently, supply chain risk management has become a recognized and well-established field, resulting in the development and dissemination of new models, tools, and techniques to understand and manage supply chain risk.

The purpose of this handbook is to capture and provide business professionals, researchers, and students with a collection of cases that illustrate how organizations can assess and manage threats to business continuity, while providing insights into practices that can create robust and resilient firms. Like all developing fields of study, supply chain risk management draws on a range of disciplines and fields. The contributing authors approach this subject from different perspectives, thus enriching the collection of cases. The cases have been selected to appeal to professionals in a range of sectors, from healthcare to aerospace, while retaining a core focus on supply chain risk management.

To provide a background to risk and supply chain risk management, the editors deliberately avoided prescriptive definitions of concepts, preferring instead to encourage contributors to explore the concepts, models, and theories appropriate to their specific sectors, case study contexts, and disciplinary perspectives. This approach is intended to contribute knowledge and understanding into the extensive practice-oriented fields. The remainder of this introduction explains the structure of this handbook, including the rationale for structuring the collection of case studies in two key parts.

SUPPLY CHAIN RISK MANAGEMENT

Before entering into a discussion on supply chain risk, it is important to provide the reader with some background on the term *risk*. The word risk is derived from the early Italian word *risicare*, which means *to dare* (Bernstein, 1996). However, the term's meaning has evolved over time, and today it means different things to different people, depending on their individual perceptions of the world. A key component of risk is *choice*. Bernstein (1996) maintains that risk is about choice: "...the actions we dare to take, which depend on how free we are to make choices, are what the story of risk is all about."

Risk encompasses both the possibility of loss and the hope of gain. Nevertheless, in looking at how organizations perceive risk, it is the negative connotation of risk—loss rather than gain—that seems to preoccupy managers. This is especially the case with large engineering projects, such as petro-chemical plants and nuclear power stations, where the consequences of failure can be catastrophic, effectively illustrated by cases in Part I. Not surprisingly, the emphasis on negative consequences is the area where most development work has been carried out on formal risk assessment procedures, as demonstrated by cases in Part II.

In the United Kingdom, the Royal Society (1992) established a working party to investigate risk and risk assessment. It stressed the negative elements of risk, defining *risk* as "... a combination of the probability, or frequency, of occurrence of a defined hazard and the magnitude of the consequences of the occurrence." In research, too, risk has continued to be discussed as the *severity of adverse effects* and the *potential for unwanted negative consequences*, which may have an "effect on the achievement of the project's objectives."

It is important to note that risk is context-dependent. Therefore, risk can be defined as a subjective expectation of loss; hence, the greater the probability of loss, the greater the risk for the individual or organization. Furthermore, depending on context, there may be significant gains expected from taking a risk; therefore, risk cannot only be defined as a negative or unwanted expectation.

This raises an important question that many researchers appear either not to be aware of or prefer to avoid: is risk something that can be objectively measured and agreed upon by all concerned or is it something which is subjective and based on individual perception? The issue of whether risk can be measured objectively or whether it is based on a subjective viewpoint will have a significant impact on how the various parties in a supply chain relationship perceive and attempt to manage risk.

The viewpoints on risk range from the scientific perspective, which sees risk as objective and measurable, to the social constructionist perspective, which sees it as being determined by social, political, and historical situations. Taking the latter perspective, it has been argued that the nature of any potential loss, its significance and the estimated chance of it occurring, are personal to the individuals concerned, for example, the result of risk-taking can be perceived as positive by some, but negative by others, giving risk a subjective dimension. But there are many engineers and physical scientists who tend to see risk as objective, quantifiable, and manageable.

Over the years, a number of well-used tools for quantifying and managing risk have been developed. These include: failure mode effect analysis (FMEA), cost benefit analysis (CBA), and risk benefit analysis (RBA). Although accepted by many managers, they have been criticized for removing the element of human judgment from decision-making by disguising underlying assumptions with mathematical formulae.

The debate between those who see risk as objective and those who see it as subjective is an ongoing one, which will not be resolved in this book, if indeed it is resolvable at all. It is necessary, though, to recognize that such a debate is taking place, and that it does have significant implications for how risk is seen and managed. It is also necessary to recognize that most people who are studying supply chain risk management do not appear to recognize that there is a debate over its nature. While most contributors use terms such as *perception* and *perceived* (Cousins, et al., 2004; Kraljic, 1983; Williamson, 1979), indicating a subjective rather than objective perspective, others use *probability* (Harland et al, 2003), indicating a more objective perspective. Nevertheless, the issue of whether risk is a subjective or objective construct does not appear to be acknowledged in the supply chain literature. Whether one views risk from a subjective or objective standpoint, the key question for organizations is: How can risk be managed?

There seems to be general agreement on what the risk management *process* should be, and it typically combines the following three stages:

- Risk Identification—determine all risk factors that are likely to occur on a project.
- Risk Analysis—understand the likelihood and extent of the most significant risks.
- Risk Evaluation—decide on the most appropriate management response for each risk/combination of risks and which party is most appropriate to manage each of the risks identified.

Most professional bodies that deal with risk take the view that:

Risk management should be a continuous and developing process which runs throughout the organization's strategy and the implementation of that strategy. It should address methodically all the risks surrounding the organization's activities past, present and in particular, future. It must be integrated into the culture of the organization with an effective policy and a program led by the most senior management. It must translate the strategy into tactical and operational objectives, assigning responsibility throughout the organization with each manager and employee responsible for the management of risk as part of their job description. It supports accountability, performance measurement and reward, thus promoting operational efficiency at all levels. (IRM/AIRMIC/ALARM, 2002, 2).

Therefore, though risk assessment is important, and although there is general agreement about the risk management process, there is much debate and disagreement as to the validity and usefulness of the tools and techniques that have been developed to operationalize the process. In practice, it has been reported that top business leaders tend to prefer approaches to risk management that combine subjective and objective measures because it allows them some freedom to maneuver rather than being pushed into making decisions based solely on numerical analysis.

Another reason why top managers may wish to keep their options open is that risk can impact the various stakeholders in a business differently. For example, the personal risk to an individual foreign exchange trader speculating on currency fluctuations may be small, but the risk for the person or body whose money is being used for the speculation may be large. Therefore, managers may need to balance the interests of different stakeholders rather than seeking to minimize risk altogether. In any case, given that there is no consensus as to the most appropriate strategies for managing risk, even if it were possible to calculate the nature and likelihood of a particular risk, it is unlikely to be clear how best to respond to it.

It is not surprising to see writers shifting the focus of attention away from analyzing and managing risk at the level of individual customers and suppliers, and toward the understanding and management of risk at the level of the entire supply chain. It can be argued that supply chain risk management, as opposed to supply chain management, is appropriate terminology to define the long chain of decisions that result in the production of goods and services, as these are accompanied by an equally long chain of risk. The increasing globalization, complexity and dynamism of supply chains are leading to greater exposure to risk from political and economic events; hence, disruption to supplies in one country can quickly spread through an entire global supply chain. An example is the sharp increase in world oil prices caused by the disruption of U.S. oil production brought about by Hurricane Katrina. The contributors have provided cases that illustrate global supply chain risks and disruptions to supply caused by natural disasters in Part I. Hence, risk management should focus on positioning the organization to try and avoid such events, and to develop strategies to manage the impact of them should avoidance not be possible. This is where the design of appropriate tools and techniques becomes an important issue, and we have outstanding case examples of these in Part II.

There is no doubt that managing supply chain risk has become a vital activity for most organizations, particularly as supply chain risk is unlikely to lessen in the near future, given the increasing trend toward globalization. Globalization has exacerbated supply chain risk, and the need for suitable tools, approaches, and methods to manage risk has never been greater.

STRUCTURE OF THE BOOK

This book comprises a collection of cases, each designed to illustrate dimensions of effective practices that firms engage in to manage supply chain risk. The cases have a practical orientation, designed to illustrate how practicing managers and students can create processes, systems, and approaches to reduce the likelihood and financial impact of risk in their firms and supply chains.

Reflections on risk management suggest that supply chain risk management is a very diverse and complex field of study, incorporating a variety of perspectives and arguments concerning appropriate responses to anticipated and realized risks. There are two distinctive groups of factors highlighted within this text. First, the identification, mapping, and managing of risks in global supply chains, and second, the design and application of appropriate tools and techniques to evaluate and mitigate such risks. As such, this handbook is divided into two parts:

- Part I: Managing Risk in Global Supply Chains
- Part II: Tools, Techniques, and Approaches

There are several emerging themes within each part, illustrated by the collection of case examples provided. Although cases have been allocated to the most appropriate part, it is inevitable that some cases apply across themes in both parts. For example, a case may present the context and structure of a global supply chain and develop the elements of the framework by providing a specific approach for managing the global supply chain risks. Each Part commences with a brief introduction and explanation of the themes, followed by short summaries of each case explaining the relevance and contribution to the themes of the Part. Each case is then presented.

OBJECTIVE OF THE BOOK AND TARGET AUDIENCE

As alluded to previously, supply chain risk has become of primary concern to many businesses today. Firms have become more dependent on their suppliers and customers for financial success. However, processes and performance are often difficult to assess outside the boundaries of the respective firm, potentially leaving the firm vulnerable to the unknown. This handbook provides business professionals and students insight into practices that can result in creating more robust and resilient firms in the face of supply chain risk. The aim of this book is to provide illustrative case examples of how firms can proactively manage risk in order to improve overall business performance.

There are currently several books that exist which focus on various aspects of supply chain risk. However, to our knowledge, there is no comprehensive collection of diverse practices that managers can adopt to manage supply chain risk other than this one. The intended audiences are professionals, experts, academics, and researchers who are working, or intend to work, in the fields of supply chain risk management, business continuity management, strategic management, or business management. Additionally, select BA and MBA programs that have a focus or concentration in supply chain management are other intended audiences. This handbook may be used in the classroom to inform students about how supply chain risk manifests itself in firms, as well as to provide a set of tools that they can adopt or potentially suggest to future employers.

REFERENCES

Bernstein, P. (1996). *Against the Gods: The Remarkable Story of Risk*. Chichester: John Wiley.

Cousins, P., Lamming, R. C., and Bowen, F. (2004). The Role of Risk in Environment-Related Initiatives. *International Journal of Operations and Production Management, 24*(6), 554–565.

Harland, C., Brenchley, R., and Walker, H. (2003). Risk in Supply Networks. *Journal of Purchasing and Supply Management*, 9 (2), 51–62.

Kraljic, P. (1983). Purchasing Must Become Supply Management. *Harvard Business Review, 61*(5), 109–117.

Royal Society. (1992). *Risk: Analysis, Perception and Management*. London: Royal Society.

Williamson, O. E. (1979). *Transaction Cost Economics: The Governance of Contractual Relations*. New York: The Free Press.

Part I

Managing Risk in Global Supply Chains

INTRODUCTION TO MANAGING RISK IN GLOBAL SUPPLY CHAINS

There is considerable evidence that the failure to manage supply chain risk effectively can have a significant negative impact on organizations. The consequences of supply chain risk include not just financial losses but also interruption to operations, reduction in product quality, damage to property and equipment, loss of goodwill with customers and suppliers, damaged reputation with the wider public, and delivery delays. There is also evidence that economic, political, and social developments over the past decade appear to increase the chances that disruptions will occur as supply chains become more complex.

Even in established supply chains, issues such as terrorism, disease outbreaks, and natural disasters all have the power to disrupt supply chains. In addition, we live in an era of rapid change in technologies, swift advances in product markets, customer expectations for better products, lower prices, and quicker response times. Add these all together and it can be seen why the potential risks facing supply chains have grown exponentially.

Chapters 2 and 3 serve as introductions to the theme of global sourcing and risk management. Chapter 2 by Ila Manuj and Paul Dittmann investigates the current state of risk management in global sourcing and the barriers to incorporating risk considerations in global sourcing decisions. Chapter 3 by Josef Oehmen presents the case of three Swiss small- and medium-sized enterprises and the risks they face in their global sourcing decisions from China. Collaboration and coordination are key challenges in managing global supply chains, but there is little guidance for managers on how to orchestrate cooperation along the supply chain to reduce risk in transportation networks.

Case studies serve to explain how collaboration and cooperation are important. Chapter 4, by Michael Smith, details how the Chamber of Commerce in Asheville, NC has worked with major manufacturers in the region to create a transportation alliance. The case specifically shows how cooperation among firms can serve to address supply chain risk that is beyond the control of a single firm, and how coordinated action can be obtained.

The collaboration theme is also the topic for discussion in Chapter 5 by Simon Burtonshaw-Gunn and Malik Salameh. The chapter identifies and reviews the potential risks and opportunities that the international company Blue Sky Aviation encountered in trying to enter the Chinese aviation supply chain market. The case describes a series of high level strategic options considered by Blue Sky Aviation in establishing a strong presence in the Chinese aviation market through strategic collaboration.

Another innovation, performance-based logistics (PBL), is a relatively new concept in healthcare supply chain management. In Chapter 6, Jerry VanVactor reveals that PBL is a good method for risk management in contingency supply chains, and describes how refined supply chain processes can enhance and better enable healthcare operations throughout southern Afghanistan. The author examines modes of transportation, evolving requirements, challenges associated with wartime healthcare operations, and efforts related to localized risk mitigation, which can be applicable to a wide array of healthcare operations that are subject to various forms of emergency management and contingency-based operations.

In Chapter 7, by Bjørn Egil Asbjørnslett and Odd Torstein Mørkve, a case of risk acceptance for greenhouse gas emissions and energy consumption in maritime supply chain systems is presented. This is an emerging and vital area of supply chain risk due to the potential impact and exposure to risks of natural disasters. Continuing with the theme of maritime risks in Chapter 8, Arben Mullai and Ulf Paulsson present a qualitative analysis of a major oil spill in the Baltic Sea. This case describes the second largest oil spill reported in the Baltic Sea region and investigates it to enhance the understanding of maritime risks. The chapter proposes several measures for improving risk management in the maritime industry, which could be useful to supply chain professionals operating in this field and to academia. The chapter may also serve as a platform for considering a detailed quantitative study of the risks in the Baltic Sea region.

Chapters 9 and 10 present cases from the oil, gas, and energy sectors. Chapter 9, by Wojciech Machowiak, describes the political risks in contemporary supply chains using the case of a natural gas crisis. The case reveals that it is impossible to completely avoid or eliminate political risk in supply chains, particularly when external forces interfere with businesses and use it as a weapon to accomplish political aims. The case provides insights into how risks can be minimized through diversification, scenario planning, and knowledge of government legislations.

Chapter 10, the final chapter in Part I, by Çağrı Haksöz and Özgür Arslan, describes the procurement risk management practice of the Enerjisa Group, one of the leading Turkish energy organizations. An in-depth survey of procurement specialists of Enerjisa reveals interesting insights into the risk perceptions and hedging strategies utilized by the procurement teams at Enerjisa.

CURRENT STATE OF RISK MANAGEMENT IN GLOBAL SOURCING

Ila Manuj and J. Paul Dittmann

INTRODUCTION

There is a general trend of increased global sourcing. As sourcing becomes more and more global to attain benefits such as low cost labor, cheaper raw materials, and access to technology, it also faces a higher number and degree of challenges. These challenges include issues related to currency fluctuations, political changes, economic changes, long and variable lead times, increases in inventory, quality considerations, inventory ownership, and availability of legal recourse, to name a few. Trade journals, magazines, and academic journals are replete with anecdotes and examples of well-managed as well as inadequately-managed global sourcing, and interesting cases of how companies suffer from setbacks and improve their global sourcing. A well-known example is the much publicized and researched case of Ericsson's supply risk management program that was set up after a second tier supplier plant caught fire and caused major production delays.

However, from the perspective of a typical supply chain executive, not much is known about the *general* level of sophistication in global sourcing, particularly when it comes to including risk considerations in the decision-making process. Such knowledge may be useful for companies to benchmark the effectiveness of their global sourcing process. Not all companies need to strive to improve global sourcing on all fronts. Knowing what is important to others facing a similar environment and how they cope with it may be valuable in deriving an agenda for improving the process. To this end, this chapter explores global sourcing from a risk management perspective. The first objective of this chapter is to answer the question: What is the current state of risk management sophistication in global sourcing decisions?

To answer this question, a database of supply chain audits from numerous companies was consulted. Insights from these in-depth audits revealed a surprising lack of sophistication when it came to incorporating risks in global sourcing decisions. Including risks is critical because they play a significant role in meeting both efficiency and effectiveness targets of global sourcing decisions. Ignoring risks may compromise business continuity and impact stock performance. Most supply management professionals understand these critical risk factors.

However, as the consulted database revealed, professionals do not always incorporate risks in their decisions. Why is this so? An understanding of factors that hinder incorporation of risk considerations in global sourcing decisions can help practitioners explicitly account for such barriers. The second objective of this chapter is to answer the question: What are the barriers to incorporating risk considerations in global sourcing decisions?

The supply chain audits mentioned earlier were conducted by senior doctoral students and professors. Through this nexus of practical and academic knowledge, several suggestions were provided to the participant companies that may be useful for practitioners in making risk management decisions that are more holistic in nature. Therefore, the third and final objective of this chapter is to develop a framework for incorporating risk considerations in global sourcing decisions focused primarily on overcoming the barriers that hinder incorporation of risk considerations in global sourcing decisions.

To accomplish these three objectives, the chapter is organized as follows. First, a brief description of the database and methodology on which the chapter is based is provided. Next, a discussion of the current state of global sourcing with respect to risks is provided, that also elaborates on risks and factors that act as barriers to the incorporation of risk considerations. Next, a framework for explicitly incorporating risk considerations in global sourcing decisions is provided. The chapter concludes with a summary of key points.

CURRENT STATE OF RISK MANAGEMENT IN GLOBAL SOURCING DECISIONS

A database comprised of the supply-chain audits of 10 companies was consulted. The 10 audits consisted of over 250 interviews that generated extensive and rich data on supply chain practice. The companies audited include leading companies (seven out of the 10 companies are Fortune 500 companies) operating in retail, cosmetics, aircraft manufacturing, and other industries. Table 2.1 provides a brief profile of the companies and the number of interviews conducted at each company. These

Table 2.1 Profile of participating companies

Company pseudonym	Description	Number of interviews
AeroCo	Over $40B annual revenue. Provider of aerospace services including electronic systems, aerospace information systems, information technology services, and aeronautics products.	28
PartsCo	Over $2B annual revenue. Primarily North American provider of automotive parts, selling products to independent dealers, wholesale distributors, regional and national retail chains, and large retail chains with operation in over 5 countries outside of North America.	38
PowersCo	Over $10B annual revenue. Global leader that designs, distributes, and services diesel and natural gas engines, and electric power generation systems with operations in more than 30 countries.	65
BeautyCo	Over $1B annual revenue. Global manufacturer and seller of beauty and skin care products that sells and distributes its products through various distribution channels in more than 100 countries worldwide.	38
VisionCo	Over $40B annual revenue. Multinational company specializing in healthcare, medical devices, diagnostics, and consumer healthcare products; has presence in over 50 countries.	48
LifeCo	Privately held company involved in design and manufacturing of lifestyle products and sells products through mass merchant outlets, online retailers, farm and home stores, and catalog and mail order catalogs with presence in more than 15 countries worldwide.	42
CarsCo	Over $80B annual revenue. Global manufacturer and seller of automotive vehicles, parts, and services and related components.	26
FarmCo	Privately held company specializing in machinery equipment manufacturing primarily servicing municipal, power, industrial, chemical, commercial, and agriculture markets with a presence in over 50 countries worldwide.	32
ElectroCo	Over $10B annual revenue. Global firm providing engineered electronic components for consumer and industrial products, network solutions and telecommunication systems with presence in over 50 countries worldwide.	36
LunchCo	Over $5B annual revenue. Retailer specializing in food products, consumer goods, health and beauty, and merchandise items.	50

companies were selected because of their broad global footprint and excellent financial history. Moreover, they were expected to be at the cutting edge of strategic supply chain management and therefore, promising in terms of providing information on state-of-the-art global sourcing.

The audits covered several areas such as logistics, inventory management, sales forecasting and demand management, purchasing, information systems, store operations, product management and merchandising, finance, sales, marketing, and human resources. It is important to note that in almost all audits, participants mentioned concepts such as risk, failures, and vulnerability more frequently in the context of sourcing than in any other context. An interesting implication is that managers responsible for global sourcing perceive their area of operations to be more susceptible to risks than their counterparts in other departments. This chapter describes the current state of risk management in global sourcing decisions by providing descriptions of risks and barriers as identified from the companies in our sample.

TYPES OF RISKS

The fact that a wide variety of risks exist in global sourcing was evident and obvious to all sourcing managers interviewed. The main origins for risks include some traditional sources and newer sources that have recently become more prominent considerations. Traditional sources include political issues such as stability, customs issues such as duties and tariffs, and cost issues such as currency fluctuations. Relatively newer considerations include factors such as cost of increased inventory, qualitative cost of bad quality (for example, poor customer relationships), security issues, faster product obsolescence, rising wage rates in developing economies, port congestion, increased lead times, and generally rising transportation costs. A common theme running across the interviews suggests that risks most salient to professionals dealing with global sourcing in our sample can primarily be categorized into cost risks, quality risks, and lead time risks. More recently, with interfaces becoming increasingly complex and with the changing global landscape, security risks have also become a critical issue. Table 2.2 provides a list of risks most important for different organizations as well as barriers (discussed in the next section) to incorporating these risks in global sourcing decisions.

Cost Risks

A major risk from the cost standpoint is the exclusion of some important components of sourcing cost that make up the total cost of a global sourcing decision. The most common example in our sample was that inventory risks were not fully considered in making sourcing decisions. In the 10 organizations included in the sample, almost half the firms made sourcing decisions based on landed cost per unit that included the transportation costs, but did not include the additional costs of inventory risks such as in-transit inventory, stock-outs, obsolescence, and damages due to long and variable lead times. Other sources of cost risk not included in the decisions were currency fluctuations, rising wage rates in low-cost sourcing regions, cost of ensuring security, expedited air freight due to natural disasters and port congestion, and the cost of intellectual property loss.

Table 2.2 Risks and major barriers

Company pseudonym	Risks and related challenges	Major barriers
AeroCo	Security, single sourcing, supplier price risks, lead times.	Lack of training (related to supplier relationship management) Focus only on cost while ignoring service and quality issues (and lack of total cost focus) New product introductions (lack of standardization among parts and components for new and different products)
PartsCo	Forecast risks, supplier pricing risks, supplier capacity	Regional parochialism Focus only on cost while ignoring service and quality issues (and lack of total cost focus)
PowersCo	Lead time, inventory, lack of flexibility, network design challenges	Regional parochialism (lack of global organization focus) Focus only on cost while ignoring service and quality issues (and lack of total cost focus) Lack of visibility
BeautyCo	Single sourcing, transportation costs, quality, supplier capacity, supplier service, untimely deliveries	New product introductions (high frequency) Lack of information sharing (primarily internal) Lack of global organization focus (lack of total cost focus) Lack of training (related to supplier relationship management)
VisionCo	Forecast, inventory, lead time, lack of flexibility	Lack of integration (primarily internal information technology integration) New product introductions (high frequency)
LifeCo	Lead time, supplier capacity, single sourcing, inventory, customer service	New product introductions Lack of visibility Regional parochialism Focus only on cost while ignoring service and quality issues (and lack of total cost focus) Lack of information sharing Lack of training (related to supplier relationship management)

Continues

Table 2.2 (*continued*)

Company pseudonym	Risks and related challenges	Major barriers
CarsCo	Single sourcing, quality, supplier reliability, supplier capacity, network design	Lack of integration (primarily internal and related to information technology) Lack of information sharing (primarily external with suppliers) Regional parochialism Lack of training (related to supplier relationship management) Focus only on cost while ignoring service and quality issues
FarmCo	Lead time, quality, transportation cost, untimely deliveries	Regional parochialism Lack of training (related to contract negotiation, supplier relationship management, and single versus multiple sourcing decisions) Focus only on cost while ignoring service and quality issues (and lack of total cost focus)
ElectroCo	Lead time, inventory, single sourcing for some and too many suppliers for other parts and products, customer service, forecasting	Focus only on cost while ignoring service and quality issues (and lack of total cost focus) New product introductions (lack of sourcing considerations) Regional parochialism Lack of integration (primarily internal)
LunchCo	Inventory, lost sales, forecasting, increase in global sourcing	Lack of training Lack of integration (both internal and external)

Quality Risks

Another significant risk is that of quality. It was evident from the interviews conducted that quality risk in global sourcing is a concern. In our sample, quality problems with global suppliers, such as the lack of capacity to replace defective parts and materials, were a routine occurrence. The implications of quality problems go beyond suppliers' capacity limitations and also add to the internal costs such as air freight. Although the cost benefits of sourcing from a low-cost region often come initially with a trade-off in terms of quality, global suppliers quickly need to achieve high-quality levels.

In addition to quality, other aspects of service such as supplier lead time reliability are routinely disregarded even though every manager with sourcing responsibilities indicated that service risks should be explicitly incorporated. Collectively, quality and reliability can have a significant impact on manufacturing costs and lifetime service costs of company-provided warranties, resulting in a direct impact on total supply chain costs. One participant narrated the following incident that summarizes the service risks related to global sourcing in his/her organization:

> "One of our suppliers was very responsive (in the region), but then we moved to a supplier in China to get a better price and added 6-8 weeks of transit time and often had to ship via airfreight. I wonder if we ever saved anything. The longer lead-times have cost us. People are hesitant to say it, but we didn't save a thing."

Lead Time Risks

The third critical risk is increased and variable lead times arising from lack of control over the lead times due to issues such as customs, port congestion, capacity constraints, and geopolitical issues. On the one hand, global sourcing often generates significant cost reduction; on the other hand, none of the companies in our sample demonstrated any sophisticated analysis for quantifying and factoring lead time risks into decisions. This tradeoff between the *cost* of lead time risk and product cost needs to be balanced carefully. Increased lead time not only increases inventory, but directly impacts the service level provided to customers.

Security Risks

Several security risk considerations have started to grab the attention of global sourcing professionals such as information systems security, infrastructure security, and freight breaches from terrorism, vandalism, crime, sabotage, and piracy. Global freight movement is dependent on elements of infrastructure security risks that are a mix of public and private utility services. Waterways, airports, and communications are a few examples. This increases the likelihood of violating the integrity of cargo and products. Such violations may lead to the loss or adulteration of goods. Even scarier is the potential exploitation for criminal purpose such as smuggling human beings and weapons inside containers.

TYPES OF BARRIERS TO INCORPORATING RISKS

There were several items that stood out in the interviews in terms of the factors that hinder incorporating risk considerations in sourcing decisions. Most notable in the context of *global* sourcing were regional parochialism, focus on cost as the driver of global sourcing decisions, lack of visibility, lack of information sharing, increased rate of new product introductions, rigidity to change single or dual sourcing patterns, and lack of training (see Table 2.2).

Regional Parochialism

Regional parochialism refers to the prevalence of local metrics that are regionally aligned and essentially focused on lowering regional purchase costs rather than being optimized at a global level. Too many locally determined metrics that are not strategically aligned to overall organizational goals lead to suboptimal decisions, both from cost and risk perspectives. A typical initiative launched by the managers in our sample to overcome the problem of regional parochialism was to centralize all global sourcing responsibilities. However, an explicit consideration of global trade-offs was missing. Another initiative was centralizing assembly operations in a single region. However, this can increase freight bills as everything needs to be brought into one region and distributed worldwide. One promising approach was a regionalization strategy that focuses on sourcing and assembling products in the region they are consumed. This may be a good strategy for several organizations, both from cost and risk perspectives.

Cost as the Main Driver of Sourcing Decisions

Another barrier to incorporating risk considerations is a single-minded focus on per piece cost as the main driver of a sourcing decision. A majority of the organizations in our sample included transportation costs as a part of the total sourcing cost. A few also added a buffer, usually a percentage of the total transportation cost, in case shipments needed to be expedited due to some risks. That is, only a couple of companies included the impact of risks on transportation costs, and those who did could not confirm that their estimate of the buffer was valid. In some cases, inventory costs were also factored in, but the analysis was rudimentary.

Cost reduction (and thus lower price for finished products) is important. In fact, lower cost through continuous improvement is a core element of most successful supplier relationship initiatives. However, as is vastly acknowledged, a transactional approach focused only on cost has a limited effect on service and quality risks and other service risks, and sets the stage for adversarial relationships. The following quote from one manager interviewed aptly reflects the observations of most senior global professionals in our sample:

> "Currently, there is no analysis of total cost of procurement, particularly on supply from China. The decisions are made on a piece price basis that leaves BeautyCo with no way of judging what the true impact is on the company per-

formance. Transportation costs, mainly air freight in response to shortening the lead-time, is not considered in the sourcing decisions. Other supply chain costs, such as inventory cost, are not fully considered in making the decisions for the offshore sourcing. And the cost of risk is also not included in the analyses."

There was also pressure from top management on global sourcing because *other firms were doing it* and targets were set up to achieve certain dollar values worth of global sourcing on a quarterly or yearly basis. Those who questioned such targets were considered as not willing to work hard and *make it happen*. There was a tacit performance incentive to make the *global sourcing figures look good*. And, one way to do so is to focus only on basic costs. As one executive mentioned, "People monkey with the numbers to make themselves look good."

Lack of Visibility

Lack of visibility, and at times, lack of access to relevant information in a timely manner is a barrier to conducting accurate analysis and making informed decisions. Even when risks are known, lack of access to, or availability of, relevant data makes it difficult to incorporate risks in decisions. As discussed earlier, some executives add a certain percentage to their estimated total cost as a buffer for *risks*. There is no rationale for this number, but a *feeling* based on past experience. This, though better than ignoring risks, is not an adequate solution. A quote from a manager at PowerCo is illustrative of the viewpoints of several managers in our sample:

> "We still don't have global visibility for sourcing. We still don't have a good way to evaluate sourcing decisions. We focus on a piece of it without understanding the total cost."

Lack of visibility can come from several sources, such as problems with capturing data, lack of information systems integration, lack of information technology capability at the supplier, and most importantly, a deliberate lack of information sharing. This is partly due to the lack of technology integration, but often it is the result of the silo-oriented mentality and lack of trust. Interestingly, managers from two different companies stated that it was their company that was causing supplier issues because, "either we are not giving them the right design or the information that they need." In particular, one manager mentioned that, "since the suppliers can't get numbers from CarsCo, they have to make their own estimates." It is redundant to mention the extent of forecast risks at the supplier's end and inventory risk at the company's end that lack of visibility can be responsible for. Timely information sharing can alleviate several risks or enable managers to proactively manage risks.

Increased Rate of New Product Introductions

More frequent and higher numbers of new product introductions are also barriers to providing adequate attention to risks. Customers are becoming more demanding, both in terms of newer and more customized products, as well as demanding more aggressive lead times. As a response, many manufacturers are continually introducing a bevy of new products that increases complexity for suppliers, that, in turn, increases lead time risks. One manager stated, "New product ideas get in the way of [a] supplier's ability to deliver products on time." Inconsistent supply increases manufacturer, as well as customer, inventory and inventory-related risks. Even in these leading companies, during the product design phase, there was little consideration of sourcing-related risks, such as lead times. In addition, lack of part/component commonality leads to delays related to reworks and extends the already long lead times.

Rigidity to Change Sourcing Patterns

The pros and cons of single versus dual sourcing have been extensively discussed in academic journals and business magazines. Sourcing managers in our sample had significant knowledge about the appropriateness of different options under a variety of operating and environmental conditions. For example, managers were aware that adopting dual sourcing as a part of risk management strategy, or having a back-up supplier closer to where the materials are needed, were effective ways of mitigating stock-out risks. Conversely, managers from one company expressed concern about having too many suppliers. Similarly, managers in companies with worldwide manufacturing were inclined toward regional or local sourcing, specifically sourcing in regions where manufacturing is done for better control and more knowledge of risk sources. However, we found that companies tend to get *stuck* in their traditional way of doing things. In the company mentioned earlier, where too many suppliers were a concern, nothing substantial was being done about it.

Lack of Training

Another barrier relates to lack of training. Procuring is a complex profession and requires a great deal of training and experience. Add the complexities and risks within global sourcing, and the importance of expertise greatly increases. Lack of training can lead to poor supplier quality management, supplier management with an emphasis only on price negotiation, inadequate competitive bidding processes, and incomplete total landed cost analyses. All of these factors, that may involve lack of training, eventually increase the risk in the supply chain, emanating from global sourcing decisions.

FRAMEWORK FOR INCORPORATING RISKS

Based on the audit reports, suggestions of auditors, initiatives being considered or implemented by the companies in our sample, and existing knowledge in academic as well as trade journals, a two-step process may be employed to actively incorporate risk considerations in global sourcing decisions. The first step deals with the identification of risks and barriers. The second step provides recommendations for strategies appropriate for different types of barriers.

Step 1: Audit the Global Procurement Process

The first step is to identify risks and barriers by conducting an audit of a recent important global sourcing decision. The objective is to find out if the cost savings indeed matched the targets or expected savings. The answer in most cases is likely to be, "No." Regardless of whether the savings are greater than or lower than expected, this exercise will suggest opportunities to pursue better sourcing operations. The risks that cause the gaps between expected and realized savings should be identified. Then, these risks need to be linked with the barriers that prevent the firm from doing a rigorous risk analysis. To offer an example for this process, Table 2.2 provides an extensive but nonexhaustive list of risks identified for several companies, and the barriers that interfered with accounting for these risks in global sourcing decisions.

To illustrate the audit process, an example from RiskPro (a pseudonym) provides a rigorous global sourcing process. In RiskPro's framework, the first activity in the audit process is to identify risk categories. The company identified 10 areas of risk, namely procurement, transportation, quality, supplier inventory, supply process partners, such as 3PLs and brokers, customs, legal, information systems, service, and overall business. For each of these categories, a risk *owner* is identified by the upper management team. Each *owner* is then responsible for creating a list of risks that may impact his or her area of responsibility. Based on dozens of risks identified by all owners, the company came up with six major groups of procurement-related risks, namely lost components, delay in delivery, damaged components (transportation damage), quality of components (design and manufacturing quality), landed costs of components, and risk of legal complications. This list is similar to the four categories of cost risks, quality risks, lead time risks, and security risks identified earlier in the chapter.

For *each* risk identified by the owner, he or she needs to undertake a detailed analysis and provide the following deliverables:

1. Place each risk into one of the six categories
2. Verify and validate, based on discussions with other risk owners, that risks are appropriate for the assigned category
3. Based on discussions with other risk owners, look for risks which overlap.
4. Assign probability to each risk factor
5. Estimate financial impact of adverse outcomes of each risk
6. Determine strategic impact of risk; for example, shut down of a supplier factory can impact product availability and consequently relationships with trade partners
7. Develop mitigation strategies for higher probability and impact risks and for high strategic impact risks

The analysis Steps 1 through 5 are summarized in Figure 2.1. In this chart, the vertical axis represents the event probability, and the horizontal axis represents the total impact of the risk. The length and placement of arrows within this matrix represents the distribution of risk across the dimensions of probability and impact. The size of the circle represents the combined effect of probability and impact. For example,

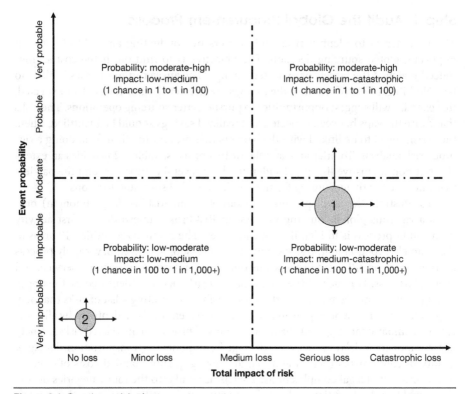

Figure 2.1 Creating a risk chart.

Circle 1 in Figure 2.1 represents a risk that has improbable-to-moderate probability with a tendency toward moderate risk, and a potential for serious loss. The size of the circle represents a fairly big effect. Circle 2, on the other hand, represents a small effect with a risk that has no loss and is improbable.

Each risk owner develops a chart for his/her area. See Figure 2.2 for an excerpt from a chart developed by the owner of the procurement category. For the procurement category, the owner identified five major risks and plotted them along the two axes based on probability and impact. The size of circle reflects the total impact of risk. Next to each circle, the risk is stated.

The next step in the audit process is to link the risks to the barriers that are potential reasons for the exclusion of risk considerations. That is, for each circle, the related risk is identified and linked to the barrier that causes the risk to exist.

Circle 1. Risk of cost price creep and raw material fluctuations. *Barrier*: Rigidity to changing sourcing pattern and lack of training (related to writing contracts).

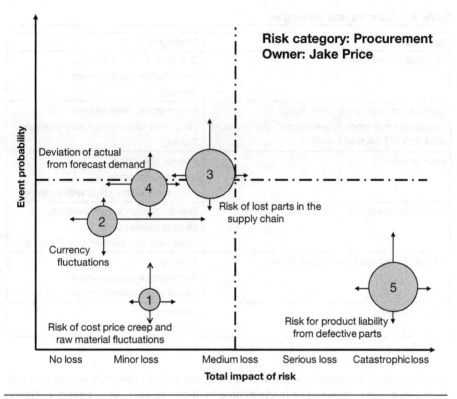

Figure 2.2 Excerpt from procurement risk chart.

Circle 2.   Currency fluctuations. *Barrier*: Lack of total cost focus and lack of training (related to computing total cost for a sourcing decision).

Circle 3.   Risk of lost parts in the supply chain. *Barrier*: Lack of visibility.

Circle 4.   Deviation of actual from forecast demand (due to demand spikes and inability to respond due to inflexibility). *Barrier*: Lack of standardization across products.

Circle 5.   Risk for product liability from defective parts. *Barrier*: Cost as the main driver of sourcing decisions.

Once the audit is complete, the next step is to identify strategies to mitigate these risks.

Step 2: Identify and Implement Appropriate Strategies

Based on the identification of risks and associations of these risks to the barriers, several strategies may be adopted. Table 2.3 presents barriers discussed earlier along with the strategies to overcome these barriers. These strategies are primarily assembled

Table 2.3 Barriers and strategies

Barriers	Strategies
Regional parochialism	Global organizational focus Performance measurement Training
Cost as the main driver of sourcing Decisions while ignoring service and quality issues (and lack of total cost focus)	Performance measurement Long-term relationships with suppliers Training
Lack of visibility	Internal integration External integration Long-term relationships with suppliers
Increased rate of new product introductions	Standardization across products Internal integration Staggered new product introductions
Rigidity to change sourcing patterns	Training Performance measurement Global organizational focus
Lack of training	Training Performance measurement

together from the suggestions of auditors, academic journals, business magazines, and strategies being considered or implemented by the companies in our sample. Figure 2.3 presents strategies to overcome barriers in the context of RiskPro, the company used to illustrate Step 1.

Global Organizational and Total Cost Focus Through Performance Measurement

Sourcing decisions must be based on the greatest benefit to the overall firm and should be reasonably independent of regional profit-and-loss considerations. Given the scale of global operations, disproportionate growth in global supply, as well as demand markets, volatile transportation costs, and most important, service and inventory issues, require an approach that takes a global view. Part of reducing regional parochialism is implementing new metrics that ensure that sourcing decisions are made on a global total corporate landed cost basis and account for risks. In addition to sourcing, transportation, and inventory costs, more sophisticated analysis may include considerations such as impact of service quality on manufacturing flexibility and the impact of product quality on production.

When a decision is being made to source from another country, a complete landed cost analysis and risk analysis is in order. Sometimes, the costs of moving to a foreign supplier (longer lead times, less flexible supply chains, and more in-transit

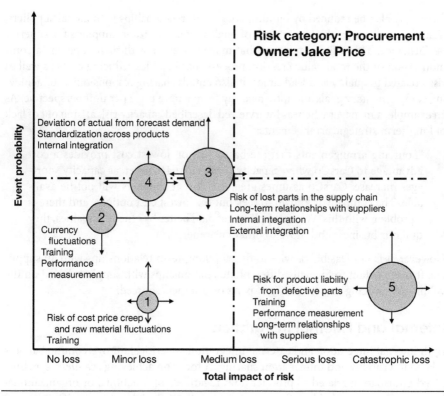

Figure 2.3 Example of a completed chart

inventory) could outweigh the benefits of lower prices. Rules and work arrangements as well as performance measurement must be devised such that they reward people who bring up concerns related to risk rather than viewing such people as roadblocks. Owing to the effort and dedication required to devise and manage a good performance system, it is easy to understand why many firms have not made significant progress in this area. However, the overall effort in such a system may be worthwhile because a good performance measurement system often leads to better decisions and higher performance. As an interviewed manager stated:

> "We have to overcome the regional parochialism. It forces us to make suboptimal decisions. We have too many locally determined metrics that are not strategically aligned. We need to take a global perspective on what's best for the company overall."

Long-Term Relationships

A global focus on performance measurement systems based on landed cost helps address barriers related to regional parochialism and cost focus. In addition, a cost focus may also be reduced by building long-term relationships with global suppliers, training suppliers on the importance of quality, and rewarding suppliers for superior performance. This attitude requires that managers share with their suppliers a common vision of the total value creation process that includes reducing costs as well as risks related to quality and lead times. It also entails sharing responsibility for achieving complementary goals and moving away from a pure price per unit perspective. As an example, a manager who was interviewed described capacity risk arising out of lack of long-term strategic arrangements:

> "Sourcing arrangements that are based just on lowest cost provides a cost advantage to CarsCo when capacity is available. However, as capacity shortages increase, CarsCo assumes greater risk that suppliers will not be available. The company is known to seek out the lowest cost options, and there is a problem with this. When suppliers get paid better by other companies, they quit our business and move to other customers."

However, it is not feasible or wise to develop long-term relationships with all suppliers. It is important to formally differentiate relationships with suppliers based on the volume of sourcing and criticality of parts or products sourced.

Internal and External Integration

Both internal integration and external integration are critical for overcoming barriers related to visibility and information sharing. A focus on achieving seamless, synchronized information related to product flow, regardless of functional or organizational boundaries, can enable identification of risks, collection of data to quantify risks, and proactive risk management. However, achieving integration requires extensive organizational and cultural change. In particular, internal process integration requires a fundamental commitment to process excellence throughout an enterprise in a coordinated effort.

Only two firms in our sample demonstrated a good grounding in process management concepts of Lean and Six Sigma, which, in these firms, were employed primarily as tools to compress sourcing lead times. Lack of integration hinders the ability of managers to make worthwhile contributions. One manager expressed concern that she does not know who to *bring to the table* during the new product development process due to lack of supplier performance and supplier capability feedback. It is fundamentally important to ensure that appropriate information regarding supplier performance is collected, and that the impact of that supplier's performance on the firm's performance is analyzed and documented. This information must be shared with all relevant managers who can then integrate the information into product design and sourcing decisions.

In addition, improved visibility permits managers to better understand inventory performance. It is well established that supply excellence can be achieved by linking horizontal product/service flows into a seamless, synchronized operational flow to satisfy customer requirements. Visibility within and across organizations creates synergies resulting from the pulling of all areas toward the same goals and objectives. From a global sourcing perspective, this enhances overall firm performance by reducing risks and lowering overall procurement costs.

Standardization Across Products

Standardization of components across products and brands, as well as use of available (rather than custom manufactured) parts, helps to reduce risks and enable greater supply chain efficiencies. Sourcing risk considerations must be explicitly incorporated in the product design phase. Product development engineers must be sensitized to the opportunity for strategic buying of items across products that have a high commonality of parts or use parts available in industry as a significant source of cost savings. For example, an executive from a cosmetic company mentioned that moving to the use of common bottles across different brands instead of redesigning *similar* bottles improved forecasting accuracy. Other major advantages from a risk perspective are lower costs variability and therefore lower cost risks, reduction in inventory risks and lower stock-outs.

Staggered New Product Introductions

Wherever possible, moving to staggered new product introductions should be explicitly considered. Spreading out new product launches allows for more time to consider risks and therefore improves the quality of sourcing decisions. Moreover, the lack of supply chain visibility can seriously compromise the ability to make informed sourcing decisions for new products. By staggering the introduction of new products, managers can take their time in making decisions about who to use in the manufacturing process.

Training

A final consideration is the training of global sourcing professionals in multiple areas. Important areas include:

1. Supplier quality management with emphasis on sourcing from low-cost regions
2. Relationship management with emphasis on service issues in addition to price negotiation
3. Conducting competitive bidding processes
4. Conducting total landed cost analyses of suppliers with emphasis on the impact of lead time on inventory cost, cost of quality, and risk of change in cost
5. Use of analytical tools to make single versus dual sourcing decisions; and
6. Measuring supplier performance.

The last item—measuring supplier performance—deserves elaboration. Training and tools to measure supplier performance in terms of order cycle time length and variance, and setting up risk-reward sharing methods, can help alleviate operational risks. Most companies in our sample, tracked specific metrics that would enable them to penalize the supplier. However, the ability and willingness to leverage this performance information for improved sourcing decisions was missing. To critically evaluate existing sourcing patterns, managers must be trained and provided with analytical tools to critically evaluate these decisions. In addition, performance measurement must encourage and reward the use of novel concepts. Finally, providing training on the latest government security initiatives, such as the Container Security Initiative and the Customs Trade Partnership Against Terrorism, can reduce risks in the sourcing process.

SUMMARY

The state of risk management in global sourcing decisions is sophisticated and complex. An analysis of current practice, based on an audit of 10 leading global organizations, revealed that risks most salient to sourcing professions in a *global environment* may be divided into cost, quality, lead time, and security risks. An analysis of these risks reveals certain barriers that hinder the incorporation of risk considerations in global sourcing decisions. These barriers include regional parochialism, focus on cost as the driver of global sourcing decisions, lack of visibility, lack of information sharing, increased rate of new product introductions, reluctance to change single or dual sourcing patterns, and lack of training. Based on suggestions of auditors, academic journals, business magazines, and strategies being considered or implemented by the companies in our sample, six strategies were discussed. The strategies include a global organizational focus, total cost focus through performance measurement, long-term relationships, internal and external integration, staggered new product launches, and global sourcing manager training. The discussion provided a framework for global sourcing managers to evaluate risks in their global sourcing decisions, link the risks to barriers, and design strategies to overcome these barriers to make more robust and less risky global sourcing decisions.

3

THE SUPPLY CHAIN RISKS OF GLOBAL SOURCING

Josef Oehmen

INTRODUCTION

The most important newly industrialized country in the world is the People's Republic of China (PRC). It shows a number of unique features and developments that make it attractive for Western companies as a sourcing market, production site, and sales market. The continuous and stable growth of China's GDP led to a catch-up race with developed economies: in 2008, China's GDP was US$4.42 trillion, exceeding the GDP of Germany. While smaller than the U.S. GDP by more than a factor of 3, China's GDP grew by 9 percent in 2008, compared to 1.1 percent for the United States.

The results summarized in this chapter are based on case studies conducted at three Swiss small- and medium-sized enterprises (SMEs) from 2007–2009. The supply chain risks of China were grouped according to the main effects on supply chain performance goals:

- Total costs too high
- Delivery reliability
- Insufficient quality
- Damage to company reputation

For each category, the companies developed a main scenario in the form of a cause-and-effect network. It explained how single risks relate to each other and cause a greater total risk. Ultimately, all performance measures translated into *cost*, as depicted in Figure 3.1.

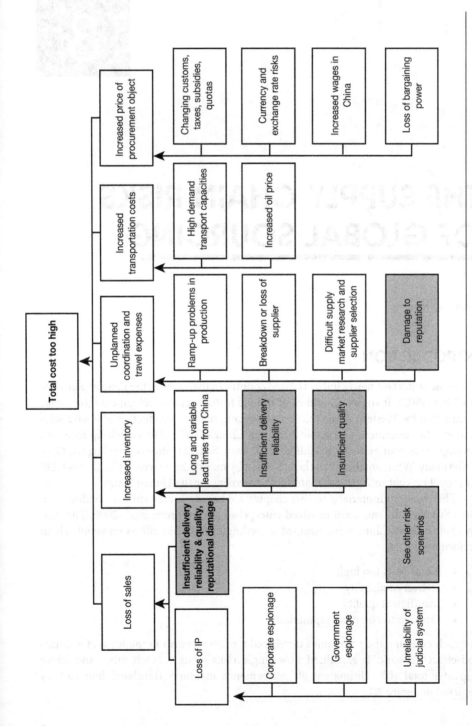

Figure 3.1 Risk scenario: total cost too high.

RISK SCENARIO *TOTAL COST TOO HIGH*

The first risk scenario *total cost too high* in Figure 3.1 is the largest in scope of the scenarios. This is due to the fact that it integrated the other three scenarios, and attracted the highest attention of the three Swiss cases. On the top level, five risks were identified: the loss of sales, increased inventory, unplanned coordination and travel expenses, increased transportation costs and increased price of procurement object.

LOSS OF SALES

The potential of lost sales due to supply chain risks when sourcing from China has four risk scenarios that feed into it, including the loss of intellectual property, which will be discussed in detail in the next section. All three other main risk scenarios—insufficient delivery reliability; insufficient quality; and damage to reputation—may also lead to a loss of sales. If delivery dates cannot be met because a product or component from China arrives late, a customer might step back from a contract. If prospective customers become aware of delivery problems, they might not consider the company at all.

The inability to deliver causes penalty payments by the company to its customers, but this is only a risk if the company cannot forward these penalty payments to the supplier. It not only depends on the contractual agreements and the financial stability of the supplier, but also on the reliability of the local judicial system to enforce the contract, which will be discussed after the loss of intellectual property. Insufficient quality leads to lost sales, as unsatisfied customers will not be back. The same is true for reputational damage that will lead to concerned customers or a loss of prospective new customers.

LOSS OF INTELLECTUAL PROPERTY

Protection of their intellectual property was a main concern for the companies in the three case studies. The loss of intellectual property leads to a loss of sales, as competitors enter the market and unique selling points of one's own products are lost. Two situations are possible: corporate espionage and government espionage. Corporate espionage occurs during a buyer-supplier relationship, where confidential material is obtained illegally or used against contractual agreements. Government espionage addresses the focused obtaining of strategically relevant technology information via their intelligence services that were restructured accordingly at the end of the Cold War. Western technology companies—small, mid-sized and large corporations alike—are prime targets for industrial espionage. The yearly damage through lost sales is estimated at €20 to 30 billion for Germany alone. China and Russia with their developing economies are the most active countries in the practice of espionage. Today, 20 percent of all German companies have been victims of industrial espionage, with a 10 percent annual increase in incidents of espionage.

UNRELIABILITY OF THE JUDICIAL SYSTEM

China's legal system largely stopped functioning during the Cultural Revolution (1966–1976). Law schools were closed, courts stopped working, and the Ministry of Justice was also closed. As a result, the current legal system is only about 30 years old. The consequences are that the developing formal legal system is still competing with an established system of personal relationships (guanxi), and corruption is a problem. The qualifications of professionals vary greatly, as many open positions had to be quickly filled; the job candidates were often drawn from the military and lacked the appropriate education. Also, the size and political structure of China as a quasi-federation make it hard to implement national laws and harmonize national and local legislation. This leads to additional risks, as experience gathered in one part of China might not be directly applicable to other provinces.

These conditions lead to several problems for Western companies: it might be difficult to get an objective ruling during litigation and the laws may not be entirely clear (due to local versus national laws, or to regional protectionism). After obtaining a favorable ruling, it may not be possible to enforce. However, the situation greatly improved with China's accession to the World Trade Organization (WTO). The establishment of a stable judicial system is high on the political agenda. The state of the legal system in the developed coastal areas today is fairly reliable; however, there remain great deficiencies in the rural provinces.

INCREASED INVENTORY

An increase in inventory leads to additional costs via an increase in bound capital and the associated capital costs, as well as an increased risk of obsolescence of the stored components (depending on the component and the speed of the final product's life cycle). An increase in inventory is caused by the necessity to increase safety stocks. The fundamental reason for increasing safety stock is a heightened insecurity regarding the availability of components if they are delivered from China. The delivery lead times are longer (both by sea and air freight) compared to truck shipments inside Europe. Additionally, delivery lead times might be more volatile in case the inland routes between the production site and the air or seaport are unreliable, or when the demand for transportation exceeds the available capacities. Another reason to increase safety stock is insufficient delivery reliability of a supplier and insufficient quality of the supplied goods.

UNPLANNED COORDINATION AND TRAVEL EXPENSES

Unplanned coordination and travel expenses describe the additional costs for management and professional personnel dealing with unexpected problems regarding

Chinese suppliers. Ramp-up problems during the start of production usually require a significant amount of an increased workforce on short notice. Not only are additional costs incurred by travel expenses and the compensation for the employees, but the expertise and contribution to their regular jobs will also be missed and may cause problems, especially if they had to leave on short notice. A breakdown or loss of a supplier might not only lead to penalty payments, but it might also require a huge effort on behalf of the purchasing department to find a suitable replacement. The supply market research and supplier selection of Chinese suppliers is much more complex for a Germany or Switzerland-based company than a similar process for a local supplier. As the selection requires (at least temporarily) a presence in China, it causes significant travel expenses.

INCREASED TRANSPORTATION COST

The transportation costs are driven by two main factors. The first factor is the demand for transportation capacities. As the fleet supply of freight ships changes slowly due to the investment costs and production lead times (currently, over 10 years, as the shipyard capacities are also limited), the first main cost driver is the demand for transportation capacity.

The second factor influencing shipping rates is the oil price, as fuel prices account for 25 to 35 percent of the operation costs of a ship. Due to these reasons, the price for sea freight changed dramatically in the last few years. The Baltic Exchange Dry Index fluctuated in 2008 between 11,793 and 663 base points, a factor of almost 18. Air freight shows smaller fluctuations, in 2008 between 138.5 and 162.6 base points, equaling around 17 percent. However, the two indices cannot be directly compared, as the first captures the prices that the transportation vehicle operators charge, and the latter the final customers' prices. These are decoupled via long-term contracts and third-party logistics providers.

INCREASED PRICE OF PROCUREMENT OBJECT

Possible causes for an increased price of the procurement object include changes in customs regulations and quotas between China and Europe, and changes of taxes and subsidies inside China. One example is the sudden reduction of export tax rebates in June 2007. These were originally announced only two weeks in advance with little detail as to which product categories were actually affected. Due to the ensuing international irritation, some reductions were later postponed. Export rebates are a form of subsidy for certain products. The same effect can occur on the importing side through changes in import quotes. One example is the *bra war* in the textile industry in 2005, when Europe tried to limit the import of certain Chinese textiles after the worldwide WTO trade liberalization earlier in the year. The other three main risks are a price increase through an increase of the Chinese currency *renminbi* (RMB), increasing wages in China, and a loss of bargaining power.

CURRENCY AND EXCHANGE RATE RISKS

Fluctuations in exchange rates are one of the major risks in international supply chains. Exchange rates between currencies have quickly changed by multiples of 10 percent in the past. These changes translate directly into price changes sourced in this currency. Larger corporations can naturally hedge against this risk by leveling sourcing and sales volumes between currencies. Other options include financial hedging of exchange rate risks, but these are not easily available for Chinese currency (RMB) hedges. A short-term *hedge* is also possible by transferring the risk to the supplier by agreeing on a price in the sourcing company's local currency, e.g., US$ or €. In the mid- to long-term, the influence of the exchange rate deviations will be so strong on the supplier that prices will be renegotiated.

In terms of the exchange rate, China is a somewhat special case. Most experts agree that the RMB is strongly undervalued, thus providing an indirect export subsidy by the government to the Chinese economy. The RMB is not freely traded, but the exchange rate is controlled by the People's Bank of China (the Chinese central bank). Between July 2005 and the beginning of 2010, the Chinese currency appreciated more than 20 percent against the US dollar. It is also apparent that the central bank discontinued the appreciation of the RMB after July 2008 due to the worldwide economic crisis. The question remains what the *right* exchange rate is. Based on an analysis of purchasing power parity, different experts argue that the RMB is still undervalued by 40 to 200 percent, making the price of most procurement objects after an appreciation unattractive.

INCREASED WAGES IN CHINA

Low labor costs are one of the main arguments to relocate labor-intensive production steps to China. Compared to Western Europe, there are great cost advantages, especially for low skilled labor. In the developed coastal areas of China, support workers are cheaper by a factor between five and 10; technically skilled workers and university graduates (engineers and business support staff) by a factor of 3–4; and employees with a significant level of experience by a factor of 1–2. However, these figures are contrasted by a steep yearly increase in labor cost of 10 to 15 percent, or 50 percent and more if highly skilled employees have to be hired away from a competitor.

RISK SCENARIO *DELIVERY RELIABILITY*

There are three main reasons that cause a significant decrease in delivery reliability (see Figure 3.2): the ramp-up phase is especially critical when new products are

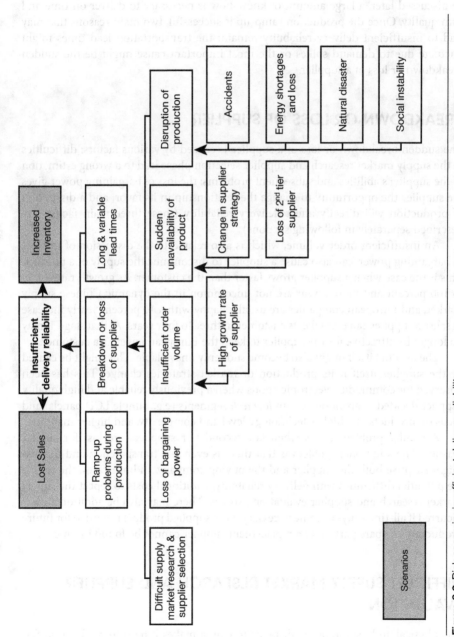

Figure 3.2 Risk scenario: insufficient delivery reliability.

introduced or the production of products with a seasonal demand is restarted. As will be discussed later, a large amount of know-how is necessary to deliver on time and with quality. Once the production ramp-up is successful, two main reasons that may lead to insufficient delivery reliability remain: the transportation lead times might fluctuate due to demand spikes or the most important cause might be the sudden breakdown or loss of a supplier.

BREAKDOWN OR LOSS OF SUPPLIER

The sudden breakdown or loss of a supplier is caused by various factors: difficulties in the supply market research and supplier selection phase lead to a wrong estimation of the supplier's abilities and subsequent problems; the loss of bargaining power gives the supplier the opportunity to change the relationship in its favor; and a disruption of production will directly affect delivery reliability (these three main factors are described separately in following sections).

An insufficient order volume, which is also related to the discussion of the loss of bargaining power, can also cause a supplier to discontinue the supply of a product. This is the case when a supplier grows faster than the customer. As growth rates of 50 to 100 percent and more a year are not uncommon in the dynamic Chinese supply market, and European companies are usually happy with a 10 percent yearly increase in sales, a supplier can overtake its customer in three to four years. At that stage, it may no longer be attractive for the supplier to keep the European buyer as a customer.

The product itself might also become suddenly unavailable. This might be caused by the supplier itself if its production or market strategies change. This has been observed for commodity electronic goods when a previously reliable and high quality supplier decided to abandon certain *low tech* segments (e.g., simple LCD panels) and focus on products of a higher technology level and complexity, and higher margins.

A similar problem arises when key second tier suppliers are lost for similar reasons. The additional problem is that there is even less transparency, and the loss might surprise both the supplier and the buying company. In both cases, the results are potential difficulties with delivery reliability, additional costs to repeat the supply market research and supplier evaluation process. There may also be additional costs incurred if all-time-buys become necessary if the supplied product is needed for future production or spare parts, and a replacement supplier cannot be found in time.

DIFFICULT SUPPLY MARKET RESEARCH AND SUPPLIER EVALUATION

The physical and psychological distance to China makes it hard to perform professional supply market research and supplier evaluations. The involved risk is high, as the selection of the wrong supplier can lead directly to problems regarding delivery reliability, quality, and finally, cost. Having one's own procurement employees in China is the optimum solution from a performance perspective. This mode ensures an efficient information exchange and a high level of transparency and control of the sourcing company. The problem for small enterprises is the high level of associated costs that make this option only viable in cases of very high sourcing volumes. The alternative is to use external service providers. Using external service providers can lower the level of (fixed) costs for small companies considerably, but also diminish transparency, information exchange, and the level of control.

LOSS OF BARGAINING POWER

The loss of bargaining power during a buyer-supplier relationship with a Chinese supplier can cause a major cost increase and decrease in delivery reliability. Power is understood as the difference in the mutual dependence between buyer and supplier. It can also lead to the loss of the supplier, if the supplier is no longer willing to accept the customer's cost, quality, or lead time demands. If the customer wishes to keep the supplier, it often means accepting an increase in the price of the procurement object. The loss of bargaining power does not occur in the beginning of these relationships: the supplier is often interested in gaining a reference customer to attract more business. Also, if a new contract is technologically challenging, the supplier often benefits from a know-how transfer and builds up new production abilities, attracting even more customers.

RISK SCENARIO *INSUFFICIENT QUALITY*

If the quality of the products delivered from China is insufficient, the two main consequences are a loss of sales (if the customer notices the quality problems), or an increase in inventory to provide a buffer against low-quality production batches (see Figure 3.3).

The two main risks regarding product quality are insufficient design adaptations of the components and unreliable production processes at the supplier.

INSUFFICIENT DESIGN ADAPTATIONS

The risk of insufficient design adaptations refers to the redesign of components that have been sourced locally or were manufactured in-house. This can involve minor changes to drawings to adapt them from prior standards (e.g., ISO, BS, or DIN) to Chinese GB industrial standards. Larger changes may involve the redesign to fit the production capabilities and experience of the Chinese supplier. Redesign of components and connections may become necessary to optimize the production costs. This may mean, for example, changing snap joints to screw joints, as snap joints are more

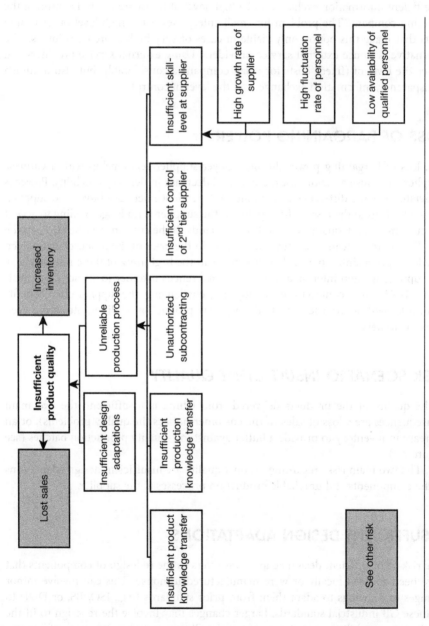

Figure 3.3 Risk scenario: insufficient quality.

expensive in production, but screw joints are more labor intensive in assembly. Due to the lower labor costs, screw joints might be the better decision for a Chinese supplier. If the necessary design adaptations are not made, this might result in the misinterpretation of the drawings by the Chinese supplier, resulting in low quality and high scrap rates. The same is true if the quality requirements set by the sourcing company do not reflect the technological or know-how level of the supplier, or the negotiated price level.

INSUFFICIENT SKILL LEVEL AT SUPPLIER

It is a major risk if the level of skill of the operators and the management team at the supplier are not sufficient. If the supplier is experiencing a high growth rate, new employees must be integrated into the company and quickly trained to do their jobs. New hiring not only binds capacities of the already trained operators and management, but also increases the amount of people with only a basic level of experience. The demand for qualified personnel is high, and there are several challenges in attracting these people.

The main problem that HR professionals identify is a fundamental lack of suitable candidates, namely, a severe lack of qualified personnel on the market. Once a candidate has been identified, the three main challenges are the competition with high profile companies (usually large international brands), the inability to pay a competitive salary, and a lack of opportunities for the candidate to advance their career in the future.

Also, the fluctuation rate of personnel is usually a lot higher in China than in European companies, and a turnover of 20 to 30 percent is not uncommon. Most affected are employees that have been employed for 1–2 years at the supplier—they account for 43 percent of the total turnover. Interesting to note is that long-term employees who have stayed with a company for more than 5 years, are highly unlikely to change their employer.

RISK SCENARIO *DAMAGE TO REPUTATION*

Damage to a company's reputation leads to a decrease in sales when customers are lost, and it can lead to a large amount of unexpected work to rectify the problem and the public perception of a potentially damaging incident.

Nonconformance to regulations, insufficient communication management in the aftermath of non-conformance, the *Made in China* label on a company's products being exploited by the competition, and ethical concerns of the public might become a problem (see Figure 3.4).

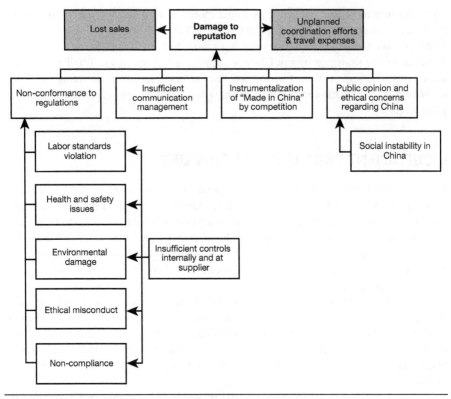

Figure 3.4 Risk scenario: damage to reputation.

NONCONFORMANCE TO REGULATIONS AND INSUFFICIENT COMMUNICATION MANAGEMENT

The most severe reputation risks that arise from incidents in China are due to insufficient internal controls and insufficient controls at the supplier, combined with an insufficient management of an incident and its communication in the aftermath. In addition to the indirect costs via lost sales and increased coordination efforts, other high costs and legal consequences might occur as a direct result of nonconformance to regulations.

The violation of labor standards addresses issues such as forced labor, child labor, discrimination in the workplace, working hours, minimum wages, and overtime compensation. Health and safety issues may arise from problems with emergency management, occupational injuries and illness, machine safeguarding and workplace safety, the safety management system, or the sanitary infrastructure. Environmental damage may arise from the emissions of waste water, solid waste, and air emissions, or problems in the areas of safeguarding of chemicals and hazardous materials, environmental management system failures, obtaining environmental permits, and compliance with the reporting requirements. Unethical behavior of the supplier or company representatives refers, for example, to problems with corruption, bribery, fair business practices, protection of intellectual property, or the disclosure of other confidential information.

ENVIRONMENTAL DAMAGE

The environmental situation in China has deteriorated dramatically with the country's economic development. In parallel, the awareness of ecological problems and sensitivity toward them is rising in the Chinese population. A recent example includes the banning of free plastic shopping bags from supermarkets, which was apparently fully supported by the affected consumers.

In 1972, China's basic position during the first U.N. Environmental Conference was that we will not stop eating because we are afraid to choke, and we will not refrain from developing our industry because we are afraid to pollute the environment. In 2005, after the successful industrialization of the coastal areas, the Chinese Secretary for the Environment, Pan Yue, said in an interview:

> "Of course I am pleased with the success of China's economy. But at the same time I am worried. [...] Acid rain is falling on one third of the Chinese territory; half of the water in our seven largest rivers is completely useless, while one fourth of our citizens do not have access to clean drinking water. One third of the urban population is breathing polluted air, and less than 20 percent of the trash in cities is treated and processed in an environmentally sustainable manner. Finally, five of the ten most polluted cities worldwide are in China."

China is not only affected by pollution, but also strongly by the risks of global warming, and since it became one of the main CO_2 producers in the world, climate protection is one of the most important environmental goals in China. The rising environmental consciousness in China poses a risk if the environment is endangered in the production process as such, or through accidents. On the other hand, it also offers a chance to generate a positive image and positive publicity, both in China and in the home markets, if environmentally sound production practices are required from the supplier.

SOCIAL UNREST

The question of potential social unrest in China remains one of the largest single risks, not only regarding the delivery reliability of Chinese suppliers, but also regarding peace and stability in Asia. Social unrest would also affect public perception of

China and, by association, potentially damage a company's reputation. According to the Chinese Ministry of Public Security, the number of incidents of social unrest increased by a factor of 10 between the years 1993 and 2005.

Several factors contribute to social tension and each of them has to be closely monitored in order to be aware of the current situation and risk exposure. Income inequality might be one trigger for social instability and unrest. The Gini coefficient is a measure that describes the inequality of the distribution of income. The higher the coefficient, the greater is the income inequality. Between 1993 and 2005, it has increased from 0.42 to 0.47. This can largely be attributed to the faster development of the coastal regions than the western provinces in China. Related to the question of income are concerns regarding high inflation rates of food and their impact on social stability.

The Chinese social system is also under immense pressure. The large number of migrant workers in the industrialized coastal areas remains a concern and these workers often lack proper payment, medical care, and social insurance. Also, due to the government's one child policy, the number of working people in China will probably peak within the next 10 years, confronting China with a massive problem of an ageing society and leaving large holes in Chinese social security systems. The growing Chinese middle class is also increasingly sensitive regarding environmental problems (discussed previously), as are the larger numbers of farmers if their livelihood is threatened. The last possible contributing factor to social unrest is the tension between some of the 56 different ethnic groups living in China. The tensions regarding Tibet feature prominently in the press; other critical issues include the tensions in Xinjiang with the Muslim Uyghur minority, and most prominently, the unresolved issues surrounding the status of Taiwan.

SUMMARY AND STARTING POINTS FOR MITIGATION MEASURES

This chapter outlined the supply chain risk management process and especially the supply chain risks that three Swiss small- and mid-sized enterprises faced when they made the decision to source from China. Their motivation was to take advantage of the low cost structure in China, gain access to a growing market, or to simply have a source for a component from where it is available in the global market. The risk management process itself consisted of the three phases of risk identification, risk assessment, and risk mitigation. The two most important tools used to identify and understand supply chain risks were: the risk matrix, where risk causes are mapped against risk effects and risk scenarios, where single risks were put into a cause-and-effect relationship to understand the dynamic aspect of supply chain risks.

Four risk scenarios were examined, addressing the main risks of: the total cost being too high, insufficient delivery reliability, insufficient quality, and damage to the company's reputation.

What were the most important risk mitigation measures for the three Swiss enterprises? While the risk exposure of the companies might be similar, the importance of a risk differs from company to company, as do the mitigation measures. Both are often strongly dependent on each company's product portfolio, strategic position within the industry, markets that are served, cash reserves, management culture, the knowledge and experience of its employees, and many other factors. However, some general themes emerged from the cases:

- Identifying and assessing the risks was often a great benefit and mitigation measure in itself. By creating transparency, many risks were addressed in the day-to-day management of their supply chains.
- Transparency regarding possible supply chain risks also allowed for strategic decision making: What is the biggest loss or longest interruption we might face? What loss or interruption are we willing to expose ourselves to? Can we retain backup capacities *at home* in case we decide to come back?
- Intellectual property rights protection attracted significant attention. This risk was usually addressed by high-level decisions on what to source from China. Additional good *housekeeping* practices on IT and organizational security were introduced, as well as taking full advantage of legal options available in China, such as prosecution of IP infringements and registration of patents in China.
- Another risk that was taken seriously and, therefore, considered in detail to develop risk mitigation measures was the management of bargaining power in buyer-supplier relationships, as well as ensuring the adherence to social and ethical standards in the supply chain.

This case example of sourcing from China demonstrates that entrepreneurial decisions are not based on choices with the least amount of risk, but on choices where risk and return are in balance. Sourcing from China will always involve more severe risks than sourcing locally, but the expected returns are also higher. It is important that risk management activities are carried out with the focus of adding value to the company's activities by enabling better entrepreneurial decisions.

NOTES

This chapter is based on the PhD thesis of Oehmen, J. 2009. Managing supply chain risks—The example of successful sourcing from China. Diss. ETH No. 18536, Eidgenossische Technische Hochschule (ETH) Zurich.

Parts of this chapter were published in Oehmen, J., A. Ziegenbein, R. Alard, and P. Schönsleben. June 2009. System-oriented Supply Chain Risk Management. *Production Planning & Control* 20:343–61.

4

TOO BIG FOR THE INDIVIDUAL FIRM: CREATING COOPERATIVE NETWORKS TO SOLVE DIFFICULT SUPPLY CHAIN RISK CHALLENGES

Michael E. Smith

Readers are surely aware that supply chain management (SCM) represents a relatively new approach to orchestrating the creation of customer value. Within supply chain management, supply chain risk management (SCRM) is a recent addition to the arsenal of the supply management professional. The relative youth of attempts at such risk management and its study has implications for how we approach this important work. In this chapter, we will explore how the unfolding development of SCRM impacts how we think about supply chain risk and its management, particularly with respect to risk that is beyond the immediate control of the purchasing (or focal) firm or that occurs outside the dyadic relationship between the focal firm and individual suppliers. Further, we will examine a group of firms that have come together in a cooperative approach to dealing with elements of risk beyond the control of the individual firms. This case should provide readers with steps that they can take to develop similar opportunities to recognize and mitigate supply chain risk sources that can have substantial impact on performance.

LIMITATIONS OF CURRENT APPROACHES TO SCRM

A rich literature in perception and decision making suggests that we tend to overestimate the extent to which we have control over circumstances and that we also tend to focus our attention on aspects of the environment over which we believe that we have influence. For supply chain risk management, these biases impact our having a tendency to focus on risk at the level of our suppliers, so that we attend to elements of risk associated with the behavior of a specific supplier, i.e., we tend to examine the supplier and not the environment that surrounds the relationship with the supplier. This bias results in far more attention to the performance of suppliers than to the linkages that we have to our suppliers. Supplier behavior may be more amenable to our efforts at control than are the diffuse elements of the network that serves to support the movement of materials and information between the organizations. It is much easier for us to comprehend and direct a specific relationship than to address the vagaries of the connections in the complex webs that serve to bring value to those relationships in today's supply chains.

Additionally, we tend to address our concerns as if they were specific to a given supplier instead of being general. We may display this tendency when we add suppliers in response to concern about supplier performance. This response will work if the performance deficit is unique to a given supplier, but prove ineffective if the deficit is the result of risk factors that are common to all suppliers for a given commodity. An example of such shared risk is present for certain metals or metal components where disruptions may result not from the behavior of any given Tier 1 supplier, but may instead result from the conditions under which raw ore for some constituent of the alloy is obtained.

In such a case, the risk would appear with all suppliers for the commodity instead of being localized to a single supplier, and the addition of suppliers to the supply base would do little to ameliorate exposure to this risk. In this form, the risk to be addressed is present in the industry, i.e., industry risk, and is beyond the control of individual firms. This lack of control at the level of the individual firm can extend beyond industries, to have an impact on the entire supply base of our focal firm. Such global impact can result from disruption at the level of critical infrastructure, such as the severing of access to communications networks or disruptions in transportation networks. Currently, there is little guidance for managers regarding dealing with risk beyond the level of the individual supplier.

SCRM AS A DEVELOPING ENDEAVOR

Most of the emphasis in SCRM has been placed on aspects of risk where the individual firm can impact the level and probability of risk exposure. For example, we focus on selecting better suppliers, or on spreading the risk by increasing the number of suppliers. In a slightly more mature approach, we might work to develop our suppliers and focus on ensuring their continued commitment to the relationship with our firm.

However, as our endeavors mature, we encounter situations where the level and probability of risk exposure may well be beyond the immediate control of the individual firm. Further, such risk may also not be effectively managed by dealing with dyadic relationships between the firm and a given supplier. Instead, greater sophistication in SCRM will require that we move beyond risk experienced at the individual level (which we can call *independent risk*) to risk that is shared among many firms (which we can call *shared risk* or *common risk*). Generally, actions taken at the level of individual firms or by pairs of firms (the dyadic relationships that supply management professionals have become used to managing) will not provide much value in addressing this type of risk.

The time has come for us to realize that healthy progress in the development of SCRM depends on our moving beyond limitations inherent in our approaches. The future of SCRM will require us to learn to apply cooperative social action among groups of firms to manage and influence risk experienced at general levels affecting industries, regions, nations, and even the global business.

FREIGHT TRANSPORTATION AS A SOURCE OF SHARED RISK

An example of risk that is beyond reasonable control by individual firms or even pairs of firms can be seen as arising out of problems in our transportation networks. A number of factors contribute to increasing variability in the performance of freight transportation networks, and this variation has served to increase the risk of poor performance and disruptions for buying firms. However, many of the sources of variation are systemic and beyond the control of individual firms. Such sources of risk include increasing transportation costs due to volatility of fuel costs, rapid shifts in the amount and direction of shipping demand, inadequacy of shipping capacity, capacity constraints, and failing transportation infrastructure. Buddress and Smith (2010) have suggested that the compounding of these factors present shippers with an impending perfect storm in logistics that may have profound impact on supply chain performance in the future. Further, while the recent global recession has provided a level of relief to some of the challenges that shippers have faced, efforts by transportation companies to adjust to their economic challenges have meant that transportation capacity remains in short supply and may be further constrained as growth emerges in the recovering economy.

Taken together, the various forms of supply risk have greatly increased both the probability that firms will experience negative impact on their operations because of events with their roots in transportation networks, and the level of potential damage has dramatically increased. At a time when many firms are operating with low levels of inventory, the arrival of shipments at their destinations is subject to incredible amounts of variation. Forecasting of pricing and performance in transportation represents a substantial risk to firms that are, in many cases, already stressed by difficult economic conditions. To further complicate matters, it is the general case that addressing the factors contributing to transportation-based risk requires the aggregated action of a number of parties involving multiple organizations, and often on a level that crosses political boundaries. This calls for a level of cooperation that is often novel in how firms think about approaching problems.

It is challenging for a firm to find means to participate in the kind of cooperative action that is necessary to reduce the uncertainty, and hence risk, that is present in our transportation networks today. Even such activity as lobbying the government for the improvement of regional transportation infrastructure, such as improved regional highways, is generally rendered more effective by the banding together of business interests. Beyond advocacy for better infrastructure, cooperation among businesses also has the potential to improve leverage with transportation firms and drive more efficient utilization of freight transportation assets. The author's research suggests that while cooperation would seem to be an obvious approach to addressing supply chain risk that is beyond the control of a buying firm or its suppliers, it is difficult for most businesses to orchestrate such concerted efforts. The next section will describe how the Chamber of Commerce of Asheville, NC has worked with major manufacturers in the region to develop a transportation alliance.

THE VALUE OF COOPERATIVE EFFORTS

The Western North Carolina Transportation Alliance represents a voluntary gathering of shipping interests on a regional basis. As the concept has taken hold, the Transportation Alliance has developed to include a number of smaller organizations, including service firms, and has grown to include membership and involvement of firms in multiple states. While the Alliance is relatively new, it mirrors similar efforts in other areas, and shows initial success in reducing risk for member firms.

For example, one member business that is involved in light manufacturing, packaging, and distribution risked losing the flexibility associated with the services provided by their less-than-truckload (LTL) freight provider, and joined the Transportation Alliance as a way to address this risk. As fuel prices increased and the economy slowed, this business, like many in the U.S., risked the loss of this service as smaller independent trucking firms reacted to the changing industry conditions. In particular, business models based upon the utilization of similar trucking services were faced with potential for price increases, and even potential complete loss of the service. (According to industry data, in 2008 alone, 3,065 trucking firms with five or more trucks went out of business, and a considerable number of owner/operators left the industry.)

The Alliance's members recognized that some of this risk could be addressed by leveraging cooperative relationships with other businesses in the region. Realization of available capacity for both inbound and outbound shipments reduced risk exposure for this business, and helped to ensure that they could preserve a substantial portion of the flexibility that they had enjoyed through utilization of independent owners, and do so in a cost-competitive manner.

Such cooperative efforts potentially address risk associated with cost, availability, and performance in freight transportation. Essentially, better utilization of freight assets allows regional businesses to overcome and mitigate many of the uncertainties resulting from the confluence of major risk sources in our transportation networks. The greatest value of such activity among businesses is that it can be accomplished without major capital investments or the need to wait for government action (as is required for meaningful investments in transportation infrastructure).

DEVELOPING COOPERATIVE EFFORTS

The Western North Carolina Transportation Alliance started as a college project. In order to complete the requirements for a college degree, John Franklin, who is a key account manager for Volvo Logistics North America, needed to complete a project related to the company that he worked for, and the project had to also provide benefit to the community in which the business was located. Franklin took the project as an opportunity to address issues associated with shipping containers that were only transported full in one direction. He realized that better utilization of transportation assets could reduce costs by ensuring utilization for both incoming and outbound freight, and he realized that if shippers cooperated, they could coordinate shipments.

In addition to the utilization issue, Franklin wanted to work toward more predictable freight transportation for area manufacturers. His experience suggested that a substantial portion of logistics costs could be reduced if planning could be extended to a 5- to 7-year window, but such planning efforts would require a level of predictability that is not generally available to individual firms.

Volvo is a member of the Asheville Area Chamber of Commerce, so Franklin presented Ray Denny, Vice President for Economic Development of the Chamber, and Clark Duncan, newly hired as Director of Business and Industry Services, with a concept that many transportation challenges could be improved if local firms would only talk together and commit to sharing information. A critical element of the concept was the belief that a substantial portion of the transportation challenges faced by individual firms could be made much better by exchanging knowledge and data relating to transportation needs and plans. The key challenge was to build infrastructure that could accommodate such cooperative efforts. This led to the formation of the Western North Carolina Transportation Alliance (WNCTA), with an inaugural meeting early in 2008.

The purpose of the WNCTA was identified as seeking practical solutions for improved production and distribution processes, greater efficiency and cost effectiveness, and improved highway safety while reducing emissions. The approach used to accomplish these ends has been to develop a shared understanding of the business and logistics needs of the members. Along with the exchange of information between manufacturing firms with large volumes of freight movement in the area, the WNCTA has also become a place for discussion of transportation needs in the area, including regional infrastructure issues, and a forum for presentations by experts in topics of interest to the members. Taken together, these areas of emphasis have led to an evolving understanding of how private-sector efforts can address real transportation needs without requiring large amounts of capital investment or the involvement of public agencies. At a time when it is often difficult to find resources to undertake large projects, it has proven beneficial for members to find less resource-intensive approaches to alleviating risk rooted in the challenges associated with the transportation networks necessary to supporting supply chain exchanges.

Since the initial meeting, it has become clear that the WNCTA has provided a forum that has been successful in promoting the desired exchanges between businesses, and firms have begun to cooperate to reduce deadheading of containers and trailers. Further, it has become clear that the membership can band together to enhance the ability to influence policy makers and legislators to address serious transportation needs within the region. While collaborative efforts have only recently begun to gain traction, membership in the WNCTA has recently shown growth, and the members noted advantages in reacting to the pressures associated with the recession and efforts at preparing to face transportation challenges that are likely to emerge with economic recovery, including severely taxed transportation capacity and price pressures.

Franklin notes that the involvement of the Chamber of Commerce was an important element in implementing an alliance that could promote cooperative efforts. While it may seem obvious that a company should link with other firms that are shipping large amounts of freight, making the connections can often be challenging. The Chamber helped Franklin locate and link to potential members. Often, staff at the Chamber obtained contact information for key managers, and even made the initial telephone calls. Duncan, with the Chamber, also facilitated organizing meetings, coordinated the logistics of the general membership meetings, provided administrative support, and provided critical resources including meeting space in a neutral setting. For most supply management professionals such assistance may represent the critical element if an approach such as the WNCTA is to get started.

With the formation of the Western North Carolina Transportation Alliance, the Chamber stepped into unique territory. According to the Senior Vice President for Engineering Services for North America's largest freight transporter, the Alliance represents a unique effort. Further, research has shown that economic development authorities like Chambers of Commerce in North America tend not to be proactive in supporting attempts at inter-firm cooperation. For example, an international study reported in 2003 that while inter-firm cooperation was a major thrust in economic development efforts in some countries, in the United States, such cooperation was rarely supported as part of economic development efforts by groups such as Chambers of Commerce (Beer, Haughton and Maude 2003).

Thus, although the involvement of the Chamber was seen by WNCTA members as critical to the formation and early success of the Alliance, such activity is not typical

of organizations that may be best positioned to help supply management professionals adopt this approach to dealing with vexing supply chain risk challenges. In fact,
a lack of understanding of supply chain management generally, and transportation
issues in particular, may serve to make it difficult for staff members of a Chamber
of Commerce or a similar organization to understand the importance of inter-firm
cooperation, and thus limit their initial interest in facilitating such interaction. This
suggests that supply management professionals interested in establishing collaborative
approaches to dealing with SCRM may face the need to institute a substantial education effort in order to gain the assistance necessary to obtain the required resources.

Supply management professionals should begin to educate staff members in
economic development organizations and business advocacy groups about the importance of supply chain management and SCRM. Among these groups, Chambers of
Commerce may represent a particularly important partner in seeking to establish
cooperative efforts to manage such large and pervasive sources of risk as those found
in our transportation networks. Chambers serve their membership and can operate
outside municipal or local footprints. This may be particularly important when seeking approaches to dealing with large issues, like transportation networks, that are not
contained within the boundaries of local jurisdictions.

SUMMARY

As SCRM becomes more mature as a business process, it is natural that we should
begin to recognize that many of our most important sources of risk are beyond the
immediate control of the focal firm, or even the focal firm in concert with individual
suppliers. Realization of the importance and difficulty of dealing with large and systemic areas of risk should prompt a search for new models for understanding and tack-
ling supply chain risk. These new models should include more cooperation between
firms facing similar challenges, and this cooperation will need to involve groups of
businesses across broader regions, i.e., crossing political and physical barriers as well
as spanning other boundaries that may limit the range of cooperative efforts.

As illustrated by the development of a transportation alliance to deal with risk
rooted in challenges associated with modern transportation networks, well-targeted
efforts by a supply management professional can bring about inter-firm cooperation
that has the potential to address the risk exposure of firms, even when the source of
risk is beyond the control of the individual firm. As in the case of the Transportation
Alliance, while cost reduction may often serve to spur interest in such efforts, the benefits of cooperative efforts can bring about results on many different levels, including
the ability to better influence public policy.

As in the case of the Transportation Alliance, the facilitation of a partner outside
of the business interests involved may help to bring about inter-firm cooperation.
However, to obtain awareness and interest from groups that could serve as good
facilitators, it will often require that supply management professionals take on an

educational role. Clearly, education of the staff at the Asheville Area Chamber of Commerce played an important role in their participation in establishing the WNCTA. Now that the Chamber has achieved better understanding of the importance of SCRM and related issues, the benefits may extend well beyond the immediate transportation-related cause. Beyond addressing particularly vexing concerns with supply chain risk, greater understanding may also serve to bring increased, beneficial attention to the importance of supply chain management in the success of firms and in economic performance generally.

While the WNCTA is a new organization that has only begun to show the nature and extent of benefits possible through inter-firm cooperation, participants in the group are clear in extolling the value of membership. This is an initiative that can be undertaken to resolve some of the really big problems that businesses face in many areas.

REFERENCES

Beer, A., G. Haughton, and A. Maude. 2003. *Developing Locally: An International Comparison of Local and Regional Economic Development.* Bristol, UK: The Policy Press.

Buddress, L., and M. E. Smith. 2010. Organizations facing a logistical conundrum. *Inside Supply Management* 21:22–25.

5

DEVELOPMENTS IN ORGANIZATIONAL PERFORMANCE THROUGH STRATEGIC SUPPLY CHAIN COLLABORATION

Simon A. Burtonshaw-Gunn and Malik G. Salameh

INTRODUCTION

As marketplaces are increasingly competitive and the rate of innovation continues to increase there is a need to manage growing complexity as companies widen their influence by looking at international supply chain management to gain a competitive advantage. While this is likely to cover the provision of goods or components, at the more strategic level the integration of an organization's people supported by the right corporate culture allows technology to capture and manage raw data and information at an unprecedented rate. Clearly, organizations have to recognize, respond to, and satisfy the requirements of their customers if they intend to stay in business and benefit from future growth through repeat business. In support of this corporate objective, supply chain management (SCM) has, for many companies, developed from the older function of purchasing to now embrace planning, implementing, and controlling all of the suppliers to the organization with a view to delivering a more integrated service to its customers. However, with a greater realization of the global economy a number of organizations are unable to compete by using solely their own resources and have to look for alternatives to gain a competitive advantage.

For many companies, both products and services have increased in their complexity and value, and as such, pursuing new business opportunities often involve accepting a greater level of risk. The inevitable consequence of such competitive pressures is to pursue high-risk business and winning opportunities by the formation of partnerships, especially when circumstances are surrounded by high levels of uncertainty. Examples of this are seen in the European aviation sector where a number of international partners design, develop, and manufacture major component assemblies for a complete aircraft with no one company, or indeed, one nation able to afford the development costs alone. For large organizations in particular, the attraction may be to form a strategic alliance or joint venture, providing organizational performance advantages to all parties through the development and realization of business synergy.

One form of strategic alliance, usually resulting in the formation of a new company, is a merger between two willing organizations that are usually developed from resource constraints among one or several of the cooperating entities. An example of this was the merger between Marconi Defense Systems and British Aerospace in 1999 with the formation of BAE Systems for the defense market. Typically, this type of alliance occurs when funding is needed to capitalize on a company's technological opportunity, or alliances are formed in order to reduce barriers to market entry; the latter is often synonymous with exploring new international markets. It should be noted that this type of alliance is formal and should only be considered when the parties concerned have a good working knowledge of each other, share a number of cultural synergies, and are prepared to give the new organization their full commitment, both financially and managerially.

Instead of forming a new special purpose company (SPC) or joint venture, an alternative approach is for organizations to develop their capabilities to be able to meet the requirements of current and future customers. Then, they can provide benefits from working closer within their respective supplier base.

This chapter uses a case study that identifies and reviews the potential risks and opportunities that the international company Blue Sky Aviation encountered in trying to enter the Chinese aviation supply chain market with a special focus on the acquisition and realization of airport prime contracts. While recent developments have encouraged Western companies to operate in China, at the time of this study the Chinese aviation sector was a difficult market to address because of a number of technical, financial, and social reasons, often resulting in multinational companies in various sectors having little success in terms of market penetration. Moreover, where this commitment had proved rewarding, it had required a long-term business strategy to gain a valued long-term return. Intrinsic to success in this example was the selection of the correct Chinese partners to provide necessary guidance and assistance, and helping to overcome bureaucratic and cultural hurdles. The case study discusses a series of high-level strategic options that were considered by Blue Sky Aviation in establishing a stronger presence in the Chinese aviation market through strategic collaboration.

Blue Sky Aviation's business vision was to develop stronger political, commercial, and industrial relations in China to support and best position itself to secure contracts in civil aviation and, in a longer timeframe, in defense sectors when European defense trading restrictions were removed. In the short term, as a preferred industrial partner, contracts would be confined to civil aviation or non-contentious defense equipment, with a medium term focus on a *commercialization* route for the funding of Chinese airports. The long-term strategy concentrated on positioning the company for the emergent opportunities that would arise once the Chinese market became available to Western defense companies.

The company had a number of existing contracts within the Chinese aviation market, which had previously afforded the company a certain level of market presence. However, the contracts had in some cases been to the detriment of the company's credibility and corporate profile. Indeed, the company had established a reputation for the manufacture of major aircraft components under license in China, but these contracts had failed to realize the business growth potential, value, or profitability expected. It should be noted that while this chapter reports on actual business considerations, the company name has been changed and some aspects have been omitted for reasons of confidentiality.

UNDERSTANDING THE INDIGENOUS AIRPORT MARKET AND OPERATIONAL ENVIRONMENT

For both economic and political reasons, air travel in China until thirty years ago was rare, with only one airline and both the airports and airspace being controlled by the military. As a result of *Opening Up* policies, an increasing part of the airspace had been gradually given over to civilian use or transferred to dual usage. The larger airports dominated in terms of passengers handled with the five largest airports by passengers believed to account for about half of all domestic passengers, and with international passengers also highly concentrated. Airport development was one of China's top priorities, and foreign direct investment often took the form of ownership of a particular service function such as ground handling or catering.

To assist Blue Sky Aviation's understanding, a detailed market analysis was undertaken of the commercial airports in China, identifying 254 airport projects, of which 143 were fully operational civilian airports, with the remainder encompassing dual purpose military and civil usage, purely military usage, or future proposed airport developments. Factors such as capacity constraints, passenger throughput, and demographic criteria had been considered when selecting target airports as supply chain partnership prospects. This research identified key differences between China and the UK in regards to an airport's status and how it functioned, as shown in Table 5.1.

Table 5.1 Market analysis of airports in China versus UK

Market finding . . .	Meaning that . . . .
An airport in China has a much higher status than in the UK and is held in much greater esteem.	In China, the airport is seen as the window of a city or the country.
An airport in China has much more control over its development than a UK airport.	In the UK, community and environmental pressure can delay or stop airport developments.
When an airport was developed in China, there was often no pressure to prove that it would be profitable.	An airport in China is often being built as a political symbol of local and national pride, not a market requirement.
Airport management structures are very different.	In China, every person working on the site is an employee of the airport and under tight management control.
Airports in China provide social services.	An airport often provides residential accommodations for employees, and operates schools, hospitals, cinemas, and pension systems on their behalf.
Civil aviation authorities in China have much more power than in the UK.	Authorities in China control air transport policy and run many institutions, including universities and research institutes.
Airports in China were facing fierce restructuring at the time of the study.	Consolidation into different airport groups—with an initiative to place airports in the hands of the local government.

A high level strategic analysis of the aviation sector in China using a SWOT (strengths, weaknesses, opportunities, and threats) format was undertaken and is presented in Table 5.2.

As a consequence of the market understanding, a set of corporate business objectives for securing significant business over a ten-year period was developed with the intention of growing the business in a low risk way through tactical market positioning opportunities. Penetrating this market at a prime contract level from the outset was considered to be high risk, and exceedingly onerous because of the time-scale for projects (often taking a number of years to win a contract in China) and the significant investment implications. By acting as a support organization, it was felt that this would prove far less restrictive in terms of barriers to market entry, also enabling Blue Sky Aviation to offer professional advice in the early planning stages of airport programs in the following areas:

- Formation of core prime contracting team
- Recruitment of key personnel and capabilities
- Supplier partnership agreements
- Management processes for prime contracting
- Risk management tools and protocols
- Life cycle management

Table 5.2 SWOT analysis of aviation sector in China

Strengths	Weaknesses
• Company name, credibility and global status	• Blue Sky's perception that airports are noncore business by internal stakeholders
• Proven core competencies in airport developments	• Unwillingness to fund any form of long-term business development activity
• Proven prime contract management capability gained through other international projects	• Ineffective market research, market analysis and customer analysis through in-country presence
• Company's funding capability	• Organization performance focused; therefore, financials need to show short-term return
• Risk management capability	• Understanding of economic regulation and macro environment including political, legal, social, cultural, technical and economic factors
• Large scale program/contract integration experience	• No large-scale successful regional experience
• Existing partnerships	• Credibility linked to other aviation projects
• Substantial expertise with JV's and strategic alliances	• Company could come under pressure to produce results because of the high cost of being in country, making it more difficult to slowly adapt to prevailing market conditions
• Balance sheet strength	• Joint ventures may be a suitable option in other parts of the Blue Sky's portfolio, even with a large equity stake in China; they can often be an uneasy marriage
• Blue Sky's capability to innovate and provide strategic and tactical solutions for technically complex high value projects in difficult markets	• Unreasonable demands from local suppliers and officials require trust and confidence in the Chinese partner's local expertise, to solve these problems with joint ventures in mind

Opportunities	Threats
• Leverage for other sales/services directly or indirectly through airport prime, such as radar, aircraft, equipment, and training	• Lack of high-level political support; considered essential to have the highest level relationships
• Build long-term strong relationships and regional presence for the company	• Lack of inclusion in the five year planning horizon may constrain business and market opportunities, unless business opportunity under consideration can be shown to be critical in the five-year development plan timeframe

Continues

Table 5.2 (*Continued*)

Opportunities	Threats
• Planned economy and five-year plan provides opportunities, both within and external, to the plan	• Intellectual property infringements have proved taxing for all foreign investment organizations, especially under Chinese law and in the maintenance of harmonious JV relationships
• Scale of deliverables and associated risks provide some good barriers to entry	• Business capture costs much higher than human capital costs
• Chinese partner is key enabler to success; Blue Sky has strength to leverage high level UK Government support	• Equity stake may have to be hard cash and not partially provided through the value of human capital and knowledge (more prominent in less developed provinces)
• CAAC (Civil Aviation Authority of China) injecting more commercialization into airport systems using private finance; to include hotels, rail links, ground handling, concessions, cargo terminals and maintenance facilities (no equity limit applies to these airport services)	• Lack of visibility of PRC government's latent needs, wants and desires could restrict the success rate of securing new business
• Merger and consolidation amongst the top and 2nd & 3rd tier airlines respectively, due to safety or financial health reasons may provide a source for a JV partner (CAAC rationalizing member airlines into three main groups)	• Targeting airport developments outside of key metropolitan and favored tourist areas may prove high risk as these have historically accounted for 95% of traffic volume
	• Acting in accordance with indigenous supply chain capabilities may prove a hindrance because of the maturity of the systems utilized
• Much needed expertise in airport operations (including safety) not just commercialization consultancy could provide a tactical entry point to the Chinese market	• Gradual abolition of special privileges and incentives to foreign investors in an attempt to level the playing field between foreign and domestic companies
• Debt-for-equity swaps may provide solutions to possible partnership issues for indebted enterprises that have good prospects and wide networks (may require management influence from investor to be successful)	• Historical legacies such as the *cradle-to-grave* guarantees of employment will have an impact on long-term business partnerships and the level of protectionism (very prominent in Civil Aviation industry—a privileged status)
• Chinese subsidiary of a foreign investment organization will allow it to be listed on the Chinese stock exchange	• Chinese dependency on political decision making

BUSINESS ANALYSIS

On the basis of market research, a partnering value proposition was developed, covering the areas of the prime contracting arena, which Blue Sky Aviation believed it had both the credibility and core capabilities to participate in, to develop existing and new airports in China. This high-level prime contracting approach offered:

- Airport facilities management
- Airport business opportunities
- Airport business community
- Private Finance Initiative (PFI), Build Operate Transfer (BOT), and Concessions
- Interface between contractors and government independently
- Interface and risk sharing by managing the prime contract
- Contingency planning and business continuity
- Integrated risk management

In examining the business strategy options, a total of 16 major factors were considered, as shown in Table 5.3.

In order to satisfy internal stakeholders and governance, it was necessary for the company to institute a partnered support performance management system against identified key performance indicators (KPIs), which were shared and specific to the regional business development aspirations of supply chain partners. These included the following:

- Financial performance
- Timeframe adherence
- Risk management
- Delivery of offset obligations
- Resource utilization and allocation

This case study provides an account of the considerations for market development from a strategic management perspective, and in particular, highlights that even when a partnership approach is an attractive approach, it is not without risk. Indeed, the business strategy options presented in Table 5.3 have particular risks associated with them, and are presented using the traditional PESTLE (political, economic, social, technological, legal and environmental) approach:

Political

- Vulnerability of Blue Sky Aviation's Chinese projects because of the UK government's foreign policy guideline changes for doing business with Chinese government agencies due to environmental or geo-political factors.
- Currently, airports generally obtain more financial support than local industries as they are funded from the Chinese Central Government. Any change in this funding would undermine their business attractiveness.

Table 5.3 Business strategy options

Strategic Option	Details
Airline Partner option	Partner with airline/airline group who could then purchase an airport. Large scale program/life-cycle management contract experience essential in absorbing high business capture costs and as a financial shield against any gradual abolition of special privileges and incentives to foreign investors.
Airport Partner option	Partner with an airport that already had an equity stake in another airport. Blue Sky Aviation's funding capability gave it access to projects where the scale of deliverables and associated risks provide some barriers to entry for the competition.
Airport Consortium option	Partner with an airport which was likely to be taken over by an airport consortium. For the first three strategies existing successful partnerships throughout Blue Sky Aviation's global network would help build necessary, strong, long-term relationships and corporate presence.
Airport Function option	Investing in an airport function with existing evidence of foreign ownership (e.g., ground handling). Blue Sky Aviation's risk management capability would have assisted in appraising such investments by means of a cost/benefit analysis; testing other areas of the supply chain as sources of opportunity.
Indebted organization option	Invest in an indebted organization—exchanging debt for equity to gain greater market presence. Blue Sky Aviation's substantial expertise of joint ventures and strategic alliances would have assisted with issues such as intellectual property rights infringements. Their proven innovative and tactical solutions would help mitigate cultural and operational issues such as cradle-to-grave employment.
Dangerous goods considerations	Set up a centralized security agency for the issuance of certificates for the transportation of dangerous goods, thus providing for a need which would gain the company high level Chinese Government approval.
Civil Aviation University	Investment in the Civil Aviation University, leveraging Blue Sky Aviation's name, credibility, and global status, making it a good partner organization for the Civil Aviation University and helping to establish a school for airport management training.
Training organization	Creation of a new business in parallel or partnership with an aircraft training organization. Blue Sky Aviation's global network of existing successful partnerships and strategic alliances, such as their share in an international aircraft manufacturing program, would assist in any such joint training venture.
Wider investments	Investing wherever opportunities exist to include other aviation related areas or industries through pilot/pathfinder projects. Blue Sky Aviation's global presence and diversity of product portfolio and service provision profile would enable it to capitalize on adjacent market opportunities outside of civil aviation to gain market presence and a greater regional operating footprint.

International airport group partner	Combine Blue Sky Aviation's capabilities in a joint venture with a recognized international airport group. This would be an airport group that had a demonstrable track record of international airport projects and, thus, could provide them with the necessary credibility, and skills for market entry, in conjunction with the right Chinese partner.
Consultancy advice	Support role offering strategic consultancy advice. This would give visibility and a proliferation of knowledge of the company's capabilities and would provide a foundation from which to build up the scale and scope of future activities within the Chinese aviation market, or by partnering a consultancy that has existing presence in China.
Manufacturing	Utilizing Blue Sky Aviation's wing manufacturing facility that operated under license in China as a means to access key Chinese suppliers in such areas as construction, logistics and respective technologies—important in mitigating unreasonable demands from the indigenous supply chain.
Investing in a Chinese partner	Identify a Chinese partner who may need greater balance sheet strength in order to grow holistically. Blue Sky Aviation could provide the required financial strength to expedite such growth in return for market access.
Third party revenue	This would involve establishing a new business operation in China with an appropriate Chinese partner capable of marketing and exporting its capabilities in a third party revenue generation capacity. Furthermore, this would act as a center for excellence in the South East Asian aviation market.
Pilot schemes	Pilot Blue Sky Aviation's airport prime contracting capability on major internal programs, while undertaking various strategic positioning activities, such as pure consultancy, until such time as market conditions offer the best business winning opportunities.
International consortiums	Blue Sky Aviation could provide a bridge for companies keen to invest in China that are otherwise prevented from doing so due to poor political relations between the two countries. This may mean the investment represents a lower financial risk for Blue Sky Aviation.

- The lengthy nature of the business capture cycle for the Chinese market means that it is reliant on medium-to-long-term market forecasts that may be inaccurate and also beyond Blue Sky Aviation's strategic planning horizons.
- Conflict of interests with the partnering organization as to where to invest and the nature of the investment.
- Restructuring of product or service offerings may act as a catalyst in shifting focus of core business to defense rather than commercial aerospace business streams.

Economic

- Underestimating the level of investment required due to weak due diligence because of lack of resources or time available prior to collaboration
- Inability to leverage the requisite level of capital necessary for the upfront investment costs involved at the infancy of an airport prime contract, either internally or from financial markets
- Impact of financial difficulties for the indigenous partnering organization because of domestic market conditions or governmental policy
- Downturn in business in other parts of Blue Sky Aviation portfolio leading to a withdrawal of equity investments and business development activities in the Chinese domestic market
- Blue Sky Aviation's main board would withdraw corporate funding due to corporate performance concerns, partnership restrictions, or lack of investor confidence
- Procurement and manufacture of assets required to deliver an airport prime contract may be negatively impacted by exchange rate fluctuations
- Insufficient contingency provision, risk allowance, and profitability exist within this new business due to transparency concerns in commercial pricing process

Social

- Resistance to change resulting from indigenous airport management having too strong of a hold over their employees through provision of residential accommodation for employees, and often operating schools, hospitals, cinemas, and pension systems on their behalf
- The acquisition of an airport prime contract may necessitate additional investments in order to gain approval—including airport employee housing and schooling
- The extent of Blue Sky Aviation's risk exposure with regard to asset management is predicated on the fact that an airport is a business with high fixed costs, which could undermine achieving the required return

Technology

- Offset may prove to be a critical and decisive factor in securing an airport prime contract award. However, inability to discharge such obligations may result in the cancellation of further downstream opportunities, including defense contracts.

- Strong Blue Sky Aviation management control applied to *close a deal* too quickly at the expense of managing expectations and delivering on commitments.

Legal

- Program duration involved in long-term Chinese projects may mean that Blue Sky Aviation could be committed to a long-term financial commitment from which it cannot extricate itself if the wrong strategic alliance is chosen
- Prime contract organizational governance and life cycle management culture may prove too restrictive and risk averse to approve prime contracts
- The impacts of legislative, regulatory, and environmental changes in civil aviation internationally are likely to heavily influence programs with extended durations—especially airport prime contracts
- Ineffective negotiation and scoping of prerequisite terms and conditions means that the contract conditions binding Blue Sky Aviation to either a JV partner or any form of investment vehicle may disadvantage the company

Environmental

- Failure of joint venture relationship or SPC, resulting from unwanted international and regional bad press through poor media management
- Market predictions arising from feasibility studies may in some cases be improperly ratified, and as such, present an overly optimistic picture of future growth potential
- Blue Sky Aviation's civil aviation plans could be frustrated midterm if the group feels that further investment would not bring the company closer to its desired long-term objective of a defense contract

For many organizations, managing supply chain risk is focused on the negative impacts on a business—ranging from intangible elements, such as goodwill with customers and suppliers, reputational and brand damage, to more easily quantifiable consequences, such as financial losses and continuity of business operations/service delivery. However, it is hoped that the principal benefit of this case study has been to encourage the reader to perhaps adopt a broader perspective on supply chain risk assessment and analysis, not limiting it to a product of the business impact versus likelihood risk equation. As discussed, this case study can offer a perspective as a source of business opportunity, market entry, and—if economic, political, and social developments are effectively addressed—a potential source of competitive advantage, as shown in Figure 5.1.

The airport prime contracting arena, because of its complexity, strategic nature, and funding requirements, provides a good example to highlight the importance of

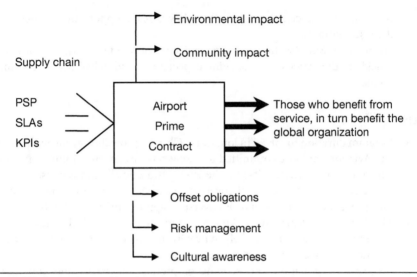

Figure 5.1 Strategic considerations and outputs.

reframing supply chain risk and mitigation and to consider other factors that can be influential in varying the risk profile of organizations and their management practices. If these factors are considered holistically, they can offer operational efficiencies without compromising service excellence and enabling greater market access, a clear case of *de facto* greater organizational performance.

However, as illustrated in Figure 5.1, for this approach to be effective it must be used to recognize and address latent customer needs and expectations, cultural pressures on and from suppliers, and the competitive drivers that exist within any supply chain by gaining a thorough understanding of the marketplace. Traditional strategic management tools such as SWOT and PESTLE analysis can be powerful in helping to develop this type of supply chain context and customer intelligence. Of equal importance is analyzing the business's existing core competences and how they can be integrated with the supply chain in a demonstrable way while satisfying environmental and community pressures—whether through delivery of other contractual obligations or culturally responsible business practices.

In the final analysis, developing greater organizational performance through strategic supply chain collaboration cannot be done by chance; it demands a conscious, proactive, and structured analysis to ensure that the planned supply chain partnerships can mutually benefit from complementary skills, competences, and resources to deliver enhanced performance—while respecting each party's fiduciary duties when sharing information that may be privileged or confidential, or in protecting their intellectual property. This SCM approach requires trust, strategic alignment, and willingness to share appropriate performance measures and indicators that can be analyzed on a regular basis and used to address poor performance. Such measurement further reinforces the benefits of collaboration and increases the partnerships' ability to respond to operational pressures and emergent risks.

CONCLUSIONS

This chapter has focused on how collaborative working and SCM can make a strategic contribution to organizational development and competitive advantage. From the discussion, it is apparent that incorporating SCM into the corporate life cycle presents a number of challenges and collaborative supply chain risks that need to be proactively addressed. The case study drew on business practice to present an account of the considerations for market development from a strategic management perspective, and in particular, highlighted that, even when a supply chain partnership approach is regarded as an attractive and appropriate entry vehicle, this strategic choice is not without risk.

With a general move by businesses to performance management hierarchies and careful monitoring of KPIs, allied to continuous improvement, it is suggested that supply chain partnering supports this approach, where performance can be witnessed in terms of quality, delivery, improved client satisfaction, and greater flexibility. In looking specifically at large-scale SCM programs aimed to bring about organizational performance improvements, the cultural and organizational changes will need to be strategically managed through an integrated change management approach. However, this too will need to be flexible enough to adapt to changing competitive environments. A phased change management approach is suggested that addresses the political, economic, social, technological, environmental, and legislative factors that will be changed both at local and at the partnership level. It is stressed that the actions required to implement a major change program are not an isolated activity, but should be regarded as being part of a new culture aimed to improve business performance for both the buyer and supplier organizations.

Where such supply chain partnering takes the form of an alliance over the long term, there will need to be a significant organizational investment (both intellectual and developmental) to help foster and encourage a culture capable of embracing significant change. Once such a partnership reaches a mature state, it is suggested that benchmarking can be used to generate innovative ideas and process improvements and lead to further increases in business performance. By seeking to benchmark the success of the organization's implementation against local and/or global organizations undergoing a similar scale of transformation, the opportunity may exist to modify jointly owned supply chain and risk management processes to take into account any such changes in the operating environment. Additionally, benchmarking comparisons will often show how much progress the partnership organization has made, where future efforts need to be targeted, and a means for checking the continued applicability and relevance of newly implemented processes and changes in accordance with the planned operational business objectives. The experience of many organizations has shown that strategic partnering—like large-scale cultural change—is unlikely to yield the full performance benefits in the short term, and that these benefits may only be realized over a longer timeframe, such as a five- to ten-year period, and only then with the right culture and management support.

6

PERFORMANCE-BASED LOGISTICS IN CONTINGENCY HEALTH CARE OPERATIONS

Jerry D. VanVactor

Health care is a specialized genre of logistics and supply chain management. Ensuring customer-demanded goods and services are available to support daily health care operations is a focal point for a wide variety of both clinical and nonclinical customers (Schneller and Smeltzer 2006). A gamut of reasons contributes to the specialization and idiosyncratic nature of health care-related supply chain management.

Many products related to health care involve short shelf lives, where if an item is not used by a certain time, the product is no longer any good or cannot be safely used in patient care. Examples of short shelf life products include blood, some pharmaceutical products, medicinal solutions, and laboratory reagents. Another reason for health care supply chain specialization involves the potential for stock-outs and supply chain shortages, creating significant negative consequences for end-users. Disruptions in a patient's treatment regimen, resulting from supply chain shortfalls, can lead to an exacerbation of injury or even death in some instances. Health care logistics professionals, like in other supply chains, are continually seeking opportunities in attaining value chain enhancements such as collecting better data, improving visibility, reducing inventory requirements, and streamlining processes to create more efficiency in health care supply chain operations.

Logistics operations go far beyond the hospital storeroom and involve a wide range of responsibilities that tend to be somewhat confusing to many health care practitioners. Logistics and supply chain management are complex issues that yield inherent complexities along with the nature of the service provided, technical efficiency, and effectiveness. Managing large numbers of specific, specialized medical line items becomes a challenge due to operational tempo, dynamic health-related conditions, and the needs of a multifaceted customer base involved in various aspects of patient care. While many health care organizations do attempt to employ this type of supply chain management strategy, enhancing operations through a performance-based approach in a contingency theater of operations is the focus of this chapter.

A contingency theater of operations is defined by joint (more than one branch of service) military publications as involving a geographic location wherein an anticipated situation could involve military forces in response to natural and man-made disasters, terrorism, subversive activities, military operations by foreign powers, or other situations (U.S. Department of Defense 2006). Many of these elements are daily occurrences in Afghanistan today. As can be discerned, planning among such a disparate array of personnel provides some of the most prominent challenges for logisticians. Crisis events are extremely unpredictable and can occur when they are least expected.

Health care logistics management in contingency-based operations tends to be reactionary and based on erratic data rather than on deliberate, synchronized future demand forecasting. A contingency-based scenario involves any unexpected crisis event that creates a disruption in a supply chain, creates a significant threat to a population's safety and security, and can trigger an immediate requirement for an irregular amplified logistical response (Miman and Pohl 2008).

PERFORMANCE-BASED LOGISTICS EXPLAINED

Supply chain management, regardless of the industry, encompasses the planning and management of all activities involved in sourcing, producing a product, delivering, procuring, and returning of items into a supply chain. Effective supply chain management entails coordination and collaboration with multiple stakeholders, including multifaceted value chain partners that involve suppliers, intermediaries, third-party service providers, and downstream customers. In Afghanistan, this includes an array of joint (U.S. Army working with sister services), multinational (coalition) forces, and interaction among third party logistics agencies. As scenarios change and the operational environment continues to evolve, requirements may also change and evolve.

Performance-based logistics (PBL) management, a relatively new concept in health care supply chain management, is one method of employing risk management. The most appropriate and well-understood metric should relay PBL strategies to complement the understanding of both supply chain professionals and nonsupply personnel (Sols, Nowick, and Verma 2007). Strategies for implementation must be comprehensive, closely integrated, and require continual dialogue and synchronicity among multiple stakeholders.

PBL management strategies represent a capabilities-based approach to supply chain management and link resources to value chain activities. Through the employment of PBL tactics, supply chain managers are better enabled to assess the costs involved in effective supply chain management and more prepared to coach and train end-users when necessary. Performance-based approaches to supply chain management provide more flexibility for stakeholders to make necessary trade-offs that balance performance, time, and available resources, and allows stakeholders to be more creative and innovative in respective approaches to supply chain management practices. By inculcating PBL strategies and tactics, a transition occurs in supply chain management techniques that represents a change from telling various stakeholders what to do and how to do it, to telling them what needs to be achieved and relying on their institutional knowledge and experience to make the change happen.

A value chain perspective should be the lens through which a performance-based approach to supply chain management links various stakeholders—each agency affecting others along a continuum of logistical preparedness. An evaluation of the entire sequence from equipment or material manufacture to the end user, using effective value chain analysis, can create a supply chain that is more responsive to various customers' needs (Burns 2005). Through effective PBL management, the assumption is that organizations can develop strategic advantages through collaborative, strategic alliances with adjacent firms that can benefit from addressing problems through information sharing among trading partners (Burns 2005).

PBL management describes supply chain management as a complete package of services and support; an integrated, affordable, performance package designed to optimize readiness through long-term support arrangements. Within these arrangements are defined lines of authority and responsibility for the various stakeholders involved. PBL focuses on results; however, the focus is not strictly concerned with material resources. The material resources are only a portion of supply chain effectiveness. Effective supply chain management must take into account the coordination of all the different aspects of a value chain from the initial manufacture to supply, production, and distribution of products to the customer as quickly as possible. This must be done without losing the quality of a product or customer satisfaction, while continuing to keep costs low.

There are several goals related to employing a performance-based approach to contingency supply chain management practices. PBL represents a supply chain management approach to reducing costs related to noncore services. However, the emphasis in health care will be placed on core services. Core medical services are often defined as those processes or procedures that a qualified physician determines as required to assess, prevent, treat, rehabilitate, or alleviate a given health concern or problem. Professional experience, consensus, or scientific evidence that is available and related to a given condition often supports decision-making processes related to core services. While logistics management performs most effectively under the leadership of professionally trained managers, accurate customer demands and consensus aids in establishing greater efficiency. Metrics, related to supply chain performance, determines the success or failure of the value chain's practices or processes. Arguably, core services must work in concert with noncore services to enhance efficiency throughout a health care organization.

PBL strategies are becoming more common as associated concepts represent clear benefits for multiple, multifaceted stakeholders (Sols, Nowick, and Verma 2007). This is evident in a contingency-based environment such as in Afghanistan, where customers can range from a medic assigned to a maneuver unit to full-scale hospitals operating in support of other organizations. In between, there is a gamut of forward surgical elements, evacuation units, veterinary detachments, and preventive medicine detachments, to name a few. Each customer will produce a variety of requirements, and each will expect a supplier to provide real-time information about orders, the location of products as material moves between locales, and accurate in-transit visibility to permit continuity that is more effective in the care provided throughout an area of responsibility.

Some of the uniqueness involved in contingency-based logistics lies within the inherent uncertainty involved in the management of the supply lines of communication, the network of transportation modes and avenues available for the movement of supply, and the resulting impact on upstream and downstream supply and demand. In Afghanistan, specifically, the roads are haphazard, and moving supply from one locale to another by ground can prove problematic. One example was when a warehouse sent supplies to a remote location by ground convoy and the supplies never arrived at their destination until almost one month later. The cause for delay was related to inter-tribal conflicts and fighting occurring along the route upon which the convoy was moving. Once this situation was discovered, at around a two week delay, the order was reprocessed and sent via air transport so that the medical organization requesting the resupply could continue to operate in their respective area of responsibility. Had the customer communicated more effectively with the supplier, the warehouse could have identified an alternate shipping medium and expedited the order faster, amid unexpected delays.

Only by ensuring customer satisfaction will supply chain managers instill the trust necessary for end users to adequately rely on distribution resources. Building a degree of trust within nonsupply chain professionals can become a logistics manager's challenge. Collaborative supply chain practices create redundancy and overlapping knowledge bases that enhance opportunities for improvement and innovation. Employing management driven cross leveling of materials is one example of how PBL can influence health care supply chain operations.

Employing a PBL strategy can result in meeting customer demands much closer to the point of use and can minimize the order-ship time required for receiving critical supplies. The resultant data reflects faster ship times, less lead times, and higher customer satisfaction rates. For example, if one of the multiple supply nodes in Afghanistan could not fill an order, the regional distribution center in Qatar would then fill demand according to the availability of supply and could access worldwide distribution resources on the customer's behalf.

IMPORTANCE OF PERFORMANCE-BASED LOGISTICS

Supply and demand disequilibria often arise from unexpected surges in demand, resulting from situations that can create spikes in requirements. Such is the case in contingency-based operations as much as during routine, status quo supply chain operations, and perhaps more so in contingency-driven scenarios where the unexpected can become the routine. Effective business case analyses need to be developed to support smart decisions that provide optimized support to end-users (Devries 2004). For example, health care practitioners are prepared, in a combat scenario, for many types of situations involving U.S. and coalition incidents, but are sometimes surprised at the extent and magnitude of injuries produced by random acts of terror. If the event is a short-term, pinpoint response, the issue related to resupply may be the mere access to communications media to submit demands related to the event. If, however, the event progresses into a prolonged fight and troops are required to sustain a battle scenario, commanders may have to place priorities on other commodities such as food and ammunition instead of medical supplies, depending on the scenario.

Multiple stakeholders involved in health care supply chain management tend to misunderstand decision processes, competing priorities, political realities, and regulatory requirements. Many health care organizations have limited capacity and experience in forecasting contingency-related demands, procurement, and supply chain management practices (Levine, Pickett, Sekhri, and Yadav 2008). The shortfalls that result from factors such as inexperience, lack of foresight, apathy, and lack of regard for other extra-medical stakeholder requirements can create difficulties in making accurate predictions of demands and can be somewhat costly in forging the critical partnerships necessary to generate trust among stakeholders.

Collaborative Communication Strategy

According to Nachtmann and Pohl (2009), there is a tendency for health care provider organizations to not collaborate well with partners among other sectors of a supply chain and to rely on preferential items without evaluating the associated cost of acquiring them. This approach can lead to limited visibility for end-to-end performance measures by supply chain managers desirous of enhancing logistics operations.

Successful partnerships, characterized by improvements in cooperation, collaboration, and information sharing, potentially reduce overall total logistics costs and can lower organizational operating costs. A continual assessment, through the establishment of a performance-based approach, yields a complex trade-off regarding the benefits of effective supply chain operations; the benefits do not always come without a price. Embedding multistakeholder information sharing in a wider set of regulatory and governance media include relationship controlling, monitoring of dependence and reliance upon other stakeholders, and trust building mechanisms. Collaborations facilitate the sharing of tacit and explicit knowledge. Customer-supplier relationships play a significant role in developing organizational ability to respond to dynamic and unpredictable changes and these relationships are often a source of innovation enhanced by an open sharing of new ideas and information.

In one instance, supply chain personnel received a request from a doctor requiring several bottles of Zocor® (20 mg tablets). Zocor is a brand named drug used in treating hypercholesterolemia and reducing a patient's risk of death related to cardiovascular disease. When the warehouse personnel began processing the order, the cost of the drug was approximately $27,000 per 1000-tablet bottle. A search of supply catalogues and consultation with a pharmacist allowed supply personnel to determine a suitable substitution with a generic brand of the same drug (Simvastatin, 20 mg tablets) at a cost of approximately $38 per bottle. A collaborative conversation with the prescribing clinician permitted the supply chain personnel to save the U.S. government over $85,000 with one pharmaceutical request.

Cost savings do not always happen, and in many instances, the supply chain professionals are unsuccessful in convincing clinicians of the value of saving money by using alternative solutions. One such example is doctors prescribing Ambien CR®. This drug, a Schedule IV narcotic and controlled substance used in the short-term management of insomnia, costs approximately $90 for a 30-tablet bottle. A suitable substitution of Zolpidem tartrate (generic for Ambien) is available in 100-tablet bottles for approximately $3.50. Despite the findings, the clinicians preferred the name brand Ambien to the generic brand, despite differences in cost.

LOGISTICS FOOTPRINT

Regional health care planning can be a multicriteria decision-making problem in Afghanistan that comes with inherent risks related to the operational environment. Factors related to performance-based logistics management include criteria related to transportation, distribution, IM/IT, security, and national infrastructure. Another critical factor involves security throughout shipment. In Afghanistan, security involves multiple factors, from ensuring that loads were not overtly labeled to prevent piracy and pilferage to military intelligence summaries concerning hostile threats along a planned route. Closer to the distribution node, monitoring and evaluating benchmarking data becomes important and is dependent upon established organizational supply chain protocols. On the opposite end of the spectrum, end-user information related to customer identities, locations, and preferences has to be maintained and updated periodically to aid in the management of expectations; different customers invariably have different needs throughout the area of operations.

One simplistic resource planning strategy throughout Afghanistan involves placing supplies closer to potential customers when, and where, possible. While distance is a subjective concept, attempts are made, as applicable, to decrease the distances between the distributor and downstream customers. In a vein of risk mitigation, distance concerns the measurement of travel between a point of origin (supplier) and a point of destination (customer). As shown in Figure 6.1, the further a customer is from the source of supply, the more likely errors can occur. By simply allowing for a more efficient management of supply chains, many distribution shortfalls are preventable.

Distances may not be the only factor in measuring the tenability of ground transportation when managing supply chains in a contingency theater. Road networks, such as ones seen in some rural parts of the United States, do not exist in Afghanistan. Many times, trucks traverse the country on roads that are unmarked, laden with antipersonnel and tank mines, and unexploded ordnance; the roads can easily be destroyed by wind, rain, or animal and human foot traffic, and sometimes lead nowhere. As indicated earlier, ground fighting and battle space is an ever-present reality where tribal discontent and terrorism is an everyday occurrence. Planning considerations related to the movement of material from one location to another should include these types of scenarios.

Inventory

Inventory seems to be one of the first variables looked at by nonsupply professionals and could be considered one of the most prudent means of mitigating supply chain risks. Many customers and supply managers feel that safety stock and pre-configured loads are a means to prevent shortages and stock-outs. In fact, a cyclical, routine aggregate study of customer order histories and organic demands helped in risk mitigation more than excessive stock maintained on hand at given locations. While assembling preconfigured loads (push packs) that the manager has seemingly prepared for contingencies, the excess inventory that is now tied to those loads becomes a risk if the loads are not needed and the items inside the packs remain unused. Especially within health care operations, if the material has potency and dated items, the chance increases that inventory will be lost due to nonuse.

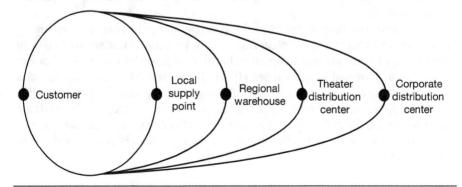

Figure 6.1 Supply line affects.

Capacity

Warehouses are not mobile; storage locations represented static, immovable objects throughout an area of operations. Warehouses tend to have limited means for expansion. Seldom is extra space set aside for contingency storage within the health care organizations for the enhancement of operations or the mitigation of surge requirements.

By developing strategies incorporating redundancy into existing supply lines the capacity of the organizational supply lines increases and more robust capabilities for operational support for medical organizations is available throughout the country. One location, somewhat central in the theater, remains the primary hub for logistics operations. Several other smaller sites can serve as adjuncts for warehousing and distribution resources.

At each of the respective locations, medical organizations operating in defined geographic regions throughout the country identify critical items and supply nodes closest to the area of concern to begin stocking critical items. Those identified critical items then become the catalyst for establishing stock levels in each of the warehouses related to customer demands. Once item identification is complete, coordinated and collaborative efforts between the theater distribution center in Qatar and the resident medical headquarters seek alternate means of shipping to ensure a continuance of efficient flow of materiel into the theater of operations. By employing third-party logistics (TPL) agencies, arrangement of direct shipments for many of the respective locations reduces order-ship times drastically. Each of the separate locations, where supply is needed and managed at a user level, reduces the need for excess safety stock and permits a more effective operational response to customers.

Time

Time is a critical component in health care supply chain operations. Allowing more time for decision making, taking action in crises, and order production and communication are each means for mitigating risk. Especially when trauma and resuscitative care are involved, time can be availed upstream to mitigate rapidly-changing demands at end-user levels.

Criteria for deciding where to establish supply nodes involves the availability of airfields and transportation platforms at each proposed location. By buffering with time, customers are able to optimize health care provisions with added capacity and to turn around supplies more efficiently. By permitting separate agencies more opportunity to take appropriate countermeasures against delays in shipping, or when supplies were not received in a timely manner, more accurate demands are forecasted and communicated to suppliers more effectively. Suppliers can react in a timelier manner with more effectiveness by having necessary resources closer to the points of need.

OPERATIONAL AVAILABILITY

What About Risk?

Military supply chain operations routinely encounter operational risk. A definition of risk in interservice planning literature relates a probability and severity of loss linked to the mitigation of associated hazards. By continually assessing and mitigating risk, leaders are able to reduce the impact of operations on personnel and mission readiness throughout an area of interest. The degree of operational risk is not always commensurate with the nature of military operations; each operation and mission carries with it varying degrees and types of risk.

Evaluating risk factors relates directly to an organization's ability to meet mission-related objectives. The magnitude of incidents and risk generated is often unpredictable; every scenario is different and each one presents new challenges for suppliers. Supply chain leaders maintain an inherent responsibility to continually assess risks and develop mitigation strategies. Continual risk assessment is employed to communicate to operational planners and staffs:

1. Where and when risk is acceptable during an operation
2. How much risk is acceptable
3. When, if operations have to be stopped due to unnecessary risk

An effective flow of material among supply nodes and end users is facilitated by continuing to consider multiple, multifaceted variables.

The development of risk mitigation and management occurs through an organization's ability to understand and manage economic, environmental, and social risks throughout a supply chain (Carter and Rogers 2008). Because risk is inherent in the supply of, and demand for for health care goods and materials, accurate forecasting can be difficult. Definitively, failure in a supply chain can happen when the provision of adequate supply does not meet customer demands. In an operational environment related to health care, however, the nature of transferable risk cannot be explicitly defined.

Risk associated with contingency supply chain management is the potential occurrence of an incident that could result in a supplier being unable to meet a customer's demands in a timely manner. Effective planning for contingencies can mitigate this type of risk and can lead, in turn, to supply chain resilience and agility related to practices and processes. Breakdowns in a supply chain represent a risk for multiple stakeholders.

A jointly developed risk mitigation plan is necessary in a contingency-based environment through adequate demand forecasts and replenishment plans as well as processes for monitoring and adjusting plans as requirements change. Risks associated with logistical support can include variables such as:

1. Untimely deliveries associated with bottlenecks in the value chain, transportation breakdowns, and so forth

2. Losses within the distribution chain, resulting from unpredictable short-falls up and downstream
3. Intra-organizational shortfalls such as loss of power, failed cold chain management solutions, and the non-availability of supply

In this type of environment, sustainment intertwines with the ongoing evaluation of organizational strategies.

Risks associated with logistics and distribution shortfalls can be negated somewhat when functional efficiency becomes a focus in supply chain operations. In a supply chain, the efficient flow of goods and material among separated entities is better managed when risks are shared among multiple, collaborative stakeholders. Each customer has an inherent responsibility to order the right supplies for the mission of respective health care organizations. Physician preferred items, routinely problematic in health care supply chain management, are preventable through the suppliers' submission of demands for items that are necessary or already available in the supply lines for the continuance of effective health care operations.

MISSION RELIABILITY

Depending upon one's perspective as a customer or as a distributor of supply, appropriate metrics for reliability are viewed differently. Performance-based logistics management cannot involve a myopic view of processes and practices from any singular perspective because effective health care supply chain management involves multifaceted perspectives and methods for achieving common goals. By harnessing various views, customers can see an observable difference in response times, availability of critical supplies, and a willingness to include the customer's voice in change management.

Reliability plays a significant role in readiness and is a measure of the system's or process's ability to achieve mission success objectives, a metric that relates to the effectiveness of a practice. This metric applies toward the supply chain's ability to ensure the continuance of material moving between the supply node and the end customer. In many instances, the need for material within a health care organization occurs intermittently and will not require a sustained replenishment cycle. Surgical items are an example wherein items and devices are not required frequently enough to establish an automatic replenishment point, and needs may vary depending on types of surgical cases performed. In other instances, there may be a requirement to have an open order in the supply system for material to be available at all times. In this regard, lab reagents deteriorate quickly, are routinely used, and replenished frequently. In both examples, the efforts of the supply chain manager to sustain a health care organization become imperative to success.

Sustainability involves developing supply chain response capabilities that meet the developing, continually evolving needs of a customer without compromising the suppliers' abilities to meet future demand. Albeit trauma is a large portion of medical scenarios in operations, but suppliers cannot afford to deplete an entire stock to provide supplies to one customer. Building mechanisms into the Afghanistan model to ensure redundancy upstream and down for health care nodes allows cross-levelling critical supply items throughout the theater. In the event that one customer starts observing low levels of a specific high-use item, and the item is not due in for the customer, the supply chain manager can request the item from a different supply node. If that distribution point is also experiencing a shortage, the distribution center in Qatar is contacted and leveraged for an emergency resupply to a point closest to the customer requiring the materiel. The distributor, from Qatar, has theater-wide oversight and can identify items available at alternate locations within Afghanistan. By embracing and leveraging this capability, suppliers at multiple locations are able to cross-level supplies to provide adequate levels of support to multiple customer locations throughout Afghanistan.

Inherent in this concept is the responsibility of an end-user to communicate identified demands to suppliers as soon as possible. In health care, clinicians expect the timely arrival of material and supplies. Without effective communication of requirements to the distributor, and in a timely manner, it is not possible to process items for delivery. Poor demand forecasting impacts business processes in two ways:

1. High demand forecasts result in having too much inventory and increasing operational costs
2. Low demand forecasts result in a lack of inventory that can contribute to increasing costs by placing emergency orders (Martin 2007)

COST PER UNIT USAGE

Cost in medical supply is a significant component of health related expenses. One feature that shapes medical prices is the inestimable force of clinical need. This need is often a catalyst for ordering supply based on conjecture and not upon adequate forecasting. Due to the dynamic nature of medical needs, health care providers often assume that they cannot adequately forecast future demand. Analysis of the complete health care system, however, indicates that supply chain management is one area in which cost reductions can be predictable.

Logistics is one area in which theorists believe costs are reducible and more efficiency is achievable in order to provide health care at a more reasonable price. Health care supply chain costs represent an average 30 to 40 percent of overall operating costs in the management of health care organizations (Burns 2005; Flower 2008; Johnson 2008; Nachtmann and Pohl 2009). Problem areas lie in not knowing, or understanding in many instances, where fundamental inefficiencies exist. Associated costs subsist throughout the periphery of a complex supply chain.

Two core measurement issues when deciding appropriate levels of support are: (1) the valuation of outcome-related performance, and (2) the selection of appropriate performance variables (Doerr, Lewis, and Eaton 2005). Valuation of outcome-related performance involves an ongoing measurement of factors such as cost and importance. This concept can also involve estimations of operational and financial risk. Setting targets (benchmarks) can aid in propagating a more enhanced supply chain operation.

The supplier's subjective assessment of a customer's needs, and vice versa, in a contingency will yield supply chain efficiency. Relying on established benchmarks and product lines are imperative, but suppliers must be cautious concerning which metric they present to external stakeholders. In one example in Afghanistan, the theater's distributor consciously declines to present sales data to customers. Sales data represents the dollar value of supplies purchased for organizations throughout Afghanistan. Instead, the supplier presents customer demand accommodation rates that are, truly, a more realistic statistic concerning the volume of supply moving throughout the theater of operations.

Why would the distributor choose to employ this course of action? As an example, one vial of a drug named Novoseven® (generic name Factor VIIa Recombinant), a blood coagulant used in the treatment or prevention of bleeding episodes in patients with bleeding problems such as hemophilia A or B, acquired hemophilia, or congenital Factor VII deficiency, is a clotting factor that works by activating the body's organic clotting system. Used frequently by trauma surgeons in Afghanistan, the cost of the medication is around $5,000 for a single-use vial. Novoseven is invaluable in trauma cases where traumatic injuries can result in significant blood loss. Many physicians want Novoseven due to its success rate in stopping traumatic hemorrhaging once a patient arrives at a hospital. To use sales data alone would have caused a tremendous misrepresentation of how much or how frequent the medication is required. Likewise, sales data alone may cause someone to misunderstand the inherent need of such a product in life saving clinical practices.

SUMMARY AND CONCLUSION

Performance-based logistics is about results. Performance-oriented management practices describe supply chain management as a complete package of services and support, an integrated and affordable performance package designed to optimize readiness through long-term support arrangements. The focus, however, is not concerned strictly with material resources, but with capabilities and processes as well.

A performance-based approach to supply chain management operations must occur from a value chain perspective and as a link among various stakeholders—each agency throughout a supply chain influences others along a continuum of logistical preparedness (see Figure 6.1). Difficulties in health care supply chain management can arise from a lack of standardization, delays in implementing new technology, and lack of accurate data upon which to base operational and strategic decisions. Some shortfalls associated with these factors are inexperience, lack of foresight, and unwillingness to work collaboratively.

By embracing a performance-oriented approach to logistics management, PBL leverages a realization of expected operational and performance characteristics. Improvements can lead to better inventory management, fewer losses related to wasteful practices, more satisfied customers, and improved quality of care. Efficient logistics operations require the effective management of multiple tenets of logistics including warehousing, transportation, inventory, order processing, information systems, and packaging of supplies.

Health care systems are dynamic organizations with complex levels of interactivity. A gamut of reasons contributes to the specialization and idiosyncratic nature of health care related supply chain management. Health care logistics operations go far beyond the hospital storeroom and involve a range of responsibilities that tend to be somewhat confusing to many health care practitioners. Health care logistics and supply chain management are complex issues and because of their inherent complexities, along with the nature of the service provided, technical efficiency and effectiveness are often difficult to measure *a priori*. Managing large numbers of specific, specialized medical items becomes a challenge due to operational tempo, dynamic health-related conditions, and the needs of a multifaceted customer base involved in various aspects of patient care.

Problem areas related to effective and efficient supply chain management can include a lack of supply chain expertise, the need for additional user level and management training, a perceived lack of cooperation among various stakeholders, and ill-interpreted translations regarding supply chain metrics. Performance-based approaches to supply chain management provides greater flexibility for a variety of stakeholders to make necessary trade-offs that can provide a better balance among performance, time, and available resources, and can encourage them to be more creative and innovative in respective approaches to supply chain management practices.

NOTES

The views expressed in this work are those of the author and do not reflect the official policy or position of the U.S. Department of the Army, U.S. Department of Defense, or the U.S. government.

REFERENCES

Burns, L. R. 2005. *The business of health care innovation*. New York, NY: Cambridge University Press.

Carter, C. R., and D. S. Rogers. 2008. "A framework of sustainable supply chain management: Moving toward new theory." *International Journal of Physical Distribution and Logistics Management* 38:360-87.

Devries, H. J. 2004. "Performance-based logistics—barriers and enablers to effective implementation." *Defense AR Journal* 11:242-53.

Doerr, K., I. Lewis, and D. R. Eaton. 2005. "Measurement issues in performance-based logistics." *Journal of Public Procurement* 5:164-86.

Flower, J. 2008, July. *Borrow my eyes: A close, integrated look into the future of health care.* Presented at the 45th Annual Conference of the Association for Health Care Resources and Materials Management, San Antonio, TX.

Johnson, B. T. 2008, July. *An overview of supply chain best practices.* Presented at the 45th Annual Conference of the Association for Health Care Resources and Materials Management, San Antonio, TX.

Levine, R., J. Pickett, N. Sekhri, and P. Yadav. 2008. "Demand forecasting for essential medical technologies." *American Journal of Law and Medicine* 34:225-55.

Martin, J. W. 2007. *Lean Six Sigma for supply chain management.* New York: McGraw-Hill.

Miman, M., and E. Pohl. 2008. "Modeling and analysis of risk and reliability for a contingency logistics supply chain." *Journal of Risk and Reliability* 222, No. 4 463-476, 2008.

Schneller, E.S., and L. R. Smeltzer. 2006. *Strategic management of the health care supply chain.* San Francisco, CA: John Wiley & Sons, Inc.

Sols, A., D. Nowick, and D. Verma. 2007. "Defining the fundamental framework of an effective performance-based logistics (PBL) contract." *Engineering Management Journal* 19:40–50.

U.S. Department of Defense. 2006. *Joint Publication 5-0: Joint Operation Planning.* Washington, DC: Department of Defense.

7

RISK ACCEPTANCE OF GEEC® RISK IN MARITIME SUPPLY CHAIN SYSTEMS

Bjørn Egil Asbjørnslett and Odd Torstein Mørkve

INTRODUCTION

GEEC Shipping is a ship-owner operating in the short-sea shipping market of industry shipping. GEEC is an abbreviation for *Greenhouse gas Emissions and Energy Consumption*. Industry shipping means that their business idea is based on providing industrial companies with customized maritime supply chain (SC) solutions, and the short-sea shipping markets mean that they are providing regional and not intercontinental maritime SC solutions. In addition, due to the increased *green pressure* on the supply chain solutions that GEEC Shipping provides, the company has increased its focus on the environmental aspects of their operations in order to provide shipping and maritime SC solutions that have an improved environmental profile, measured by factors such as energy efficiency and emission of carbon (CO_2).

Maritime SC or maritime logistics can be defined as a logistics system in which sea transport constitutes a major part of the logistics chain. Therefore, in the design and analysis of a maritime logistics chain, the sea leg of the chain will often be the point of departure when searching for the most optimal design. A maritime logistics chain is illustrated in Figure 7.1.

As ship owners and managers of maritime SCs, GEEC Shipping is always looking for new business opportunities that can strengthen their market position. When developing a business opportunity, some risk issues for GEEC Shipping, and most of

Figure 7.1 A generic maritime logistics chain.

its competitors, are more or less taken based on gut feeling, while others are treated more formally and transparently. This was especially the case for GEEC Shipping some years ago, when they were asked to answer a tender that specifically asked for an *environmental* evaluation of the proposed green-field maritime SC solutions. This inquiry was not common to include in logistics tenders for the industry at that time.

GEEC Shipping was in this specific green-field SC development trying to determine how to best evaluate environmental risk compared to the business opportunity. More specifically, they were assessing what risk they believed that the cargo owner could accept, and specifically how to best prepare for, and deal with, the CO_2 emission profile of the SC solution, against the cost competitiveness of the SC solution.

There are several steps in assessing the best solution for a given tender considering green-field maritime SC development. First, the structure of the industrial maritime SC design is described, including the requirements of the tender and the constraints of technology and infrastructure alternatives. Second, the decision support modeling made for the tender is formed, which consists of evaluating different alternatives, outlining the difference between a cost-based optimization versus a GEEC-based optimization, and then relating this difference to a risk acceptance discussion for the maritime SC design. After evaluating the results of their decision support model, GEEC Shipping continued further modeling based on a multiobjective cost and emission basis, balancing the weight that each cost and carbon emissions measure should be given in the evaluation (optimization) of alternative maritime SC designs. This was done to reach a solution with a cost benefit trade-off that could match the cargo owner's risk awareness with respect to the carbon footprinting of their supply chain. Finally, they examined some other risk and vulnerability aspects related to the maritime SC design, as well as discussed the issues raised in the tender, given their understanding gained after the evaluation of the maritime SC system.

SC TENDER REQUIREMENTS—AN OVERVIEW

GEEC Shipping was invited to tender for a new multimodal transport system. The transport system would serve new volumes of unitized cargo from a new green-field plant into an existing market with an existing distribution network from distribution centers (DCs) to end customers. The tender document laid down the main operational requirements for the logistics system.

TENDER REQUIREMENTS

The requirements stated by the cargo owner could be summarized in the following main groups:

- Volume and volume distributions:
  - o Annual volume of approximately 400,000 load units and limited seasonal variations, which results in even delivery distribution of cargo over the planning period
  - o Delivery to approximately 25 DCs with location and annual volume defined
  - o Demand was given per regional DC, and not per port of discharge—the port was to be treated as a transshipment point facilitating the required throughput capability
  - o Each port of discharge was given a maximum and minimum volume that could be unloaded
- Sailing patterns/schedule:
  - o A list of preferred ports of discharge (could be changed if found appropriate by the shipping line)
  - o Time and frequency requirements, which includes the suggested ports of discharge with given recommended arrival frequencies, ranging from every 4th to every 7th day
  - o Suggested sailing patterns/schedules given by the cargo owner as the point of departure for the tender
- Vessels to be used:
  - o Some general requirements with regard to the vessel to be used were set by the cargo owner
  - o Truck should be the preferred mode of distribution from port of discharge and DCs
- Environmental performance of the suggested transport system:
  - o The cargo owner had started to focus on the environmental performance of its operations, so the bidders were also asked to include an estimation of the *carbon footprint* for the proposed logistics systems in addition to the cost calculations

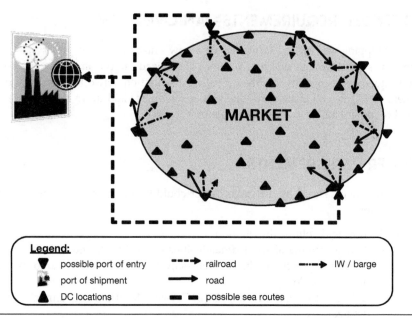

Figure 7.2 A schematic illustration of the main structure of the logistics system.

- The logistics system (see Figure 7.2) included in the tender comprised the following main elements:
  o Cargo handling in port of shipment (loading of vessels)
  o Sea transport from port of shipment to ports of discharge
  o Cargo handling in ports of discharge (unloading of vessels, cargo handling at ports, loading on trucks for distribution to DCs)
  o Transport from discharge ports to main DCs in various markets

DELIVERABLES

Due to its long lasting relationship with the customer, the business opportunity made possible by the tender, and the added environmental focus, GEEC Shipping decided to answer the invitation to tender. Based on the operational requirements defined in the tender document, GEEC Shipping would provide the cargo owner with a proposed design of a multimodal transport system, which minimized the total costs and fulfilled the operational requirements set out in the tender document. The proposed design included the following main elements:

- The maritime routes that were needed for the transport, including optimal port/terminal configuration
- The number, size, and brief outlines of the vessels needed to operate the transport system including vessel and fleet utilization

- The frequency (days between port calls) for each route that had to be served
- Total system costs and costs per load unit transported to different locations
- Total GHG emission and energy consumptions of the proposed transport system and for each mode and node included in the system
- Carbon footprint for a unit of transported cargo to different locations

In addition to the proposed design of a multimodal transport system, GEEC Shipping also included a description of alternative transport systems based on operational changes in the system. These systems included an analysis of routes, types and number of ships, frequency and volume distribution to each port of discharge for the alternative solution, and distribution from port of discharge to DCs. Each of the described alternatives was described with regard to the effect the proposed changes would have on:

- Total system costs
- Total CO_2 emission and energy consumption
- Costs per ton reduction in GHG emission for alternative transport systems
- Changes in carbon footprint for transport from port of discharge to each DC [$kgCO_2$/unit]

Based on these analyses, GEEC Shipping could provide the cargo owner both with a recommended system based on the pure cost optimization and an evaluation of the environmental performance of the proposed system, and the cost associated with improving the system's environmental performance.

MODELING THE SC TENDER SYSTEM AND REQUIREMENTS

As stated in the tender requirements, the maritime SC design included delivery of load units from a production plant to regional DCs, where short-sea shipping was both a central and required part of the supply chain. Outbound hinterland transport from plant to port of shipment would be equal in all cases, and could therefore be taken out of the consideration. The SC system design consists of vessel sailing, port of discharge calls in regional markets, unloading and port of discharge operations, and final hinterland transport from regional port of discharge to regional DC(s), as illustrated in Figure 7.3.

To model and analyze the decision support required for the tender, GEEC Shipping was engaged in the following process:

1. Establish a cost and carbon footprint baseline (*as-is*—based on cost minimization with the port of discharge structure and port call frequency given in the tender document)
2. Establish an SC design based on minimum cost optimization (cost minimization with free choice of port of discharge structure and port call frequency)

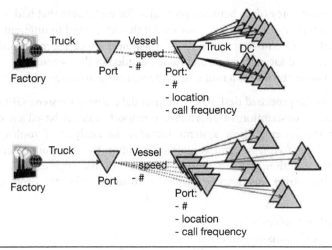

Figure 7.3 The assumed SC system.

3. Establish a SC design with minimum CO_2 emission optimization (CO_2 minimization with free choice of ports of discharge as above)
4. Risk evaluation of a cost and CO_2 emission position
5. Seeking a cost effective risk acceptance through modeling a balanced cost/CO_2 emission, in a way that meets cargo owners' need for information

All of the above factors take the requirements and constraints of the problem, as defined in the tender, into account. GEEC Shipping's modeling of the SC design would be based on a set of main cost and emission dimensions, given in Table 7.1.

The SC analytical modeling and optimization process used in this case was a key element to enabling analysis of the large number of possible maritime SC designs based on the given input requirements and the required cost/GEEC balance. The

Table 7.1 Costs and emissions standards

	Cost	**CO_2 emission**
Vessel	• CAPEX—capital expenditure (fixed per vessel) • OPEX—operational expenditure (variable)	• Fixed emission (per vessel used) • Variable emission (vessel usage based)
Port of discharge	• Port call cost (fixed) • Cargo handling cost (variable)	• Port call emission (fixed per port call) • Cargo handling emissions (variable)
Inbound hinterland to DCs	• Distribution cost (variable)	• Distribution emissions (variable)

next section provides a short introduction to this modeling, first with a cost based approach, and then with a GEEC-based approach. The purpose of the models was to support the decision making process at a strategic level, specifically whether, and how, to best design a maritime SC system that would be a long-term, viable system design that is both commercially competitive and robust with respect to expected market focus and regulatory changes concerning SC carbon-footprint measures.

Searching for Cost Effectiveness (Cost Minimum)

The starting point for GEEC Shipping's analysis was the traditional cost minimization approach. The cost minimization was carried out in two main steps. First, they had to check the minimum cost position available for a respective SC design given the preferred port structure and port call frequency requirement in the tender document. Then, the frequency requirements were relaxed, but without compromising the minimum and maximum cargo unloading requirements in each port of discharge. Thereafter, they had to ease the port structure requirement, and determine the choice of which ports to call.

A Cost Minimization Objective Function

To be able to optimize the system, a cost (objective) function had to be developed. The cost, c (objective) function took the form of;

$$c = \sum_{p \in P} C_p^P \partial_p + \sum_{v \in V} C_v^C z_v + \sum_{r \in R} \sum_{v \in V} \sum_{s \in S} C_{rvs}^O n_{rvs} + \sum_{p \in P} \sum_{r \in R} \sum_{v \in V} C_p^H q_{prv} + \sum_{p \in P} \sum_{d \in D} C_{pd}^L D_d y_{pd}$$

In short terms, the cost minimization objective function could be read as:

Total SC design cost, dc = port call cost (p) + vessel acquisition cost (c) + vessel use cost (o) + cargo handling cost in port (h) + hinterland distribution cost (l).

Or, more fully described:

Total SC design cost, c = cost of using a port (CAPEX), summed for all port calls, for all ports used in a specific SC design
+ cost of acquiring a vessel (CAPEX), summed for all vessels required in a specific SC design
+ cost of using a vessel (OPEX) in a given number of voyages on given routes with given speed in the SC design, summed for all vessels used
+ cargo handling cost in ports (OPEX) for the given vessels used, for the amount of cargo unloaded and shipped through a port, summed for all port calls, for all ports used in a given SC design
+ hinterland distribution cost (OPEX) summed for all cargo units shipped from a given port to a given DC, for all port/DC pairs.

The objective function was represented as a mathematical model, with defined sets, indices, and parameters. For example, one model incorporated the set P of available

Table 7.2 Sets and indices used in the SC decision modeling

Set	Index	Description
P	p	Set of available ports
R	R	The set of possible routes
V	V	The set of available vessels
D	d	The set of available DCs
S	s	The set of possible speed levels per vessel

ports that could be used in the design of a given maritime SC system, with the corresponding index p. Table 7.2 shows the sets and indices that were used.

MODEL CONSTRAINTS

To obtain viable results from the optimization model, in addition to the cost objective function, some constraints had to be added to ensure that the model provided a good approximation of the problem in the *real world*. Several constraints were used, and one constraint considered the volume delivered by a given ship, to a given port, on a given route, was not less than the minimum volume, nor larger than the maximum volume, allowed by the port, applied for all combinations of ports, routes, and ships in the model. This was an important requirement to adhere to the relaxation of the fixed port requirement. For example, one port had the requirement that a minimum of 100 load units could be unloaded in the port per port call.

RESULTS OF COST MINIMAL SC DESIGNS

The model was developed and run on professional optimization solver software, bringing cost minimization solutions to SC designs with resulting ports, routes, port call frequencies, unloading volumes, number of vessels, vessel speeds on given routes, and distribution volumes from given ports of discharge to given DCs. The results with respect to cost and carbon emissions footprint of the cost minimized SC designs are presented in Table 7.3. The *fixed routes* scenarios are those where the original ports required by the cargo owner were used, while the *open routes* scenarios are those where ports to call were chosen by the optimization model. *As-is* represents the cost and emission position of the given SC design before optimization.

The main improvement was achieved from relaxing the port call frequency requirements, resulting in an improved cost position from $97 million (as-is) to $63 million (FR-Cost-Min, i.e., fixed route, cost minimization). Further relaxing the requirement of which ports to use improved the cost position to $53 million (OR-Cost-Min, i.e. open routes, cost minimization). The corresponding carbon footprint (total SC CO_2 emissions) was 190, 119, and 107 thousand tons of CO_2 respectively.

Table 7.3 Results of cost minimization SC design

	As-is	Fixed routes (FR)	Open routes (OR)
Minimizing	As-is	FR-Cost-Min	OR-Cost-Min
Cost (mil. $)	97	63	53
Emission ('000 tons CO2)	190	119	107

BRINGING GEEC INTO THE DECISION SITUATION

As for the cost modeling, an optimization model also had to be developed for the SC system design based on carbon (footprint) emission minimization. The emission objective function was created following the structure of the cost model:

$$e = \sum_{p \in P} E_p^P \partial_p + \sum_{v \in V} E_v^C z_v + \sum_{r \in R} \sum_{v \in V} \sum_{s \in S} E_{rvs}^O n_{rvs} + \sum_{p \in P} \sum_{r \in R} \sum_{v \in V} E_p^H q_{prv} + \sum_{p \in P} \sum_{d \in D} E_{pd}^L D_d y_{pd}$$

As can be seen, the carbon emission objective function has the same structure as the cost optimization function. In short terms, the carbon footprint minimization objective function could be read as:

Total SC carbon footprint (CO_2 emissions), e = port call emissions (p) + fixed vessel emissions (f) + vessel use emissions (o) + cargo handling emissions in port (h) + hinterland distribution emissions (l).

Or, more fully described as:

Total SC carbon footprint (CO_2 emissions), e =
the fixed emissions added each time a port is called in a SC design
+ fixed emission from adding a specific vessel to the fleet of vessels in a given SC design
+ the variable (activity and speed dependent) emissions from the use of the vessels in a given SC design and voyage speeds
+ the variable (activity dependent) emissions from having a given activity in a given port
+ the emissions from distributing given cargo volumes from given ports to given DCs.

Results of Carbon Emission Minimal SC Design

Like the cost minimization, the carbon footprint minimization was also run on an optimization solver, returning a set of solutions other than the cost minimal solutions. The results of the carbon footprint minimized SC designs are presented in Table 7.4.

GEEC Shipping then had solutions based on two alternative approaches. The first is minimizing the cost position of the SC design; the other, minimizing the carbon footprint (CO_2 emissions) of the SC design. GEEC Shipping noticed that the SC designs based on carbon emissions minimization were able to lower the carbon emissions, but with an increased cost.

Table 7.4 Results of CO_2 minimization SC design

	As-is	Fixed routes (FR)	Open routes (OR)
Minimizing	As-is	FR-CO_2-Min	OR-CO_2-Min
Cost (mil. $)	97	65	69
Emission ('000 tons CO_2)	190	107	82

A Risk Acceptance Discussion

As the analyses showed, bringing carbon emissions into the decision discussion increased the costs of the SC design. As the SC cost position is a main parameter with respect to the competitiveness of the SC design, a question was how much the cost position could be relaxed in meeting a lower carbon emission level. The discussion of cost or price per unit of CO_2 emission was regarded as important in this analysis and decision process. Then, to be able to analyze, discuss, and recommend into a tender decision process they had to be precise in their definition, and firm on which premises they based their analysis. In addition, they had to be transparent in how they quantitatively balanced these different requirements and objectives of the decision problem, given an acceptance of the risk.

Carbon Emission Control Measures

There were three considerations that GEEC Shipping could use in approaching the handling of risk acceptance of carbon footprinting in the SC design. The first was the market approach, in which they acknowledged that CO_2 quotas were traded in a carbon market, and that they could set as a risk premium for CO_2-emission issues, the cost per unit of CO_2 traded in a carbon market. The second was carbon tax schemes. The third was based on the cost of different abatement technologies per unit of CO_2 abated that would be required to deal with the estimated growth in CO_2 emissions toward the year 2030.

A FORMAL EMISSION ASSESSMENT APPROACH

To approach these issues, GEEC Shipping used as a basis the underlying thought in the Formal Safety Assessment (FSA) process set up by the International Maritime Organization (IMO) as their approach to a transparent, proactive risk analysis process. Although the FSA process was meant as a risk based approach to novel ship designs, it had also been found useful by IMO's Marine Environment Protection Committee (MEPC) to be used for cost effectiveness considerations of abatement measures for various environmental risks, such as CO_2 emissions.

Emission Risk in the ALARP Area

A central part of IMO's FSA process was to deal with risk issues that were in the *as low as reasonably practicable* (ALARP) area. This means that the risk should be reduced as much as possible with practical measures, and where cost effectiveness criteria should guide how much ought to be used of the measure to reduce the risk to an acceptable level. The ALARP area was placed between unacceptable and acceptable risk, meaning that the risk was not fully acceptable, but should be reduced only as long as it was practical, as measured by cost-benefit criteria.

GEEC Shipping assumed, at least when trying to position their bid for the SC design tender, that CO_2 emissions could be regarded as a risk within the ALARP area. The risk consisted of the likelihood and the consequence of a given risk scenario maturing, and GEEC Shipping saw the likelihood as high, and the consequence as *considerable*, given that either a tax or fee could lead to increased operational costs. More importantly, the focus on reducing the carbon footprint in SCs could lead to CO_2 emissions becoming a positive/competitive business driver. As such, it was comparable to IMO's initial implementation of the FSA approach to evaluate the safety oriented risk in novel ship designs, by GEEC Shipping employing it to address environmental risk in novel, green-field SC designs. To assure the cost-effectiveness of the SC system design changes, they opted for three alternative approaches that could be tracked back into external processes, supporting their risk acceptance question, as outlined above.

The three alternatives were:

1. The trading scheme approach—a CO_2 allowance pricing that in those days traded for approximately $23 per ton CO_2.
2. Carbon tax schemes—approximately $55 per ton CO_2.
3. A comparison between global economic mitigation potential and projected emission increases in 2030—the global cost-effectiveness considerations of the IPCC (Intergovernmental Panel on Climate Change), a cost-effectiveness criteria (used in cost benefit assessment, CBA) for abatement technologies; $50 per ton CO_2 or $100 per ton CO_2 dependent on the targeted scale of emission reductions.

The three alternatives, with two levels in the last alternative, are shown in Figure 7.4.

In addition to these formal measures, GEEC Shipping saw that the carbon footprint labeling of products in the consumer markets were spreading in such a way so that it could be better to treat carbon footprinting proactively, as a leader, rather than reactively as a lagging participant.

Based on the three measures, GEEC Shipping opted for SC designs that could meet cost/emission trade-off of $50 to $100 per ton of CO_2 emission reduced. They decided to use the single point of $55 because it met the carbon tax level and would thereby be easy to communicate to the relevant stakeholders as a starting point.

Another question for GEEC Shipping was how to evaluate the SC designs that would meet both the cost and emission focus of the cargo owner, and base their

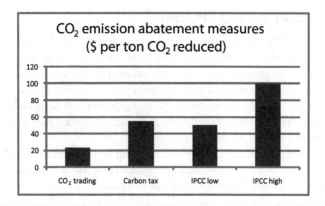

Figure 7.4 CO_2 emission abatement measures as basis for risk acceptance considerations.

evaluation in such a way that they could backtrack their analysis into decision points and a decision basis. As they had to work on their design parameters based on whether they set cost or emission as the key objective function, GEEC Shipping developed some answers in cost/emission balancing.

BALANCING COST AND GEEC

When GEEC Shipping entered into the decision making process of this SC tender, the baseline they had to compare with was the *as-is* cost and CO_2 emission position of the SC design, shown in the previous tables. They observed that both the cost and CO_2 emission position of the SC system could be improved considerably from *as-is*, even based on the fixed routes given by the cargo owner, summarized in Table 7.5.

As earlier described, the fixed routes were based on calling the ports required by the cargo owner, while the open routes were those routes where ports were chosen freely by the optimization model.

Given the restriction of specified ports to call in the fixed routes scenarios, the differences in cost and CO_2 emissions were smaller compared to when the optimization model was allowed to analyze and select routes freely as in the open routes

Table 7.5 Cost and CO_2 emissions for the scenarios with as-is, fixed routes and open routes

	As-is	Fixed routes (FR)		Open routes (OR)	
Minimizing	As-is	FR-Cost-Min	FR-CO_2-Min	OR-Cost-Min	OR-CO_2-Min
Cost (mil $)	97	63	65	53	69
Emission (thousand tons CO_2)	190	119	107	107	82

scenarios. For example, the CO_2 emission for the emission focused optimization with the fixed routes were on the same level as the emission for the cost-based optimization with open route selection, but with a considerably lower cost position ($53 million versus $65 million). Therefore, from here we will primarily address the *open routes* scenarios.

MULTI-OBJECTIVE PROGRAMMING AND THE EFFICIENT FRONTIER OF THE BALANCED SOLUTIONS

As GEEC Shipping had seen in the cost versus CO_2 emission focused optimization analyses, there were considerable cost and emission differences between the optimized SC design solutions. The question was then how to treat this in the design process of their solution and offer to the tender. Given that the cost position was regarded as the main decision parameter, the question raised was how the cost disadvantage of optimizing on CO_2 emissions could be balanced before accepting a solution.

The singular optimization of cost or emissions gave *extreme* solutions that could pose challenges in different future scenarios. To find solutions that possessed better trade-offs between the cost and emission positions, they developed a trade-off analysis model based on multiobjective programming. A multiobjective programming model seeks to find efficient solutions in which no improvement in one objective function may be obtained without degrading other objective functions. A set of these efficient solutions are used to create an efficient frontier.

GEEC Shipping had two objective functions, cost and emission minimization, and given that they had only these two functions, they were able to illustrate an efficient frontier by drawing a graph with each objective function representing the axis of the chart. The efficient frontier could then be used to identify solutions with a trade-off between costs and emissions that would be equally efficient according to their definition of the decision problem. They could then use their risk acceptance approach to seek solutions that would provide an efficient cost/emission trade-off, and equally meet their risk acceptance criteria.

The basis for the cost/emission balancing model was an objective function that introduced a balancing weight function between cost and emission minimization. The balanced objective function could be written as:

$$min\ f = \alpha c + \beta e, \text{ subject to } \alpha + \beta = 1$$

In this objective function, c is cost and e is CO_2 emission. The requirement of the weighting parameters $\alpha + \beta = 1$, ensures that the minimized function comprises cost and emission only, but that the emphasis on cost and emission can be changed, e.g., 70 percent cost and 30 percent emissions. The efficient frontier that was obtained from their cost and carbon emission model is given in Figure 7.5.

Given the illustrative representation of the efficient frontier, they could use that as a tool to support the discussions leading towards their decision. As can be seen,

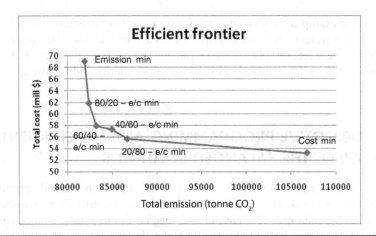

Figure 7.5 The efficient frontier of cost and CO_2 emissions of GEEC Shipping's supply chain designs.

Table 7.6 New cost and carbon emission positions with cost/emission weighted optimization

	As-is	Fixed routes (FR)			Open routes (OR)		
Minimizing	As-is	FR-Cost-Min	FR-80/20-Min	FR-CO_2-Min	OR-Cost-Min	OR-80/20-Min	OR-CO_2-Min
Cost (mil. $)	97	63	64	65	53	56	69
Emission (thousand tons CO_2)	190	119	108	107	107	87	82

the efficient frontier is a convex and strictly decreasing function, which for low cost positions shows that a marginal cost reduction would lead to a substantial increase in CO_2 emission. Then, with the cost/emission balanced modeling, GEEC Shipping found some new cost and carbon-emission positions, as illustrated with the 80/20 cost/emission weighting of the objective functions in Table 7.6.

THE COST VERSUS CO_2 EMISSION RISK PICTURE TRADE-OFF

The results that GEEC Shipping had achieved through their analyses had shown that they were able to reduce the SC cost position considerably from the *as-is* situation. Based on this acknowledgement, they proposed to open up the port call frequency requirement and port suggestions of the cargo owner to take into account the option of using other port call frequencies and other ports. Therefore, their *open routes* (OR) design would be recommended. The next question was how much one would invest in improving the carbon emission level from the cost minimal solution. They saw that moving from the cost optimal solution to the 80 percent cost and 20 percent emission optimal solution, led to a +6 percent change in cost (increase) and a −19 percent change in carbon emissions (reduction). This corresponded to a price per unit of carbon reduced of $120 per ton CO_2.

USING THE EFFICIENT FRONTIER AND THE RISK ACCEPTANCE MEASURE

The final question for GEEC Shipping was which emission position to opt for, and why. Based on the risk acceptance criteria they had defined earlier, they wanted a solution based on a cost minimal solution (SC design) that moved on the efficient frontier in such a way that they accepted a reduction in CO_2 emissions and the following cost increases, as long as the incremental cost increase per unit of CO_2 emission reduction was below the risk acceptance criteria they had decided. This resulted in a cost of approximately $55 per ton of CO_2 reduced.

The incremental changes in unit cost per ton CO_2 emission reduced were examined among various scenarios, both for the fixed and open routes scenarios. The approach was a cost benefit assessment, or CBA, where the cost was the incremental cost between scenarios, and the benefit was the reduced carbon emission between the scenarios. The situation that they observed is presented in Figure 7.6.

Figure 7.6 shows that, between the chosen scenarios, the cost increment per unit of CO_2 emission reduced varied from $50 to more than $2800. Going from a cost-minimal SC design to a SC design based on an 80/20 cost/emission trade-off, would cost $60 per ton CO_2 emission reduced in the fixed port case, and almost $120 in the open port case.

Giving their risk acceptance criteria of $55 per ton CO_2 reduced, this informed the decision makers that the CO_2 emission minimization scenario was not considered realistic in an 80/20 trade-off. However, they also saw that it was quite practical to move away from the cost-only minimum SC design, and with cost increments within the risk acceptance criteria, they could reduce the CO_2 emission and the SC design carbon footprint considerably. Then, after reoptimizing for the open route scenario, they met the $55 risk acceptance criteria in the 90/10 cost/emission weighted range. Therefore, the cost effectiveness criteria of mitigating the risk of carbon emissions in the SC design was met when optimizing with a 90 percent cost based and 10 percent carbon emission based weighting.

With this result, GEEC Shipping had considerably reduced the SC cost position, and at the same time treated the CO_2 emission and SC carbon footprint concerns as a potential risk issue for the SC design. However, this risk could be mitigated and kept within an ALARP area through following a process that was both transparent and

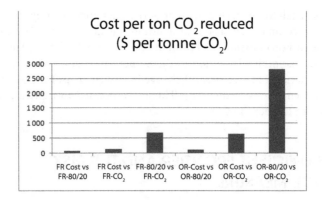

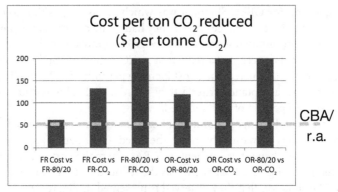

Figure 7.6 Cost per ton CO_2 reduced between given cost/emission optimized scenarios.

aimed at cost efficiency in the balancing act between a split focus on cost and CO_2 emission reductions.

CONCLUSION

GEEC Shipping felt now that they had constructively answered the question called for in the tender. However, could they have introduced other SC risks into their recommended design? The initial *as-is* SC design used 8 vessels, calling 7 ports. Their recommended solution used 4 vessels calling 9 ports. The reduction in number of vessels was a positive contribution to the risk picture, as they were able to off-load CAPEX from the solution. However, fewer vessels calling more ports require good tactical and operational route planning and management. Not just the number of ports had changed, but also which ports. To mitigate the risk potential in this, they recommended that the cargo owner change from local port agent contracts to one contract with a common port agent that had offices in all the ports used in the network. GEEC Shipping had initially aimed to search for ports that had a robust set of alternative hinterland transport modes, but had to leave that to secure the primary cost/emissions positions of their recommended solution.

Let us now come back to the initial requirements set forth in the tender. The tender specified requirements with respect to volume and volume distributions, sailing patterns and schedules, vessels to be used, as well as the environmental performance of the SC design. In their different SC design solutions, GEEC Shipping had been able to considerably reduce both the cost and carbon footprint of the SC solution and still meet the tender requirements. They had also, with a transparent, proactive risk analysis approach following IMO's FSA method, showed how a cost-minimal SC design could be changed into a design that also improved the carbon footprint of the SC solution in a cost effective manner. The cost effectiveness of the cost and carbon emission trade-off for the optimal SC design was based on treating carbon emissions as a risk for the design, and using a carbon tax approach to assess the value of mitigating the carbon emissions in changing the SC design. Through their approach, GEEC Shipping had not just met the tender requirements, but had also given the cargo owner a firm basis from which they could backtrack how carbon footprint improvements had been made in the SC design. GEEC Shipping's final tender was based on a design found when optimizing with a 90 percent cost and 10 percent carbon emission basis, meeting the risk acceptance of $55 carbon emission abatement level.

8

AN ANALYSIS OF A MAJOR OIL SPILL CASE IN THE BALTIC SEA

Arben Mullai and Ulf Paulsson

INTRODUCTION

The increasingly large quantities and types of dangerous goods transported and handled in the Baltic Sea Region (BSR) and the consequences of accidents involving these goods are concerning issues for all countries in the region. Between 300–1000 million tons of dangerous goods, including oil and oil products, gases, and a wide range of chemicals, are transported annually in the BSR Maritime transport traffic and transport of hydrocarbon products are expected to increase two and three fold respectively during the period 2010–2015 (Rytkönen et al. 2002). The increase in the maritime transport of dangerous substances is most likely to be associated with the increase of the maritime risks in the BSR.

The objectives of this chapter are to enhance understanding of maritime risks and propose measures for improving risk management. For the purpose of analysis, a case history of a major oil spill in the Baltic Sea has been selected. The case is based on the casualty investigation report and other reports prepared by the Danish Maritime Administration (DMA 2001), the European Task Force in Denmark (Vincent et al. 2001) and the Danish Emergency Management Agency (DEMA), Development and Research Unit (DEMA 2001), the authors' research report (Mullai and Paulsson 2002).

CASE DESCRIPTION

This case is the second largest accidental oil spill incident reported in the BSR. At midnight the 29th of March 2001, the tanker ship Baltic Carrier and the bulk carrier Tern were sailing on reciprocal courses in the deep water (DW) route northeast of the German and Danish waters. Both ships observed each other initially by means of radars and then visually, at a distance of 8–10 nautical miles. One nautical mile (nm) is equal to 1,852 meters.

At 00.15 hrs local time, the ships collided due to the loss of steering in the Baltic Carrier in combination with inadequate seamanship in both ships. The incident resulted in the release of 2400 tons of fuel oil into the sea. The collision took place in the western Baltic Sea, Kadet Renden, which is the water area between Germany and Denmark. The oil drifted into the Groensund area, which is surrounded by the islands of Falster, Moen, Bogoe, and Faroe (see Figure 8.1). It is an environmentally sensitive and economically important area for the local community. The Baltic Sea is the world's largest brackish body of water, with relatively shallow waters, a slow water exchange process, and a low level of biological activities. The oil spill seriously affected the marine environment and its habitats, public and private properties, and activities ashore.

RISK ANALYSIS

A key objective of every risk study is to provide decision makers with sufficient, reliable, and valid information. The risk analysis attempts to answer three fundamental questions, namely: "What has gone and could go wrong?" "What are the consequences?" and "How likely is that to happen?" These questions are known as *the triplet definition* of risks (Kaplan and Garrick 1981). The risk analysis is a rigorous and systematic process that is facilitated by specific frameworks and techniques. The analysis of the case presented is facilitated by a framework proposed by Mullai (2007). The main steps of the risk analysis are system definition, hazard identification, exposure and consequences analysis, risk evaluation and presentation, and the final conclusions and recommendations.

SYSTEM DEFINITION

The supply chain is defined as:

A network of organizations that are involved, through upstream (i.e., supply sources) and downstream (i.e., distribution channels) linkages, in the different processes and activities that produce value in the form of products and services in the hands of ultimate consumers. (*Christopher 1992, in Brindley 2004*)

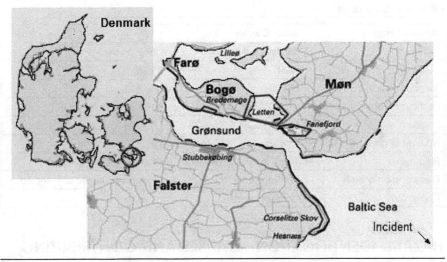

Figure 8.1 The location of the incident and the oil affected areas (DMA, 2001).

Like many other supply chains, the dangerous goods or petrochemical supply chain encompasses a wide range of activities and systems including extraction, production, storage, handling and transport, use, and waste disposal or return. By definition, transport (all modes of transport—air, road, rail, water and pipeline), which is *the flow of goods and an activity that produces value in the form of services*, is an essential component of the supply chain. The maritime transport system (supply chain) is vital to the economy of many countries and regions. Thus, approximately 95 percent of the U.S. and the Swedish foreign trade (imports and exports by weight) consists of waterborne cargo (Wetzel 2004).

A large portion of goods carried by sea are classified as *dangerous goods*. The maritime transport of dangerous substances is regulated at international, regional, and national levels. The International Convention for the Safety of Life at Sea (SOLAS 1974) and the International Convention for the Prevention of Pollution from Ships (MARPOL 1973/78) are the most important conventions dealing with shipping safety and the prevention of pollution from ships, respectively. MARPOL contains six annexes concerned with preventing forms of marine pollution from ships. Annex I deals with oil. The oil and oil products are class 3 flammable liquids, which also pose explosion, toxic, suffocation, and environmental hazards. It is a complex mixture of organic and inorganic compounds. The oil contains carcinogens, like polycyclic aromatic hydrocarbons (PAHs), and other toxic components.

Both ships involved in the incident were well equipped. Steering, communication, and navigation systems were in full working condition and well maintained. Both had valid certifications and were properly manned in accordance with relevant international regulations. Table 8.1 shows the main properties of the ships involved in the incident.

Table 8.1 Ship data

Name of ship	Baltic Carrier	Tern
Type of ship	Oil/chemical tanker	Bulk carrier
Built year	2000	1973
Tonnage (brt)	22,500	20,362
Length/breadth/draft (m)	182.2/27.3/10.9	185.5/26.0/11.1
Engine power (kw)	12,871	8,494
Number of crew	19	22
Ship owner	Interorient Nav, Hamburg	Ranger Marine SA, Piraeus
Classification society	Det Norske Veritas	American Bureau of Shipping
Registration	Marshall Island	Cyprus

HAZARD IDENTIFICATION—CAUSES AND CONTRIBUTING FACTORS

The purpose of hazard identification is to explore the causes and contributing factors by providing answers to the question "What went wrong?" The motor vessel (m/v) Tern hit the motor vessel (m/v) Baltic Carrier in the starboard side at a collision angle 50° from the stem, which later changed to 80°. The Baltic Carrier sustained a large hole through a double hull (side ballast) into starboard cargo tank no. 6 (Figure 8.2), containing 2,700 tons of fuel oil. The main deck was opened from the ship's side by 5 meters toward the centerline.

Figure 8.2 The oil released from tank no. 6 of the m/v Baltic Carrier (DMA 2001).

Both ships were responsible for the incident. However, the incident is largely attributed to the loss of steering in the Baltic Carrier. The fault tree in Figure 8.3 shows the causes and contributing factors of the collision.

Loss of steering: The Baltic Carrier lost steering just three minutes before meeting the motor vessel Tern on the reciprocal course at a distance 1.2 nm. The alarm on the steering device began sounding and flashing 35 seconds after the ship lost steering. The ship gained steering and the alarm stopped when the steering device switched from the system 2 to 1. By that time, the distance between ships reduced to 0.75 nm. The master decided to continue to port and proceeded at full speed ahead as the best alternative to avoid the collision. But, he missed avoiding the collision by 10 seconds.

Disturbance in the steering system: According to the master and third officer of the m/v Baltic Carrier, the ship lost steering due to disturbances in the steering system. In 2000, the ship ran aground near Rotterdam due to the failure in the steering system, which was caused by a loose wire in a junction box at the hydraulic unit. In this case, the investigations found no malfunction or failure in the steering system. Two weeks after the collision, another ship experienced a similar problem at a distance 9 nm northeast from the location of the collision. The rudder suddenly went hard to port while the ship was steering in the autopilot mode. The disturbance disappeared when the system was shifted from autopilot to hand steering and then back to the autopilot mode. According to the DIMA's tests, the magnetic field, due to underwater power cables connecting Sweden and Germany that pass through the area, was most unlikely to have caused any disturbance in the steering system of the Baltic Carrier. The possible cause of the technical error suggested was electromagnetic compatibility (EMC). *Electromagnetic compatibility* refers to the ability of equipment and systems to function as intended, despite unintentional reception of electromagnetic energy, or the vulnerability of equipment, and in this case, the weakness in the software of the steering device to electromagnetic interferences. But, the configuration of the magnetic field and deviation values in the area were not available in the investigation report. Any slight deviation in the magnetic field may cause disturbances in the

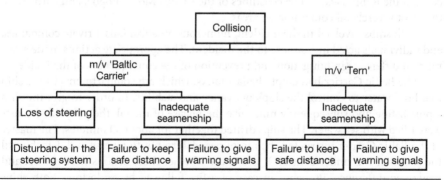

Figure 8.3 The fault tree of the collision.

systems, including the compass and the steering system. The Baltic Carrier passed over the power cables 11 minutes prior to the collision, which means eight minutes prior to the loss of steering. The tests performed onboard the ship were limited to a short period of time, and it was unclear how these tests were performed.

Inadequate seamanship—failure to give warning signals and keep a safe distance: One or two minutes after the ship lost steering, the third officer of the m/v Baltic Carrier contacted other ships in the vicinity, informing them that the m/v Baltic Carrier was not under control, switched on the not-under-command lights, and sounded the general alarm on board. But, he failed to switch off the navigation sidelights and give warning signals to other ships by sound and/or light in accordance with the international navigation rules. Both ships failed to communicate the situation and the intention of their actions in due time. A few seconds would have made a difference.

Further, both ships were unnecessarily sailing within the deep water (DW) route, which was reserved for ships that, due to their draft, could not navigate safely outside the route. The master of the Baltic Carrier stated that, due to shallow waters and dense vessel traffic, he chose to sail within the DW route. But, the incident investigation indicated that both ships had a maximum draft of 11 meters and there was no other ship in the close vicinity.

THE FATE OF OIL, RESPONSE, AND CLEANUP OPERATIONS

The fate of the oil spill determines, to a large degree, the extent of consequences. As the result of collision, the Baltic Carrier lost 2700 tons of oil from tank no. 6, of which 2428 tons spilt into the sea, 30 tons seeped into the double hull, and 242 tons ended up into the bow of the Tern. The oil slick drifted towards the Danish coastlines due to the prevailing winds and currents. By late afternoon of the 29th of March, the oil penetrated into the narrow waters of the Groensund stranding along the coastline of islands Moen, Faroe, Bogoe, and Falster. Immediately after the incident, the response teams placed booms along the most sensitive coastal areas and harbors. On the morning of the 30th of March, large oil slicks landed along the northern and northeastern coast of the island Falster. The coastlines of the islands Moen, Bogoe, and Faroe were the most severely oil contaminated areas.

Both ships involved in the incident, numerous organizations, private companies, and individuals acted in response to the incident. The appropriate actions made a significant difference in mitigation and prevention of the consequences of the incident.

The Baltic Carrier had empty ballast tanks, which are compartments in the ship that hold water to control the ship's buoyancy and stability. In order to give the ship a port listing and subsequently minimize the release of the oil, the port side ballasts were filled with sea water. The ships drifted together for about 30 minutes. The master of the Baltic Carrier instructed the motor vessel Tern not to reverse and detach until the situation was under control. It is unclear whether these actions were correct and made any difference. Probably, in case of a fire followed by explosions, both ships would have sunk. Fortunately, no fire broke out on board the ships. The ships were prepared for fire fighting. The Baltic Carrier anchored north of the DW route after the collision.

When the German and the Swedish authorities were informed of the collision, they launched response operations to control the oil spill and mitigate the consequences. The initial cleanup operations at sea were hampered and subsequently suspended due to weather conditions. In Denmark, a task force was set up in accordance with the Danish Act concerning protection of the marine environment. Many people worked hard for days in cleanup operations, including people from the municipalities affected by oil and other municipalities, the National Rescue Preparedness Corps, and volunteers from other municipal rescue service corps and local citizens.

The response teams employed different measures. Special ships equipped with grabbing devices collected the oil with a low viscosity at sea. The oil heated at 80° C was pumped to the facilities ashore. Additional barges were chartered and oil disposal sites established in order to deal with the large amount of oil collected at sea and coastal lines. The oil was collected directly from the sea by means of sludge sucking devices. But, because of the heavy weight of equipment, the oil collection by these devices was confined to a few locations with a firm ground, such as dams. The oil waste was disposed at incineration plants, whereas the oil mixed with sand, soil, stone, sea grass, and other substances was disposed at decontamination plants.

The oil contained with booms was towed close to the shore. A large part of the oil waste ashore was mechanically collected by excavators and container trucks. The oil collected and loaded manually in one meter cubic containers in inaccessible areas was airlifted by helicopter and discharged to barges at sea or disposal sites ashore. The authorities decided not to use chemicals to disperse the oil deposits. Tests showed no significant results in removing the oil by application of chemicals. High pressure water flushing was used instead where it was not possible to collect the oil, for example, in the areas with large stones.

According to the DEMA, the cleanup operations were generally efficient— approximately 90 percent of the oil spilt (2428 tons) was collected. Small oil patches floated outside the Groensund area, as far as the Swedish coast. A part of the oil spilt evaporated, diluted into the water and degraded. However, according to a survey report (2001), compared to some other major oil spill incidents, the monitoring activities of the consequences of the oil spill from the m/v Baltic Carrier incident were inappropriate both in time and extent. Due to the lack of common strategy and division of the responsibility and financing, the monitoring program was slowly developed. The survey report also pointed out the lack of acceptable criteria for PAHs in seafood.

CONSEQUENCES TO HUMANS, THE ENVIRONMENT, AND SUPPLY CHAIN IMPACTS

The incident affected the marine environment and its habitats, public and private properties, the maritime transport and various supply chain systems. Consequences to the risk receptors were largely related.

Human Consequences

Human consequences include categories such as deaths, injuries, acute or chronic illness, and other health effects. The m/v Baltic Carrier and the m/v Tern had 19 and 22 crewmembers, respectively. Fortunately, no one was killed or injured as a result of the collision. Immediately after the incident, the Danish food inspection authorities informed the local communities about the risks of consuming contaminated fish. The authorities advised people not to consume fish from the area with visible oil pollution until further instructions.

The Marine Environment

The marine environment is sensitive and economically important to the local community. The Groensund is a shallow area surrounded by islands of Moen, Faroe, Bogoe, and Falster, which have sandy beaches, slopes, and rocky shorelines. The area is rich with vegetation and it is an important breeding and sanctuary area for wildlife. The area is inhabited by the smallest Danish whale. It is an important area for industrial fishery and aquaculture, and recreation.

The county authorities and research institutions closely cooperated in laboratory and field studies on the environmental impacts of the oil spill. In the first year after the incident, samples were taken three times for analysis at many stations covering the entire affected area. A few samples were also taken during 2002. The results of analyses were compared to the natural background concentrations, i.e., the Danish and the international waters as well as the international guidelines.

The oil spill affected the sea water, sediments, and the biota (fauna and flora). It caused physical damage to the environment and had acute and chronically adverse effects to organisms. After the oil spill, high levels of PAH concentrations were found in the seawater column, sediments, and fauna (shrimp, flounder, mussels and fish). The concentrations in the fish's liver and muscle tissue indicated a recent exposure. The test results showed that the oil concentrations in the most heavily affected areas were high enough to have caused acute toxicity to pelagic crustaceans. The oil affected the growth, activity, and behavior of the marine organisms. However, the risk of long-term effects of the oil spill in the area was considered *low*.

Many birds of 23 different species were found dead or dying in the area. Birds died due to oil smeared feathers and damaged respiratory and ingestion organs. Only about 1750 birds were collected of the total amount estimated by the Gamekeeper, and the Greenpeace and county biologists of between 4000–20,000 birds dead or dying. Eiders and long-tailed ducks accounted for the largest number of dead birds. Many birds did not arrive to the area as expected. However, the population of breeding birds recovered gradually, except for waders.

CONSEQUENCES TO MARITIME TRANSPORT AND RESPECTIVE SUPPLY CHAINS

The incident generated a chain of undesirable effects with direct consequences to the maritime transport systems. In turn, these consequences might have caused domino effects on other systems within respective supply chains, namely petro-chemical and food supply chains. Like any other business unit, a merchant ship is a complex system designed to perform a value-adding activity in the form of material flows. The tanker ship Baltic Carrier loaded with 33,000 tons of heavy fuel oil was enroute to the UK. The ship lost 2700 tons of fuel oil due to the collision. The bulk carrier Tern loaded with 20,000 tons of raw sugar was enroute to Ventpils/Latvia.

Both ships were seriously damaged. The Baltic Carrier sustained serious damage to the hull (see Figure 8.2). The Tern was also heavily damaged in the stem, impairing the ship's seaworthiness, but the cargo remained intact. The forepeak ballast water tank was ripped open to the sea. A considerable amount of fuel oil from the Baltic Carrier poured into the forepeak tank and mixed with seawater. The mooring system in the bow, including the port anchor, the anchor shaft, the foundation of the anchor winches and mooring winches forward were damaged. In addition, the bulkhead between the forepeak tank and the cargo hold were damaged. The oil in the damaged bow leaked into the sea, causing minor pollution to the harbor.

Both ships interrupted their activities due to serious damage. The amounts of cargo carried onboard both ships were considerably enough to have caused disruptions to the systems of petro-chemical and food supply chains, respectively. The Baltic Carrier anchored in the nearby area until the damaged tank was emptied and temporally repaired. The ship then sailed for the shipyard for repair. Whereas, the motor vessel Tern headed for the port of Rostock, Germany, for inspection and temporary repairs. On April 9, the ship was allowed under strict conditions to leave the port and set sail for the port of destination to discharge the cargo and get fully repaired. An incident of this magnitude means a great deal, if not bankruptcy, to a small company with a few ships.

CONSEQUENCES TO OTHER SUPPLY CHAINS—THE COSTS OF THE OIL SPILL

The oil spill caused considerable consequences to other supply chains ashore, namely fishing, aquaculture and tourism industries. All categories of consequences can be measured in monetary units. The costs of risks can represent a considerable portion of supply chain costs in the form of human, environmental and property, maintenance, preventive and quality measures, and insurance costs.

Fishery: The commercial and recreational fisheries are important for Storstroem County. In the year 2000, the commercial fishery generated an annual profit of € 20 million, which included profits from fish delivered to the county and fishing activities in the Baltic Sea. After the oil spill, the fish population declined dramatically in the Groensund area. During the season of 2001, the production of fish was suspended in three aqua farms in the area due to the oil spill. The fishing gear were also affected. The loss of profits and damage to fishing gear of the local commercial fishery were estimated to be € 200,000. In addition, Japanese customers suspended the import of fish from the areas contaminated by oil.

In many similar situations, fishing activities have been banned in the contaminated areas until further notice. But no strict regulatory measures were taken in banning fishing in the case of the Baltic Carrier oil spill. The authorities concluded that the risk of increased cancer to humans due to consumption of fish in the affected area was low. However, the results of a risk analysis performed by the Danish Veterinary and the Food Administration suggested that marine organisms from the polluted areas were not suitable for human consumption for a period of several months after the oil spill.

Aquaculture and private property: In 2001, Storstroem County had seven aqua farms, of which three farms were located in the Groensund area, with an annual income of about € 9.5 million. Three out of seven aqua farms were closed down for the season in 2001. The fish stock was destroyed in three farms. The aquaculture business in the county lost € 2.7 million due to oil pollution. In addition, during cleanup operations, fields and private property, for example, fences and private roads were damaged. Heavy machines used to remove the oil disturbed habitats known for some rare species. Damage to fields and private property amounted to € 27,000 and € 67,000 respectively, or € 94,000 in total.

Tourism: It is an important industry for the local community, generating an annual profit of € 200 million per year in 2000 reports. Many local shops and restaurants depend very much on tourism. There are many summer cottages, hotels and camping sites in the area. The Groensund is a popular holiday resort and recreational site for bathing, diving, sailing, and fishing. A great number of tourists mainly from Germany, Sweden, and The Netherlands visit the area. Many Danish and foreign sailboats visit the local harbors during the summer. However, the impact of the oil pollution to the local tourism business was considered not as significant as expected. In 2001, according to the tourism industry, the influx of tourists from Germany to Storstroem County declined, whereas the number of tourists from other Scandinavian countries and The Netherlands increased.

In summary, the costs of the oil spilt to the local fishing industry, aquaculture, agriculture, and properties ashore were reported to be € 3 million. But, these costs are only a portion of the total costs of the incident. Based on nine world major oil spill cases, the amount of claims in U.S. dollars in the case of a major oil spill is estimated to be $3000 per ton of the oil spilt (Mullai and Paulsson 2002). These claims are adjusted for price inflation to the year 2001. The costs of the oil spill in the Kadet Renden are estimated to be $8.1 million U.S. dollars, excluding cargo and ship claims. Based on the International Maritime Organization, the proposed value of gross cost of averting a fatality is US$1.5 million, and the total costs of the oil spill (€8.1 million) is estimated to be equivalent to 5.4 fatalities.

Expenses paid by the governmental agencies in response, cleanup, monitoring, research and other activities are the taxpayers' money. In addition, many organizations and individuals interrupted their daily activities and participated in response and monitoring operations. These costs become a burden to a country's economy and directly affect various supply chains. Spending in risk management and regulatory control increases as the risks increase, particularly in response to major events. These incidents directly affect transport and supply chain costs as well as their reliability.

PUBLICITY, MEDIA, AND LEGAL IMPLICATIONS

This incident became the center of public and media attention for several weeks in both Denmark and Germany. Danish TV channels and newspapers showed pictures from the scene and dead birds. German tourist agencies were informed about environmental effects of the oil spill. No reactions from the public to the oil spill were reported. The data sources provide no information whether the Danish authorities filed any lawsuits or took any legal actions against the ship owners and the crews of either ship for the oil spill. However, the ship owners are liable for the consequences.

RISK EVALUATION AND PRESENTATION

The simple notion of risk is the likelihood of consequences of undesirable events. Quantification and evaluation of the risk elements based on the data contained in this case history is limited, if not impossible. Therefore, the risk elements are benchmarked against other data, relevant risk criteria, and our judgments (see Table 8.2).

The review of many other marine incident data and our risk study (Mullai and Paulsson, 2002) suggests that, in terms of the amount of oil spilt and its consequences, the oil spill that resulted from the collision between the Baltic Carrier and the Tern is the most severe oil spill to ever have happened in Danish waters and the second largest oil spill in the Baltic Sea. The aggregated risks, i.e., the combined human, environment, property and reputation risks, posed by the Baltic Carrier incident are found to be at *a relatively high level*, but within the as low as reasonably practicable (ALARP) region, as presented in Table 8.2. The following are the main facts and our judgments:

- The severity of the aggregated consequences—*weighed ranking 4.*
  o *People*: No human fatality, injury, or health effects were reported. However, according to the international standards of conversion, the estimated costs of US$8.1 million for the incident, excluding ships and cargo damage, are equivalent to around six fatalities, i.e., *severity ranking 5, multiple fatalities.*
  o *Assets*: Both ships sustained serious damage. The Baltic Carrier lost 2700 tons of oil from tank no. 6. Commercial and recreational fisheries, aquacul-

ture farms and agriculture, and private property were seriously affected by the oil spill. *The severity ranking 4, major damage.*

o *Environment:* The marine environment (seawater, sediments, and coast-lines) and fauna (shrimp, fish, and birds) and flora (vegetation) were seri-ously affected. The situations generally returned to normal one year after the incident. The concentrations of oil decreased to the natural background levels. The oil pollution did not cause any irreversible damage to the wild-life and the environment. The oil pollution was largely confined to the local area, the Groensund. *The severity ranking 3, local effect.*

o *Reputation:* The incident stayed at the center of public and media atten-tion for several weeks. The attention was largely confined to the local area, Denmark, Germany, and Sweden. The incident might have caused limited or little impact to the reputation of the ship owners of both ships. *The sever-ity ranking 2, limited effect.*

- The frequency—*weighed infrequent (B).*

The above data suggest that incidents of the magnitude of the Baltic Carrier incident are infrequent in the Baltic Sea area, including the Danish waters. The oil spills of the magnitude (in tons) of the oil spilt from the Baltic Carrier are relatively infrequent. They are likely to happen at a frequency of one incident over a period of more than ten years (see Table 8.2).

CONCLUSIONS AND RECOMMENDATIONS

In conclusion, with reference to our objectives in this chapter, attempts have been made to perform a systematic risk analysis of a major oil spill in the Baltic Sea, and thereby contribute to enhancing the understanding of maritime risk. The collision occurred as the result of an unfortunate combination of technical failure, human factor errors, and unfavorable weather conditions. Collisions are among the most frequent types of maritime incidents in this region and the world. But, an incident of this kind is extremely unlikely to happen at open sea. Due to the features of the area, a relatively small amount of oil spilt in the Baltic Sea can cause serious consequences. The oil spill seriously affected the marine environment and its habitats, local public and private properties, maritime transport systems and supply chains, such as fishing, aquaculture, and tourism industries.

The response operations made a difference in mitigation and prevention of the consequences of the oil spill. We have found that the aggregated risks posed by the Baltic Carrier incident were at *a relatively high level,* but within the ALARP region. The principal strategy for the risks located in the ALARP region is to incorporate risk reducing measures. We propose the following measures:

- Risk studies are largely limited in the region. Perform detailed quantita-tive studies on maritime risks, including the risks of maritime transport of

Table 8.2 Evaluation and presentation of the aggregated risks of the m/v Baltic Carrier incident based on the ISO Risk Matrix

Severity rating	Consequences				Frequency				
	People	Assets	Environment	Reputation	A	B	C	D	E
					Rarely occurred in industry	Happened several times per year in industry	Has occurred in operating company	Happened several times per year in operating company	Happened several times per year in location
0	Zero injury	Zero damage	Zero effect	Zero impact					
1	Slight injury	Slight damage	Slight effect	Slight impact					
2	Minor injury	Minor damage	Minor effect	Limited impact					
3	Major injury	Local damage	Local effect	Considerable impact					
4	Single fatality	Major damage	Major effect	Major national impact	Baltic Carrier Incident	ALARP Region			
5	Multiple fatalities	Extensive damage	Massive effect	Major international impact	Incorporate risk-reducing measures	Intolerable Risks Avoid/Eliminate			

Tolerable risks

Manage for continued improvement

dangerous substances for the Danish territorial waters and the entire Baltic Sea Region.

- Risk criteria for the evaluation of dangerous substances risks, and maritime risks in general, are nonexistent in Denmark as well as in other countries in the region. Establish risk criteria for individual countries and the entire region based on quantitative risk studies. The criteria will assist decision makers in risk evaluation and adequate monitoring of the situation.

- The cleanup and monitoring operations were generally efficient. However, the process was inhibited by some shortcomings. Due to organizational and budget issues, it took months until the monitoring process proceeded in a structured manner. Studies and efforts should be made to improve cooperation among national and local parties in response to incidents including oil spills. Emergency planning, equipment, organization and budget should be well prepared in advance and be in place in case of a major oil spill. Denmark and Sweden in particular are exposed to major oil spills.

- Enhance cooperation among international partners in the region. Organize meetings, training, education and exercises on a regular basis.

The risk analysis of the case presented in this chapter is based on the combination of various data sources available. Our judgments also played an important role in the risk analysis and the risk evaluation. This study may serve as a platform for considering a detailed quantitative study of the maritime risks in the region.

REFERENCES

Brindley, C., ed. (2004). *Supply Chain Risk*. UK: Ashgate Publishing Company, Farnham, UK.

Coyle, J. J., E. J. Bardin, and R. A. Novack. 2000. *Transportation*, 5th ed. South-Western College Publishing, New York.

Danish Maritime Administration (DMA), Ministry of Trade and Industry. (2001). Casualty Report: Collision on 29 March 2001 between the tanker Baltic Carrier, registered on Marshall Island and the bulk carrier Tern, registered on Cyprus. Case 199913714, Division for Investigation of Maritime Accidents (DIMA).

Danish Emergency Management Agency (DEMA), (2001) The oil pollution from the Baltic Carrier incident—cross-body evaluation and report of experience, Development and Research Unit.

Kaplan, S., and B. J. Garrick. (1981) On the quantitative definitions of risks. *Journal of Risk Analysis* 1:11–27.

Mullai, A., and U. Paulsson. (2002) Oil Spills in Oresund—Hazardous Events, Causes and Claims. Report on the SUNDRISK Project, Lund University Centre for Risk Analysis and Management (LUCRAM), Lund University, Department of Industrial Management and Engineering Logistics, Division of Engineering Logistics, Lund, Sweden. 1-160.

Mullai A. (2007) A Risk Analysis Framework for Maritime Transport of Packaged Dangerous Goods—A Validating Demonstration. PhD thesis, Lund University, Lund Institute of Technology, Department of Industrial Management and Engineering Logistics, Division of Engineering Logistics, Lund, Sweden, I:1-210 and II:1-330.

Rytkonen, J., Hannninen, S. and Sonninen, S. (2002) Sea-borne traffic in 2000 upto 2015 in the Gulf of Finland, Research Paper from the VTT Technical Research Centre of Finland, Espoo, Finland, available at http://www.vtt.fi/vtt.new/210302doc.pdf, accessed Dec 20, 2005.

Vincent, G., B. Le Guen, and S. Le Floch. (2001) "Accident of the oil tanker 'Baltic Carrier' off the Danish Coastline." European Task Force in Denmark Final Report, European Commission.

Wetzel, E.A. 2004. International Shipping: A Focus on the Republic of China: An Interview with Steven R. Blust, Chairman, Federal Maritime Commission. Review of Business 25: 5-9.

9

POLITICAL RISKS IN CONTEMPORARY SUPPLY CHAINS: THE CASE OF THE NATURAL GAS CRISIS

Wojciech Machowiak

> GAZPROM's strategic goal is to become a leader among global energy companies by developing new markets, diversifying business activities, and securing the reliability of supplies.
>
> —GAZPROM's mission statement

The mission of the giant Russian gas company GAZPROM came under serious scrutiny at the beginning of 2009. Words such as "securing the reliability of supplies" sounded more like stinging irony when on Tuesday, January 6, 2009, GAZPROM simply turned off the gas taps on the Russia/Ukraine border point of the Brotherhood pipeline, leaving some EU countries completely without a supply of gas, and others with a considerably reduced supply of gas.

Natural gas (NG) is growing increasingly important in the world's energy balance today and will continue to be important in the near future. Natural gas is a ready-to-use, clean, environment friendly, and efficient energy source that is being used for a growing scope of applications, and has therefore created a dynamic increase of interest. The fundamental applications are industrial (chemical, pharmaceutical, and other industries), electricity generation and also commercial utilization, as well as household heating.

The world's estimated Natural Gas (NG) reserves are at least about 6,254 trillion cubic feet, and more than 26% of that amount is deposited in Russia (EIA-IEO 2009 46). Russia

115

GAZPROM (Gazprom Open Joint Stock Company)

GAZPROM Group possesses the world's largest natural gas reserves. As of December 31, 2008 the Group's A+B+C1 resources were estimated at 33.1 trillion cubic meters.

With 17 percent of the global gas production, GAZPROM Group is the leader among the world's oil and gas companies.

In 2008, GAZPROM Group produced 549.7 billion cubic meters of gas. GAZPROM owns the world's largest gas transmission system; its trunklines stretch 159.5 thousand km.

In 2008, the company sold 184.4 billion cubic meters of gas to European countries along with 96.5 billion cubic meters to the CIS and Baltic states.

www.gazprom.com

Figure 9.1 GAZPROM Group.

also remains the biggest producer and exporter of natural gas. GAZPROM's contribution to the world's NG production exceeds 23 percent (EIA-IEO 2009 39). The major customers of GAZPROM are European Union countries, purchasing one quarter of their NG consumption volume. Approximately 80 percent of that amount comes from Russia via Ukraine (see Figure 9.1).

The enormous dependence on supply from Russia is thus considered to be a key risk factor in European natural gas procurement. The diversification of sources to avoid excessive dependence on one supplier, a fundamental principle of risk management, has been broken for years. For several countries the level of risk is excessive. Natural gas demand covered by Russia is: 100 percent for Finland, Slovakia, and Macedonia; 96 percent for Bulgaria; 87 percent for Serbia and Montenegro; 82 percent for Greece; 79 percent for Czech Republic; 74 percent for Austria; 64 percent for Slovenia; 54 percent for Hungary; 47 percent for Poland; 36 percent for Germany; and 25 percent for Italy (EIA-ISA, 2009). Moreover, Russia intends to increase that dependency through construction of two new big gas pipelines to Europe.

Events at the beginning of 2009 exhibited how dangerous such a policy can be. Disrupted natural gas supply chains in many countries not only resulted in stopping production, but also increased awareness of the dangers of one big supplier such as Russia, in terms of what the political risks are and the importance of managing such risks.

NATURAL GAS SUPPLY CHAIN—FROM SIBERIA TO EUROPE

There are two giant NG pipelines that are thousands of miles long supplying European countries with the gas from Russia. Both start from the Yamal Peninsula at Western

Siberia—the biggest NG reserves in the world. The first one, named YAMAL—Europe, runs via Belarus to Poland and Germany. The second pipeline, Brotherhood, runs via Ukraine and feeds countries such as Romania, Bulgaria, Turkey, Greece and the Balkan republics, also Slovakia, Hungary, Austria, Italy, France, Czech Republic and again Germany. Behind Russia's border points, gas in the pipeline is owned by the local gas operator, which is usually a state owned company. In Poland, such a company is PGNiG; in the Ukraine it is NAFTOHAZ; in Slovakia it is SPP; and similarly in other countries.

These companies distribute and sell NG in their respective countries, build and control gas stores, and also negotiate contracts with GAZPROM. The pipelines within each country are controlled by other companies, being mostly subsidiaries of both GAZPROM and local, domestic NG operators. The end link in all these NG supply chains are distributors (mostly domestic local subsidiaries of a national gas operator) selling gas to end users, who are industrial, commercial, or municipal subjects as well as households.

These simple, more or less linear supply chains, being greatly dominated by GAZPROM are significantly exposed to political risks. Usually supply chains consist of several collaborating enterprises, where one plays a basic role (e.g., manufacturer of final product) and to some extent takes responsibility for coordinating a risk management process for the entire configuration. In the natural gas supply chain, the prominent role of the main supplier GAZPROM can have detrimental political ramifications, and risk mitigation measures must thus be taken by local gas operators. An important attribute of the Russia-Europe natural gas supply chain is the interweaving of state controlled and private businesses, not always categorized as a public-private partnership.

Whereas in the majority of typical supply chains, one of the major risk sources is logistics, in gas supply this is not the case. Once completed, a pipeline rarely provides any logistical problems; thus, other risk categories play a dominant role, including political risks. The aspect that requires extraordinary imagination when managing risks in NG supply chains is the time factor. Critical situations usually need instantaneous actions adjusted to current and/or immediate needs, whereas any legal solutions and investments in the gas supply business, which are basically effective risk management measures, most often take years.

POLITICAL RISKS

Within the global supply chains of today, enterprises have to face, among many other risk categories, risks of a political nature. Political risks are identified with the possible destabilization in a country or a region where a particular business operates or is going to operate. Such destabilization may be understood as a change of the political team in power (via a democratic election, or as a result of a revolution, *coup d'etat*, domestic unrest) and also as a change in the legal regulations regarding business activities (e.g. fiscal policy), variations in the local attitude to foreign investments, and other factors within the business climate and environment. Sometimes it may also include fluctuations in the local currency which is unstable, or obstructions with the transfer of capital, acts of nationalization or property confiscation, or some forms of protectionism. All of these factors may result in losses for particular enterprises and/or the disruption of the supply chain. However, considering the political risks as potential events and decisions of a political nature negatively affecting the supply chain's functionality, we should widen the scope of the list to include all likely events and decisions having open or veiled political backgrounds or roots.

The Russia-Ukraine conflict provides us with an interesting business case, which has strong political undercurrents. In this case, the supply chain breakdown was caused not by soldiers, guns and tanks, neither embargos nor economic sanctions, but by using business as a retaliatory political weapon and as a tool applied to exert political pressure. The dispute started from financial claims and controversies. Nevertheless, the main questions asked were: What political price must be paid? What could be the ultimate level of gas transfer fees?

Political risks are complex and not easy to treat, unlike many other typical risk categories. They include factors and drivers of fundamental significance often completely out of sight of the enterprise's control. Moreover, in global supply chains, often where countries are politically unstable and/or unstable entities are involved, exposure to such risks is increased and the predictability of partners in the supply chain remains poor and limited.

THE 2009 RUSSIA-UKRAINE GAS CRISIS

The 2009 Russia-Ukraine gas crisis was not the first time GAZPROM turned the gas taps off to Ukraine, but this time it was not Ukraine alone who suffered. As a consequence of the supply halt at the Russian-Ukrainian border in January 2009, several EU countries were left completely without gas or with substantially reduced amounts of gas at their disposal. In Bulgaria (almost 100 percent dependent on Russian gas), the temperature at the time was around -20°C. Bulgaria's gas storage was sufficient only for a few days. Slovakia, with a few weeks of reserves stored, established Martial Law for enterprises at midnight on January 7th (see Figure 9.2 for a chronology of events).

Besides the numerous Russian and Ukrainian VIPs involved, EU authorities also became involved, including the European Commission's President Jose Manuel Barroso and German Chancellor Angela Merkel. Even the White House found it reasonable to warn Russia against manipulating the supply of energy resources in the region. There is no way to judge accurately who was more culpable in the affair, Russia or Ukraine. The background of that conflict was compounded by several factors, each significantly contributing to the course of events, the tactics, the entrenched attitudes, and the proceedings of the parties involved. Nevertheless, the main aspects

Chronology of events

19 December 2008—GAZPROM claims over 2 blnUSD of Ukrainian debts to be paid as a condition of gas supply continuation for 2009; USA and Ukraine sign the Charter on Strategic Partnership

23 December 2008—President Yushchenkoof of Ukraine informed that over 1 blnUSD was paid

26 December 2008—GAZPROM warns Ukraine again – all debts must be settled by the end of the year, otherwise the gas supply will be halted

30 December 2008—NAFTOHAZ made a payment of over 1.5 blnUSD; GAZPROM announces its arrangements to cut the gas supply off

31 December 2008—New agreement for gas supply from Russia to Ukraine still not signed

01 January 2009—Daily gas supply at Ukrainian border reduced by 90 mlnc.m.

02-03 January 2009—Gas pressure decreases in transit to Hungary, Romania and Poland; GAZPROM accuses Ukraine of stealing EU destined gas

05 January 2009—Economic court in Kyiv rules to ban NAFTOHAZ from continuing Russian gas transit to EU because of formal reasons

06 January 2009—Further accusations from both sides; GAZPROM cuts flow from 262 to 65.3 mlnc.m.; complete cut off at "Bulgarian" branch of the gas supply network; significant shortages in gas supply to Austria and Hungary

07 January 2009—definitive halt of Russian gas supply to Europe via Ukraine; Slovakia establishes martial law for enterprises

08 January 2009—EU, GAZPROM and NAFTOHAZ officials meet in Brussels

11 January 2009—Russian President Medvedev announced new conditions of gas supply resuming as a response to Ukrainian change in the protocol

12 January 2009—Resigning of the protocol

17 January 2009—Summit in Moscow, no results

18 January 2009—After day-long talks between Y. Tymoshenkoand W. Putin, a deal is reached and signed the next day by GAZPROM and NAFTOHAZ

20 January 2009—Gas supply to Ukraine and Europe is resumed; two days are necessary to restore full volumes; the crisis is over.

Figure 9.2 Chronology of events leading to January 7, 2009.

of the imbroglio, being concurrently considerable sources of risk, may be identified as coming from the following areas:

- *Business negotiations* of the new Russia-Ukraine gas contract, including new prices, transit fees, and such, obstructions in Ukrainian remittances, and also Russian attempts to win at the expense of its partner's troubles and Russia's pursuit of gaining further growth in its already huge domination of the gas market
- *Internal problems*—both parties were in a difficult financial condition, exacerbated by the global recession; GAZPROM faced steeply declining gas prices, tremendous credit liabilities, a large but unprofitable internal market, and

therefore had a vital necessity of further investments; Ukraine faced mounting debts, a huge drop in GNP (–14 percent in 2008), growing unemployment, and social tensions rising in the face of the flagging efforts of the main political parties

- *Political issues*—relations between both countries were never good, worsening after the *Orange Revolution* and the Georgian war, and also because of Ukrainian attempts to get closer to NATO and the EU, a prospect unacceptable to Russia
- *Legal*—long-term contracts (even beyond 2030) on gas supply seem to be disproportionately ensuring the interests of both parties; these contracts were concluded under the pressure of time and the seriousness of the situation; a ban on the reexport of Russian gas made it difficult for EU countries to help each other during trouble and is difficult to change; moreover, the principle of *take-or-pay*, applied in long-term contracts, additionally aggravated any attempts to quickly diversify gas sourcing

This background of dispute, the existence of other than business-oriented incentives, and motivated actions, mainly of a political nature, played essential roles in the course of events. Russia used that background to punish any lack of subordination from its former allies. It also never approved Ukraine's march toward NATO and EU (Marson 2009)—the life mission of President Yushchenko. Another part of the game was Russian expansion of its gas business in Europe. GAZPROM had just started two major projects of new, huge pipelines from Russia to EU—*NORD STREAM* and *SOUTH STREAM*—both passing around Ukraine. Considering the enormous costs of such an investment, GAZPROM—itself in poor financial condition—was vitally interested in gaining the EU's support and financial engagement. By attempting to portray Ukraine as an uncertain and unreliable partner, a weighty argument could be made in making these plans feasible.

On the other hand, Ukraine also frequently played a dubious and inconsistent game. First of all, it didn't pay Russia, which is inexcusable in normal business. Second, there could be some truth to the allegations that Russia leveled against it of stealing gas. Moreover, sometimes disloyally or in open opposition, Ukraine expected to be treated by Russia as a privileged country like other former Soviet republics, which many saw as unrealistic.

All of these circumstances resulted in a deeply critical situation that threatened Europe in a way it hadn't experienced for years, and in the area that is one of the most vulnerable for each economy—energy supply. Perhaps the most important result of the crisis was that it triggered two essential issues for the future. One issue is a strong awareness of the risk Europe takes in being so dependent on the Russian gas supply. The other issue is how urgent the need is for common actions aimed at diversifying energy sources and building infrastructural facilities that could assure possibilities of helping each other when countries are facing energy-supply trouble.

In this sense, especially from the long-term perspective, Russia remains likely the greatest loser in the whole affair. But Ukraine also comes out of the dispute as a big

loser, as its image as a reliable transit country faltered. Perhaps an even worse consequence, the EU may now be in no rush to tighten relations, fearing the repercussions.
Ukraine's road to joining NATO and the EU now seems to be much longer and more
difficult.

RISK MANAGEMENT—THE CASE OF PGNIG

In general, as the primary imperative in practicing enterprise risk management, we
used avoidance of loss, whereas at the supply chain level, we used the usual continuity
of supply. However, when political forces come into play, they become even more critical to business goals, and possible loss or supply chain disruption become secondary
issues. Political goals must have their price, since both Russia and Ukraine seemed to
be ready to pay. The fact that they did, may have resulted in an unexpected surplus. So
who had to care about risk management the most?—mainly those who were left without gas. One of them was Polish Oil and Gas Company (PGNiG) (see Figure 9.3).

Political risk management is basically subject to the same process that is practiced
with other risk categories. Roughly speaking, threats have to be identified, then assessed,
and finally adequate measures must be taken within the risk treatment phase to mitigate
any possible risk impact and/or reduce the likelihood of negative events. The last outcome is the most difficult to directly influence, as all possible measures leading to the
reduction of political event probability are almost completely out of the risk manager's
or CEO's influence. Thus, practically the whole core area of political risk mitigation in
such a supply chain is to reduce the possible risk impact. For all national gas operators
like PGNiG, the fundamental risk factors in the gas supply chain are:

PGNiG (Polish Oil and Gas Company)

*PGNiG is a leader in natural gas segments in Poland, including trade, distribution,
oil and gas exploration, and production as well as gas storage and processing. The
company is also the largest importer of natural gas to Poland.*

*It is a leader in the natural gas market in Poland. The core activity of the company
encompasses field exploration and production of natural gas and crude oil as well
as import, storage, trade and distribution of gas and liquid fuels. Polish Oil and
Gas Company is one of the largest and oldest companies in Poland.*

*In 2008, total natural gas sales were 13.9 bcm and total natural gas imports were
at a level of 10.3 bcm. 66% of gas comes from the east, 28% from domestic
production and 6% from the west.*

www.pgnig.pl

Figure 9.3 Polish Oil and Gas Company (PGNiG).

- *Excessive dependence on a single supplier*—in our case this is GAZPROM (47 percent of Poland's domestic NG demand; in a few other EU countries this dependence can be as high as 100 percent)
- *Insufficient stored gas reserves*—in Poland these reserves amount to only a few weeks of the country's consumption; in other countries it varies from a few days (Bulgaria, Slovakia) to a few months (Germany)
- *Lack of technological alternatives*—only in very rare cases (like in power supply) can gas as an energy carrier be instantaneously replaced by another source;
- *Limited (if any, especially within short periods of time) capabilities of increasing gas production from domestic resources*—even if they are recognized
- *Existing infrastructural facilities* resulting in limited chances of alterations in gas sourcing and making quick help from EU neighbor countries (such as aid to Poland from Germany or the Czech Republic) difficult or even impossible
- *Wrong or disadvantageous records and clauses included into gas supply contracts with GAZPROM*—like long-term validity with very limited possibilities of change and notice, the *take-or-pay* principle, and a ban on reexport.

These risk factors had already been well recognized by PGNiG—as a result of previous experiences with GAZPROM—before the crisis. It may be that not all the necessary or possible measures had been undertaken, but we have to remember that such strategic decisions as the supply of energy are usually taken by governments, and business involvement is mostly anticipated by interstate agreements. In that context, what PGNiG essentially did was rather reasonable and produced feasible results. First of all, in a critical period of a few days, PGNiG managed to arrange additional supply of Russian gas via Belarus, which significantly improved the situation in Poland.

To decrease the country's dependence on a regular supply of gas from Russia, suppliers' alternatives to GAZPROM had been considered years in advance. As early as 2001, Poland signed an agreement with Norway, irrationally noticed after the change of government. However, PGNiG may still return to that idea. An interesting development or scenario could be the adjunction to the NABUCCO (also known as the Turkey-Austria Gas Pipeline) pipeline; however, this way of diversification and subsequent decrease in political risk may appear as doubtful, as countries from which gas will be sourced are regarded as politically unstable and at least some of them are under Russian influence. The most realistic solution however expensive (as an investment that will also result in a significant increase of gas prices for end consumers) is the LPG sea terminal off of Poland's Baltic Sea shoreline. This concept is interesting as it assures a high level of resilience in the supply chain—liquid gas may be imported from any country and in variable (within technical limitations) quantities, depending on current demand.

To increase storage capacities, PGNiG has already started new investments in underground depositories, which should enable it to double recent reserves within a few years. These reserves could still prove to be insufficient, as opinions concerning the level of stored reserves are conflicting and varied after the last crisis. Looking for technological alternatives to gas to be quickly replaced by other energy carriers seems to be the least preferable solution for Poland; nevertheless, plans of building nuclear plants have been given new life again. However, such an action may be regarded as an emergency measure, not a solution to the problem of shortage as a whole.

Modernization of infrastructure was also considered as a realistic and an accepted way of improving gas safety. PGNiG has already engaged in talks with Poland's neighbors, namely the Czech Republic and Germany, and has begun technical preparations to modernize existing pipelines or build new pipeline linkages, making it possible for quick emergency sourcing from each other.

Perhaps the most difficult decision would be to change the gas contract with GAZPROM to make it more buyer-friendly. The lengthy talks on a new agreement were very difficult and unnecessarily drawn out by GAZPROM. GAZPROM realizes well that PGNiG has no real alternative but to use their gas, both today and in the foreseeable future. At the same time, Russia remembers the strong opposition they encountered from Poland in their negotiations with Europe when leading the NORD STREAM project.

In other countries involved in the 2009 gas crisis, similar measures were taken, pursuant to local needs and possibilities. Germany, The Netherlands, Great Britain, and Romania, similar to Poland, managed to increase their own gas production. Where technically permitted, EU countries were helping each other by interchanging additional volumes of gas (from Western Europe to Hungary, from Germany and Hungary to the Balkan countries, from Greece to Bulgaria, from Germany, France and Czech Republic to Slovakia. Some of them made usage of technological energy source substitutions.

What may be the most spectacular development is a significant change in the awareness of risk in strategic areas of energy safety. This change has been noticed at the level of governments and at the EU Commission, as well as among businesses and society in general. Nobody doubts that something must be done before the next gas flow from Russia is halted. The first actions from the EU Commission are establishing gas safety coordination groups and they have announced intentions to stabilize gas purchases from Russia to below 30 percent of EU demand. However, the fundamental problem remains unchanged. Effective measures mitigating the political risk of Russian sourced gas supply chain disruption, such as diversification of supply, investments, and a common EU policy, all need time and financial resources.

As this case illustrates, it is impossible to completely avoid or eliminate political risk in supply chains. Thus we have to manage them, even if they are apparently *management proof*, as shown in the 2009 gas crisis example. Many types of political risks can be insured today. In fact, this branch of the insurance industry is growing rapidly in times of globalization. However, the political risks described in this case, where external forces interfere in businesses to use it as a weapon to accomplish political aims, are not insurable.

Nevertheless, looking at the problem of political risk in a more general perspective, we still have some means to minimize such risks. Number one is undoubtedly diversification, which may significantly mitigate detrimental political measures. In political risk assessment, a technique of special usefulness is the scenario of planning and analysis. To set the scene for political risk management and subsequent strategic decisions, we should reach out to all available sources of information, including diplomatic and intelligence reports, such as the U.S. Department of State's Background Notes, and other similar reports. Also presidential, parliamentary, and local authority terms of office, political and social events, and political tendencies—all these factors affect businesses and should be analyzed and subject to monitoring, since understanding them is fundamental to the successful management of political risks.

REFERENCES

EIA-IEO (Energy Information Administration/International Energy Outlook). 2009. [26 Dec 2009].http://www.eia.doe.gov/oiaf/ieo/index.html.

EIA-ISA (Energy Information Administration/Independent Statistics and Analysis). 2008.

Colorado Electricity Profile (2008 edition), Table 5. http://www.eia.doe.gov/cneaf/electricity/st_profiles/colorado.html.

Marson, J. 2009. "$250: The price of Ukraine's independence," *The Guardian*, [26 Dec 2009], http://www.guardian.co.uk/commentisfree/2009/jan/03/ukraine-russia-gas.

10

ENERJISA: MANAGING PROCUREMENT RISKS IN THE TURKISH ENERGY INDUSTRY

Çağrı Haksöz and Özgür Arslan

> *"Even if earthquakes create huge disruptions, in the aftermath, the first move has to be made in setting up electricity generation facilities. Without it, no communication, production, heating, even warehousing is possible. We cannot move without energy . . ."*
>
> —Melih Keskin, Procurement Manager, Enerjisa

COMPANY BACKGROUND

The Enerjisa Group is 50 percent owned by Sabancı Group and 50 percent owned by Verbund. Sabancı Group is one of Turkey's biggest industrial and financial conglomerates, composed of 69 companies. Sabancı Group's fundamental business units include financial services, automotive, tire and tire reinforcement materials, retail, cement, and energy. Verbund, the largest producer and transporter of electricity in Austria, is one of the leading hydropower producers and also one of the most profitable energy utilities in Europe.

The Enerjisa Group aspires to be the leader in the Turkish electricity market as an integrated utility, and has established the challenging goal of obtaining a 10 percent market share via 5000 megawatts (MW), and 6 million customers by the year 2015. Sabancı and Verbund signed a joint venture agreement in May 2007. The agreement is based upon the principles of joint control. Sabancı and Verbund will work together in the electricity sector, except for nuclear energy investments. Enerjisa lists the strategic goals as follows:

- Turkey as a key growth market
- Generation portfolio of *hydropower, gas, coal,* and *wind power* plants with a total capacity of 5000 MW by 2015
- Target to reach minimum market share of 10 percent in the Turkish electricity market by 2015
- Privatization of the electricity distribution and generation industry in Turkey
- Expand into other fields of energy activities internationally

Enerjisa has a generation portfolio of 455 MW and construction work has started on new power plants with a capacity of 2555 MW. Enerjisa Group strives to become the market leader for the electricity sector in a vertically integrated structure, by combining generation, distribution, supply, and trading activities. Figure 10.1 displays the organizational structure of the company.

Power Generation

Enerjisa Power Generation Company was founded on April 4, 1996 to explore new business opportunities that could emerge in the energy sector, and to operate as a reliable and competent supplier of energy to its customers. In addition to the gas-fired power stations in Kocaeli, Adana, Çanakkale, and Mersin, with a combined capacity of 370 MW, Enerjisa added operating hydroelectric power plants that are located in Antalya, Mersin, and Kahramanmara regions with a combined capacity of 85 MW to its generation portfolio through acquisitions in 2007.

With the objective of diversifying the generation capacity, 9 hydropower plants with a capacity of around 1049 MW, and the Bandırma Natural Gas Combined Cycle Power Plant with a capacity of around 920 MW are currently in implementation and construction phases. In addition, the 450 MW Tufanbeyli Coal-fired Power Plant and other growth options are currently in planning and implementation status. As part of

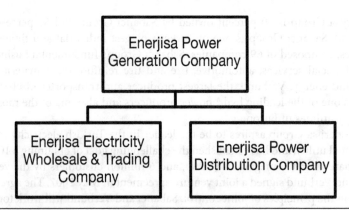

Figure 10.1 Enerjisa Group Companies (source: www.enerjisa.com).

its commitment to renewable energy, Enerjisa also has wind farm projects in different planning stages with a total capacity of 136 MW. In a bid to ease the problem of Turkey's tightening supply-demand balance, Enerjisa has put into operation the urgently needed generation capacity. In 2008 the firm had the groundbreakings of the 920 MW Bandırma Natural Gas Combined Cycle Power Plant, the 180 MW Adana Kavşak Bendi Hydroelectric Power Plant, and the 142 MW Kahramanmaras Hacınınoğlu Regulator and Hydroelectric Power Plant.

Electricity Wholesale and Trading

Enerjisa operates in the electricity wholesale market through Enerjisa Electricity Wholesale & Trading Company that was established on January 12, 2004. In addition to wholesale trading of electricity, the firm sells electricity directly to eligible customers. Opportunities to import and export electricity are also evaluated under the wholesale license. Enerjisa Electricity Wholesale & Trading has a customer oriented approach in its sales and marketing activities. With the objective of becoming a supplier preferred by its customers, the firm offers qualified services to meet the customers' expectations at the highest level, and improves its systems and processes on the basis of customer feedback. Besides wholesale and trading activities, Enerjisa Electricity Wholesale & Trading provides consultancy services to its sister companies and advises on operations in the balancing market, power plant optimization, and customer relationship management.

In order to secure the supply of natural gas and other fuels in a cost effective way over the long run, the firm advises the Enerjisa Group companies on natural gas supply contracts and other fuels for current and prospective power plants. Moreover, it helps in formulating fuel procurement strategies in the mid- and long-term, establishing fuel optimization systems and management of risks.

Power Distribution

The Sabancı Verbund Joint Venture won the privatization tender for the block sale of 100% of the shares of Başkent Electricity Distribution Company (Başkent Elektrik Dağıtım A.Ş.), on July 1, 2008, offering the highest bid at US$1.225 billion. In line with the commitment of Enerjisa becoming a vertically integrated leader of the market, Enerjisa Power Distribution, which will be holding the shares in Başkent Elektrik Dağıtım A.Ş., was established on October 24, 2008. The transfer of shares of Başkent Electricity Distribution Company was finalized on January 28, 2009. Enerjisa's objective is to make the Başkent Electricity Distribution Company the leading service company of the Turkish electricity sector, adhering to internationally accepted target benchmarks and highest customer satisfaction.

PROCUREMENT MANAGEMENT AT ENERJISA

Enerjisa performs the procurement activities under the Procurement Management Department, which has two procurement teams. The first procurement team operates for the existing power plants, coined as the *operational team*, and the second one works on the investment projects, and is called the *project team*. The firm has purchasing groups located in İstanbul, Ankara, İzmit, and Adana. The groups located in İstanbul and Ankara are responsible for both operational and project procurement. The groups located in İzmit and Adana are responsible for procurement processes of existing power plants.

For the existing gas power plants and hydropower plants, procurement management is responsible for procuring raw materials, spare parts, and chemicals, maintenance services, and other supplementary materials. Regarding the procurement process of power plant projects, responsibilities of procurement management include designing and preparing contracts and commercial specifications, opening tenders and negotiating with companies, requesting, and evaluating offers and purchasing goods and services.

MANAGING RISKS IN PROCUREMENT

In this case, we would like to shed light on the procurement risk management practices of Enerjisa. We will focus on the following topics in order to achieve this purpose.

- Procurement risk awareness: drivers of procurement risk
- Procurement risk assessment
- Risk hedging and mitigation
- Managing learning and procurement talent
- The path forward

Procurement Risk Awareness: Drivers of Procurement Risk

For Enerjisa, drivers of the procurement risk ranged from supplier related to market related risks, disruption risks, end-customer demand risks, environmental risks, regulatory/political risks, and strategic risks. In Figure 10.2, we provide a risk map that displays the perception of the procurement manager on various risk drivers and their respective *probabilities* and *impacts*. This map is constructed considering the risk drivers for the project-based procurement team. Surely, there are differences for the operational-based procurement. As shown in Figure 10.2, market related risk drivers obtained the highest score on the probability of occurrence. In contrast, supplier related risk drivers obtained the highest score on the impact with relatively low probability of occurrence. Next, we will explain these risk drivers in detail.

Supplier Related Risks

In this category, most of the risk exposure has to be managed by the project-based procurement team. As the new power plants are in progress, the suppliers in the construction sites may go bankrupt or Enerjisa might observe various supply contract breaches by the suppliers. These events will surely delay the project completion times,

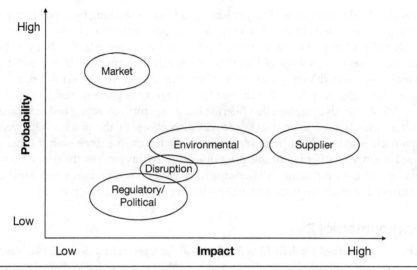

Figure 10.2 Procurement manager's risk map for project-based procurement.

which could further lead to financial losses. These undesirable events create supplier related risks, which are closely monitored by the procurement team.

Market and Demand Related Risks

Enerjisa closely watches the current market conditions in Turkey, potential imbalances in the market, and the lingering effects of the global financial crisis. Enerjisa is less exposed to foreign market risks since its investments are based in Turkey. Market risks are intimately related with end-consumer demand risks. It is known that the electricity consumption is expected to grow in Turkey. Therefore, unless demand curtailment is beyond 30 to 40 percent, investments in this industry will not incur huge financial losses. On the other hand, in the case of unexpected demand spikes, profits will skyrocket and the impact will be hugely positive. Of course, we should note that the regulator would dampen the positive impacts by balancing out the demand and the generation in such situations. As noted by the procurement manager, 2009 financial results were rosy for Enerjisa even though the national demand had decreased due to the global economic slowdown.

Disruption Risks

Disruption risks are caused by events that create a supply shortage for certain durations. Enerjisa considers carefully, different disruption creating events such as natural disasters (earthquakes, floods, fires, hurricanes etc.) and deliberate fragility of supplies created by greedy suppliers. Although the investment projects have their own debt payment service insurance coverage, Enerjisa bears all the risk of an earthquake or a possible natural disaster. On the other hand, Enerjisa has a good risk positioning by handling approximately 15–16 projects in the same portfolio. The possibility of a total loss in case of an earthquake is being reduced by increasing the number of projects. Enerjisa simultaneously considers the total risk of a portfolio of projects. This approach is very useful since a project's certain risks may negatively affect other projects or vice versa. Yet, a formal quantitative approach has not been used for managing the portfolio risk.

We should also mention that Enerjisa has a very intricate repair and maintenance culture that is used to mitigate potential disruptions in the process. One general approach is to use OEM parts and components for maintenance even if other spot market suppliers offer reasonable price discounts. In this process, the firm is very risk averse and does not want an inferior quality item or service purchased. Surely, the managerial perception is the key while selecting the maintenance providers.

Environmental Risks

This category of risks is defined as the potential damages caused by the firm toward the environment, and possible reputation and legal risks exposed due to these damages. In some cases, cancellation of generation licenses may be observed. This could further lead to the cancellation of construction processes, which is very costly in terms of finances and reputation in the market. Thus, Enerjisa is keen on managing these risks by using all the managerial power and experience to avoid such undesirable events.

Regulatory Risks

Enerjisa thinks that these risks create lower exposure when the projects are in the investment stage. Later, when power plants are in operation, changes in regulations create bigger financial losses and a hassle for not only Enerjisa, but also every other firm in the energy industry. For example, the regulatory bodies could reduce emission levels for Carbon Dioxide (CO_2) in Turkey as reductions take place all over the globe. These reductions can be handled more easily in the investment stage as design changes can be made with little extra cost and effort. However, when the plants are in operation, the added investment for the emission curtailment could be more than the initial investment and thus becomes unbearable. Unfortunately, this situation has been seen recently in various Turkish firms.

Establishment of the Turkish Energy Market Regulatory Authority (EMRA) created a better organization of regulation in Turkey. Surely, different stakeholders in energy generation, wholesale and distribution have different demands. EMRA's objective at this point was to establish a financially viable, stable, and transparent energy market. The current balancing and reconciliation system developed by EMRA was a big step toward a competitive market structure.

Political Risks

These risks are considered to have low impact and low level probability of occurrence. As years go by, it is believed that the privatization process will create a better and more flexible energy industry in Turkey. Thus, Enerjisa is quite comfortable in managing these types of risks. Surely, these risks are related intimately with the regulatory risks already mentioned.

Strategic Risks

These risks are considered to be critical. In general, they are market related events, thus also considered under market risks. In Turkey, over the past few years, there has been a rush on obtaining licenses to generate and sell electricity. Interestingly, many firms having no prior experience have attempted to initiate such enterprises. Enerjisa states that there is surely an overcapacity of proposals to the regulatory body for certain types of energy generation. For instance, Turkey's technically and economically feasible wind power potential is around 20,000 megawatts (MW). EMRA issued a call for license applications for wind power plants on November 1, 2007. After the call, EMRA received license applications totaling 78,000 MW, which was nearly twice the amount of the total installed capacity. Now, the final license distribution results are eagerly awaited. The regulatory body was surprised by such a high level of applications.

It should also be noted that, in the energy market, there are intermediary players/firms, who already purchased licenses much earlier with no intention of electricity generation. The objective of such firms is not the completion of the projects. Their intent is to sell the licenses at reasonable prices. Surely, the market once stabilized in a few years will eliminate such inefficiencies. Until then, these types of strategic risks are on the radar screen of Enerjisa.

Procurement Risk Assessment

Enerjisa uses mainly judgmental methods and heuristics to assess their procurement risks. Unfortunately, at this time, there are no formal mathematical tools designed for procurement risk assessment. However, designing such tools is currently in progress. On the other hand, Enerjisa computes the business impact of supply price/cost increases by experience-based methods. Moreover, procurement risk is explicitly considered while selecting and evaluating suppliers. In the near future, Enerjisa intends to develop the capability to assess the procurement risks using various innovative quantitative tools and techniques.

Risk Hedging and Mitigation

Operational Hedging of Procurement Risks

In this section, we first focus on the operational hedging strategies. Enerjisa uses a few operational hedging strategies to hedge the procurement risks. They are as follows:

- Setting up close relationships/partnerships with suppliers
- Establishing multiple sourcing/backup suppliers/portfolio of suppliers
- Restricting a supplier in the same region to one project/job

These hedging strategies are considered to be highly effective. They are also prevalent in different industries such as automotive, fast moving consumer goods, commodity metals, pharmaceuticals, and fashion retail. Among the aforementioned operational hedging strategies, multiple sourcing turned out to be one of the most critical operational hedging strategies in the cross-industrial survey conducted in Turkey.

On the other hand, Enerjisa is not actively using the following operational hedging strategies. The first one is purchasing speculative inventory in the expectation of price increase. In essence, not using a speculative inventory holding strategy might be a good choice. Procurement specialists seemed to understand the downside of such a strategy and its disastrous financial consequences. Second, Enerjisa does not have an internal crisis team to respond to supply disruptions. A crisis team is deemed unnecessary at the firm, since business continuity is ensured in most cases when supply is temporarily disrupted. Therefore, for example, a backup procurement specialist is not used at Enerjisa if the entire procurement department is on vacation. Yet, at some other firms where purchasing immediately affects the continuity of business, such a strategy could be effectively employed. Third, Enerjisa is not actively using, but is working on developing a methodology to create a list of prequalified suppliers to potentially reduce the costs of supplier selection and evaluation.

Financial Hedging of Procurement Risks

The use of financial hedging instruments at Enerjisa such as forwards/futures/options is limited. Financial swaps have been examined in detail as well as hedging with commodity futures. It turned out that the cost of commodity futures hedging is higher than the risk exposures mitigated via hedging. Thus, Enerjisa decided for now that hedging with futures was not a viable option.

Second, their financial hedging tool is insurance. Enerjisa purchases insurance for property, project, business continuity, and delay in start-up events. It is known that insurance is an *ex post* risk reduction method that does not preclude the potential disruptions in the first place. However, it may reduce the financial losses up to predetermined levels. Furthermore, Enerjisa also encourages its closest suppliers to purchase insurance for different purposes to share risks.

Third, designing supply contracts with beneficial terms and conditions is also effectively used at Enerjisa. A fixed-price supply contracts strategy with price renegotiation and contract breach/nonperformance penalty terms is quite common in Enerjisa contracts. Most of the contracts span 5–6 years due to long investment periods. Therefore, escalation based fixed-prices are written into contracts up to certain price caps. Once prices reach the designed price cap levels as time passes, renegotiation process begins between the two parties. If there is an impasse or the supplier breaches in some cases, financial penalties are imposed with potential litigation.

Integrated Operational and Financial Hedging

By looking at how Enerjisa overall mitigates various procurement risks, it is clear that the firm has a smart procurement risk management practice. The firm considers operational and financial hedging strategies in an integrated fashion. Not many firms have successfully applied such a strategy. Recent research also shows the value of such integrated approaches. For instance, Enerjisa is keen on using multiple sourcing strategies with price renegotiation options. Using more than one supplier for the same material/commodity is operationally hedging the supply disruption/bankruptcy/price risks. Designing price renegotiation options in the contracts reveals that using a portfolio of suppliers may require flexible pricing schemes. As time unfolds, market price may appreciate/depreciate. If the firm does not want to lose the supplier in its portfolio, provision of renegotiation on price might become a necessity. Thus, this becomes a valuable option and creates flexibility for the supplier portfolio management problem.

Last, but not least, we should note that while using multiple sourcing, monitoring the financial health of suppliers becomes more critical. It is clear that, using only multiple suppliers may not completely eliminate the negative impacts created by the suppliers in case of macroeconomic and/or environmental disruptions. Hence, it is crucial to closely monitor the overall health of the supplier portfolio as supplier defaults/bankruptcies may even be correlated under certain market/industry conditions. Enerjisa states that they have to work better at monitoring the financial health of suppliers especially for mission critical items.

Managing Learning and Procurement Talent

We will now focus on the learning and knowledge creation processes at Enerjisa. According to the procurement manager, each project is a learning process per se for the teams involved and for the individuals. Ensuring that the specialists work for more than one manager at the same time encourages cross learning among different projects. In the procurement process, a specialist is given responsibility from the beginning to end for each stage. Also, each individual is made responsible for a general-purpose concept such as design, conflict management, and such. Hence, it is clear that Enerjisa applies a *T-based learning* approach for its employees, both as a generalist and a specialist at the same time. This strategy is found to be quite effective in other knowledge industries such as management consulting and investment banking.

In order to enable effective sharing of learning and experience, specialists are asked to document their annual learning each year. This enhances the firm's know-how and know-why database and converts inferred knowledge into explicit for the completed projects.

Yet, it is noted that the work culture in Turkey seems to be the main roadblock toward such initiatives. In general, Turkish work culture reveres a, "*Work fast, finish early!*" motto, which sometimes leads to sloppy and not-carefully-thought-out results. Enerjisa strives to create a more effective work culture by establishing policies in learning and knowledge creation.

Since Enerjisa invests in different projects, in different regions, of Turkey, many interesting observations and hints are gained in time, regarding the suppliers and work ethics. Currently, there is a system being developed to rate suppliers and score the individual cases as well as provide a few sentences of critical knowledge for future projects. This system is believed to improve the supplier selection process and minimize the potential disruption and supplier related risks later. Surely, the system will also screen and filter out the dirty data that does not add value.

When we examined the talent selection and development, the procurement management stated the following four criteria in the order of importance for selecting procurement talent:

- Potential to grow and learn
- Enthusiasm
- Experience
- Market and industry knowledge

The potential to grow and learn is the main selection criterion for the firm. Junior specialists who are eager to learn and develop themselves are lured towards the growing energy industry. This makes the young firm a more dynamic and energetic environment.

THE PATH FORWARD

The future outlook is quite positive for Enerjisa. The timing and quality of shipments, commodity price risks, and supplier loss or bankruptcy/insolvency in the market are well managed for the near future. One potential risky event that is in everyone's mind is unexpected price increases in the market. For managing such a risk, Enerjisa seems to be ready with an in-depth knowledge of the market and industry, as well as continuing long-term relationships with critical partners and suppliers.

Last, but not least, as stated by the procurement manager, it is imperative for Enerjisa to establish a sound and effective infrastructure to store and share critical knowledge as new projects are developed and put into action. Storing and sharing critical knowledge requires managing a variety of supply chain risks such as infrastructure, fraud, intellectual property, and data management, as well. It is clear that development of a sound company procurement culture is crucial. Moreover, as types of risks and their dependencies increase, procurement teams have to hone their risk management skills. Hence, policies and strategies put forward the need to support both the evolving procurement and risk management cultures.

REFERENCES

Haksöz, Ç. Procurement risk perceptions and hedging: A cross-industry study in Turkey, Working Paper, Sabancı University, Faculty of Management, Turkey, 2009.

Haksöz, Ç., and S. Seshadri. Integrated Production and Risk Hedging with Financial Instruments, *Handbook of Integrated Risk Management in Global Supply Chains*, eds. P. Kouvelis, O. Boyabatli, L. Dong, and R. Li, John Wiley & Sons, Inc., New York, 2011 (scheduled).

Haksöz, Ç., and A. Kadam. Supply portfolio risk, *The Journal of Operational Risk*, Spring 2009, 4(1):59–77.

Wagner, S. M., C. Bode, and P. Koziol. 2009. Supplier default dependencies: Empirical evidence from the automotive industry, *European Journal of Operational Research*, 199(1):150–161.

Part II

Tools, Techniques, and Approaches

11

INTRODUCTION TO TOOLS, TECHNIQUES, AND APPROACHES

George A. Zsidisin and Omera Khan

As described in the title, Part II consists of various tools, techniques, approaches, and examples of how firms assess and manage risk in their supply chains. While Part I focuses on supply chain risk from a global perspective, this part takes a more granular view at the industry and firm levels to provide insight as to how organizations can prevent risk occurrence or recover quickly when problems do arise. Chapters 12, 13, and 14 examine firm practices in the financial, automotive, and aerospace industries. The final five chapters of this book provide case examples and approaches, such as incorporating information systems, strategic sourcing, and analytical tools for assessing and managing supply risk.

Part II begins with a case in the financial services/banking sector written by Kurt Engemann, Holmes Miller, and Natalie Dengler. This chapter describes a case involving a firm that created a contingency planning process in the 1980s from: (1) being an early adopter of a U.S. Treasury Department Circular emphasizing contingency planning, and (2) experiencing a large corporate loss from repurchase transactions in securities. This case describes the process of developing a business continuity strategy from initial project initiation through its evolution and deployment throughout the corporation.

The second industry-specific case in Chapter 13, written by Constantin Blome, Volker Groetsch, Michael Henke, and Christopher Tang, compares and contrasts two firms in the automotive industry and their respective approaches in gathering and incorporating data for measuring bankruptcy risk. Comparisons along various risk criteria, measures, and their subsequent effect on supply chain disruptions are illustrated.

The third industry-specific case in Chapter 14, written by Olivier Lavastre, examines the deployment and utilization of various tools and approaches in the aerospace industry. Criteria and tools are provided for helping managers choose low risk suppliers, verify their activities, secure product flows and encourage suppliers to create solutions for managing supply chain risk.

Chapter 15, written by Doug Voss and Keith Helfrich, takes a general approach in understanding how firms can utilize the information that currently resides in their firm to mitigate supply chain and network risk. The tool they describe as *Common View*, is a web-based software solution that consolidates data from multiple systems to uncover potential and actualized problems, both upstream and downstream in the supply chain.

Chapter 16, written by Cliff Thomas, provides insightful analyses into well-documented supply chain risks and business disruptions. He elaborates on several well-known approaches to ensuring business continuity, as well as describing some emerging threats and issues such as information, data security and globalization. Thomas then provides some prescriptive suggestions as to how firms can ensure supply chain continuity cost-effectively.

Supply chain risk is rarely viewed more than one tier upstream or downstream from the firm. Reham Eltantawy and Larry Giunipero present a case study in Chapter 17 of an organization that has implemented strategic supply management activities, which have resulted in reducing risk exposure at both the first and second tiers upstream in the supply chain. This case provides evidence that strategic sourcing can be effectively used to manage supply chain risk, while at the same time providing firms with overall performance benefits such as reducing inventory levels and attaining greater supply chain visibility.

In Chapter 18, Barbara Gaudenzi describes the application of an approach referred to as PRORAM (PROject Risk Assessment Method) for managing the risks associated with projects, as applied to the firm SELEX Sistemi Integrati Spa in Italy. This tool examines risk from the upstream, internal, and downstream perspectives of the supply chain. Risk factors evaluated include those associated with supplier relationships, the project definition, engineering, manufacturing, and customer relationships.

The concluding Chapter 19, written by Ulf Paulsson and Arben Mullai, describes the supply chain risk approach that three companies took in various industries and how they applied a disruption risk exposure estimation model. Each of the case's risk sources are examined from the products themselves, supply side, production, and demand side. A disruption exposure solution model is applied to all three firms, as well as the specific risk handling methods deployed by those organizations.

12

MANAGING SUPPLY CHAIN RISK IN FINANCIAL SERVICES

Kurt J. Engemann, Holmes E. Miller, and Natalie M. Dengler

Tony Rossini stared at the blank legal pad before him and smiled at the irony of his situation: As the CIO of one of the world's largest and most profitable financial institutions, he was trying to develop a list of the major business continuity challenges facing the firm as it moved into the second decade of the twenty-first century—and doing it the old fashioned way with pen and paper. "Is there a message here?" he thought. In 1983 Rossini joined *the firm* right out of college, and was assigned to work as an analyst in its money transfer department. His degree was in business administration with a minor in computer science, and his first project assignment was to assist in developing the department's contingency plan. Now his responsibilities had expanded and as CIO of the firm, he was responsible for over $6 billion of technology investments for an organization whose assets topped $2 trillion, whose net income for 2009 exceeded $10 billion (one of the most profitable banks in the United States after the 2008-09 financial crisis) and whose branch network reached over 40 percent of the U.S. population with a presence in 60 countries.

Although the firm had engaged in contingency planning before then, in 1983 the U.S. Treasury Department's Office of the Comptroller of the Currency issued Banking Circular BC 177 (OCC BC 177), which for the first time raised contingency planning to the level of the Board of Directors. Since then business continuity and resiliency had been a highly regulated aspect of the financial services industry. The firm was one of the first in the financial services industry that looked at business resiliency and had remained a leader, both in its practices and in its results, when faced with disasters. Now, the firm's Board would have to review and approve its Business Continuity

Program as it had for a quarter of a century. Tony realized that the thoughts he jotted down eventually could end up saving billions of dollars.

HISTORY OF FINANCIAL SERVICES GROWTH

The firm, like most large financial institutions, was the product of numerous mergers over the years. Initially founded at the turn of the eighteenth century, the firm counted over 1000 banks than had been incorporated in its structure since its inception. In terms of asset growth, the last twenty years were the most significant, and the firm was comprised of three major lines of business (see Table 12.1)—the result of integrating seven major banks, which had, as late as the end of the 1980s, been independent entities.

Each merger or acquisition created a set of questions to be addressed: Would the acquired or merged institution be retail focused, investment focused, or both? Would technology be centralized or decentralized? Or would it be a combination due to regulations around the world? How would centralized staff areas work together—security, business recovery, and public relations?

The firm found that as the culture of the *new* firm developed, individual areas begin to define themselves in terms of structure and staff. With each merger and acquisition, the impact of a one bank outage became exponentially greater. More customers were impacted, more transactions needed to be processed, and many large data processing systems needed to recover. To deal with these challenges, risk assessment was important in addressing the ease of system growth, ease of customer conversion, and ease of training staff.

SUPPLY CHAIN RISK

In the mid-1980s, in response to a large corporate loss stemming from repurchase transactions in a securities business, the firm established a group whose focus was

Table 12.1 The firm's businesses

CONSUMER BANKING	INVESTMENT BANKING	COMMERCIAL BANKING
Branch, ATM, telephone and online banking	Investment bank	Middle market
Credit cards	Asset management	Mid-corporate
Small business	Treasury services	Commercial real estate
Home finance and home equity loans	Worldwide securities services	Business credit
Auto finance	Private banking	Equipment finance
Education finance	Private client services	
Retirement and investing	Equity partners	

operational risk management. Among the responsibilities for managing these risks was establishing a corporate wide contingency planning program, which will be described later. This department propagated a corporate-wide focus on operational risks, which, in hindsight, was groundbreaking.

Among these efforts were projects aimed at identifying and managing supply chain risk in financial services. This involves managing the risk in a complex supply chain ranging from its suppliers to its customers, and also includes institutional entities and competitors. The firm's suppliers include traditional suppliers of goods and services, direct and indirect supplies, hardware, telecommunications, software, consulting services, and so on. In addition, the firm's operations depended upon third party networks operated by the Federal Reserve and the New York Clearinghouse. With each bank merger the impact of potential outages increased. An outage by one institution now meant that there was a significant impact to the entire financial industry. In addition, the growing importance of the Internet, ongoing increases in customer expectations for immediate service, and plans of both customer and competitors all had to be factored into a supply chain risk assessment. Early on, the firm understood this and for over 25 years had refined a process steeped in the fundamentals that support effective business continuity planning.

INITIAL PROJECT DEVELOPMENT AND IMPLEMENTATION

Following the issuance of OCC BC 177, the firm decided to develop a business continuity strategy where all domestic and global locations adhered to the same principles. The firm looked at the regulations and thought that data processing alone did little to continue the business during an outage. What was needed was a program that encompassed not only data processing, but also critical functions and subfunctions to ensure service to critical customers would continue. Identifying the critical customers was a challenge, as was determining what functions were critical. In the mid-1980s, although many functions had been automated, there were still numerous business functions where paper was *moved*, for example, check clearing where paper checks were moved, and paper could be destroyed in a disaster at any step in the process. Therefore, either the paper or a certified paper copy needed to be created in order to continue processing. Business continuity plans had to deal with both automated and paper environments, and although the specific plans could be tailored to the individual businesses, general business continuity *good practices* were built into the process, and supported by corporate guidelines and case studies.

A centralized group in the Product and Production Risk Management department (referred to below as the *planning group*) developed the *good practices* guidelines and conducted the case studies, and also served as a consulting and monitoring function during and after development of each area's business continuity plan. The following sections discuss the specifics of this process, as well as the program implementation strategy.

Project Initiation and Management

Prior to developing the business continuity planning process, some areas of the firm had contingency plans, but these varied in detail and quality, were mainly *systems* specific rather than business driven, and did not always adhere to business continuity planning good practices. A consistent approach to business continuity planning using a standard methodology with articulated standards across the entire organization was needed. The planning group, under the sponsorship of executive vice-president of the firm's Operations and Systems department, developed a methodology (described later) that was used to identify potential catastrophic events and was used to select the best alternatives to deal with the risks. This approach, while adjusted over the years, formed the conceptual foundation for how the firm deals with business continuity planning today.

To test elements of the new methodology, the planning group conducted a pilot study where the scope of the decision was restricted to the threats of fire and power failure to several critical services at operation's headquarters. Initially, management's attention focused on alternatives such as fire control modifications and an emergency generator. The planning group evaluated the costs and benefits of these control alternatives and the results indicated that the problem needed to be redefined to include other threats and other solutions, such as alternate off-site processing facilities. This was an important moment for senior management because it illustrated that systemic solutions often could be more cost-effective than just focusing on ensuring an individual system continued to function, in place. Further, all stakeholders now realized that business continuity was more than an issue of replicating computer systems, but rather, was a business-wide process where ensuring contact with customers, availability of personnel and supplies, and the ability to communicate were also critical. The offsite strategy paid off several years later when the firm experienced a fire at its operations headquarters causing the building to be evacuated for a week. The offsite processing facility picked up the slack and the firm's businesses did not miss a beat.

The result of this initial project reinforced the firm's decision that all business components must have documented and tested business continuity plans for the full range of operational and data processing resources required for service delivery. The level of service to be provided in the event of a disaster was a business-driven decision based on the cost of providing that level of service, potential losses, and vulnerability to disasters. The level of detail of the documentation was to be consistent with the business addressed, the complexity of the operating environment, service requirements, and was based on established risk management principles.

Risk management decisions are among the most conceptually difficult decisions managers face because, by their very nature, such decisions must come to grips with uncertainties surrounding highly unlikely events with major potential adverse impact upon the operation of a business. Ideally a control is both affordable and effective. To address this complexity, the planning group developed and applied a risk management methodology for business continuity management that was implemented for all business units and geographic locations. The few implementation problems that arose were overcome by presenting the approach in an intuitively appealing way and by providing the means to incorporate subjective judgment. Managers proved to be surprisingly receptive to such concepts as events, probability, expected value, and utility—as long as these concepts were presented in an intuitive rather than a mathematical framework. The approach increased managers' risk awareness and provided them with a structured way of addressing risk issues, which they also applied to other problems. As a result of the initial project and resulting methodology, the planning group was charged with worldwide functional responsibility for business continuity and information security.

Risk Evaluation and Control

A wide range of potential risks can impact service delivery in any organization. The firm's business continuity methodology included steps to identify disasters that may lead to events that cause losses, and also procedures for selecting cost justified control alternatives that reduced the probability of events and mitigated losses. Services are disrupted when the resources required to deliver the services are unavailable. Some typical threats include fire, flood, power outage, strike, civil disturbances, terrorism, acts of war, pandemics, and acts of nature. The relevance of these threats depends upon the geographic location, the structure of the buildings, and the political/economic conditions. For example, hurricanes may be a threat in Puerto Rico, but not in Switzerland. The occurrence of a disaster event may create a service disruption for a specific length of time, for example, a three-day outage disabling processing for a floor of a building. The same event could result from any one of several disruptions and disasters. For example, loss of data processing support for three days could result from flooding of a data center, lack of power, or a small fire.

Business continuity planning focused on those events that could result in significant losses. Alternatives were developed to reduce the risk or impact of an event. An alternative may provide protection against only one event or against several. Some alternatives reduce the probability that an event will occur; other alternatives reduce losses by providing some continuation of customer service during a disaster. Earnings were affected by these alternatives, just as they were by insurance. Annualized costs of the alternatives were developed and compared to the reduction in the expected annualized risk exposure. Figure 12.1 illustrates these relationships.

To identify potential disasters, it was necessary to clearly understand the service delivery mechanism. Information common to all services and other information that was specific to each particular service was collected. Specific events that could impact the functions and disrupt service were identified. Control alternatives were developed to reduce the probability of the event occurring or to mitigate the impact of the event on the delivery of service.

For the initial implementation of the program, operations managers were responsible for developing and implementing the continuity plans in accordance with

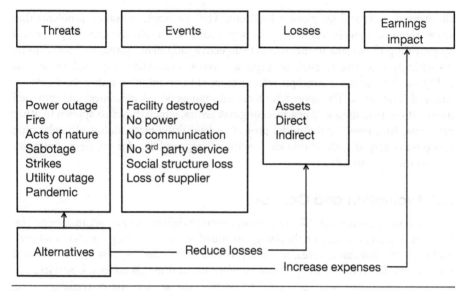

Figure 12.1 Risk overview.

business needs and the business managers were accountable for overall business continuity planning. This framework was not intended to replace management's intuitive judgment on occasions when and the results of an analysis disagreed with the manager's intuitive judgment, the source of the disagreement was isolated and resolved in order to provide proper implementation.

Business Impact Analysis

Business managers reviewed all services provided by their units to identify the critical services for which disruption would result in significant losses. Business continuity plans for critical services (for example, money transfer) addressed the full range of resources required to deliver the services. The important role of computer resources and data made business continuity planning for data centers and telecommunications links critical elements. Business managers determined when the services needed to resume and what priority transactions needed to be processed to avoid incurring significant losses.

Data collection was an important element of this process and was conducted via interviews, workshops and questionnaires. The result of this initial identification process indicated what areas required more detailed analyses. Since an objective of business continuity planning is to limit the impact and risk of major disruptions to an acceptable level, determining how long services could be deferred before unacceptable losses were incurred was an essential element of the process. For each service, business managers specified the minimum level of service required and how soon service should be provided to avoid such losses. Management then determined recovery time objectives (RTO) and recovery point objectives (RPO) from the solicited information. Given the upstream and downstream nature of the supply chain, businesses with given RTOs and RPOs, at times, required other business units to raise their respective RTO/RPO values.

Business managers helped estimate financial losses including lost fees, compensation and interest losses, penalties, and consequential damages. Management also estimated the impact on future business, including which customers would be lost to competition, how long it would take to reestablish lost business and the cost of regaining lost business. The impact on projected growth and the impact on other services also were evaluated. Finally, if business could be redirected, or if a service bureau provided a service, the magnitude of these costs was estimated.

Business impact costs involved determining direct and indirect losses. Direct losses included those losses related to the service or services for which the business continuity plan was being developed, such as loss of assets, loss of documents, personnel costs, and financial costs. Indirect losses included loss of future business and consequential damages, for example, payments that were made to offset losses resulting from failure to provide service on a timely basis.

Developing Business Continuity Management Strategies

Developing a strategy involved selecting from a set of preferred alternatives that met business continuity management objectives. For each critical business function, the available recovery alternatives were evaluated according to their costs and benefits. These included selecting from cold, warm, and hot sites; manual procedures; reciprocal agreements; work from home; quick ship; and other alternatives. Sometimes the decision was obvious—for example, when an alternative provided protection for most events and was relatively inexpensive. Occasionally, an alternative was the only one that would provide the continuation of a service in case of all major events, and the service was so vital that management could not accept its disruption. Sometimes, the additional expenditure was small because it was combined with other plans, such as when the decision to place operations at two or more locations was made at the same time as additional space was being acquired for expansion.

Because a business continuity management strategy must provide backup for all major events, a primary focus was to include off-site alternatives. Some events that resulted in unacceptable consequences, (such as the loss of key markets, restrictions from regulatory agencies, or very high losses), were reviewed and were selected, even when their costs seemed excessive. Each combination of alternatives and events was evaluated by assigning relative ratings (excellent, good, fair, poor) with respect to each criterion. These ratings provided a qualitative evaluation useful in comparing strategies. Management judgment was used in both assigning the ratings and selecting the strategy. When the selection of a set of alternatives was not obvious, a more detailed cost-benefit analysis was done.

The benefit of an alternative was the reduction in potential losses compared to a base case. Quantifying benefits required reviewing all the events for which the alternative provided some protection, and estimating how it reduced the expected loss for each of these events. All losses were considered in conjunction with insurance coverage, including self-insurance. The net benefit of an alternative was obtained by subtracting the total annual cost of the alternative from its annual benefit. The alternative with the largest positive net benefit was selected as part of the overall strategy. Sensitivity analysis was performed to determine how changes in the estimates of costs, losses, and probabilities would affect the selection of a strategy.

DEVELOPING AND IMPLEMENTING BUSINESS CONTINUITY PLANS

Plan implementation involved putting the selected alternatives into place, testing the plan, and documenting the plan. This included:

- Carrying out the changes in location, equipment, document protection, and procedures dictated by the strategy
- Establishing agreements and, where necessary, supervising construction
- Testing the plan to ensure the level of service specified could be achieved
- Maintaining the plan to ensure ongoing technological change and evolving business requirements in the financial services supply chain were incorporated
- Documenting the plan to facilitate its usefulness
- Developing action steps for the various stages of emergency response (and identifying individuals responsible for these actions)
- Documenting the steps necessary for detection, reaction, damage assessment, authorization to initiate the plan, and notification

Awareness and Training Programs

With senior management's full support, awareness and training programs were implemented. The objective was to make all employees aware of the program and enable all participants in the business continuity organization to understand their roles and be thoroughly trained. This included yearly reviews of the necessary emergency response actions and informing new employees of relevant business continuity procedures. In addition, a process was established to ensure that supervisors and managers responsible for tasks in the business continuity plan understood the overall plan, and their particular responsibilities within it. The business continuity management process increased managers' awareness of a broad range of risks and established common ground for communication regarding product, operational, and business risks at the firm.

Maintaining and Testing Business Continuity Plans

To ensure the plan was accurate, timely, and complete, reviews of business continuity plans were performed at least once a year, as well as after any major change in a service delivery mechanism. The review program began by validating the plan's assumptions and included visits to backup sites, and examination of sample documents. The objective was to ensure that the business continuity procedures suggested by the plan were being followed.

Each year all personnel reviewed the necessary emergency response actions and new employees were informed of relevant business continuity procedures. Drills were conducted at least yearly, where people and resources were mobilized, and procedures were carried out to determine how well the plan really worked. Backup sites and equipment were tested, if at all possible, and suppliers were called without prior notice, and asked how soon space and equipment would be available, if the disaster had just occurred. Service bureaus on which the firm depended also conducted drills for select firm personnel. In subsequent versions of the process, testing involved working with the New York City Office of Emergency Management and participating in their exercises, as well as financial industry-wide exercises. Using the command center structure was effective in dealing with significant events such as Y2K and Euro-conversion. Executive management participated in many tests which illustrated the importance of the testing process. If reviewing or testing indicated a weakness in the business continuity plan, the plan was modified to remedy the situation. Modifications ranged from changes in phone numbers to a complete plan overhaul.

Implementing the Corporate Program

The program was developed in several phases. Phase 1 involved researching business continuity planning methodologies used in other banks and organizations, reviewing existing business continuity plans for business units of the firm, and extensive interviews with business, operations, and information systems managers. Business continuity planning guidelines, general enough for worldwide use, but still tailored to the needs and policies of the firm, were a product of this phase. The guidelines included steps that discussed how to develop, implement and maintain a business continuity plan.

Phase 2 involved developing several *case studies*, conducted jointly between members of the planning group and the business unit. Two sites were selected: one site was a domestic operations unit headquartered in New York and the other was a business unit overseas. Each of these case studies was published (with sensitive material excised) so other domestic and international business units could use it as a template in developing their own business continuity plans. Publishing the completed plans was effective; many individuals found working from an existing case document to be more helpful than trying the construct a plan from guidelines alone. The planning group also found this method helpful in reviewing area's plans because the plans were more uniform and amenable to being analyzed by common criteria. The project's final phase was reviewing and managing the worldwide process and offering consulting support. Over time, the processes themselves became embedded in the business units and the planning groups as a reviewing body was reduced. Each one of these phases involved developing a schedule and a budget, working with teams, and reporting to executive management.

THE PROGRAM EVOLUTION

Since its initial development the program has evolved to meet the changing organizational, technological, and risk environments. Organizationally, the firm today is the product of the mergers and acquisitions of other independent banks that each had their own business continuity plans and processes in place. The challenges of integrating these plans were great and many specific details of the firm's process and enunciated guidelines were modified. The underlying principles discussed above, however, largely remain in place because these principles were specific not only to the firm, but also are the good practices followed in the larger community of business continuity professionals.

One major strategic initiative that affected the business continuity process was that the firm was outsourcing a significant amount of its data processing operations to a third party provider. Initially, the agreement, developed late in 2002, was a $5 billion deal to transfer 4000 of the firm's employees to the outsourcing organization. This strategy changed in light of a merger that provided the firm with new operational capabilities and new managerial perspectives and several years later the firm decided to wind-down the contract to bring its IT support staff back in-house, including the 4000 employees and contractors who transferred when the deal was made.

In the last two decades perhaps the major macrotechnological changes affecting financial services and modifying the firm's supply chain have been advances in telecommunications capabilities. Enormous increases in bandwidth and processing speeds have affected two sides of the business continuity equation. First, they have introduced new requirements for responsiveness and for data quantity and quality. They also have introduced new components into the supply chain that must be included in business continuity plans. Second, these changes also have expanded the universe of strategic possibilities, including that of using a broader global processing network and working at home. Microtechnological challenges the firm faced involved selecting applications, processing locations, adjusting processing capacity to deal with demand, and ensuring the ability to recover and resort backup data within limited timeframes.

This expanded network performed effectively during the events of September 11, 2001. Headquartered in New York, the firm was affected by the events, but unlike some other institutions, did not have their processing consolidated in lower Manhattan. Some firms realized that, even though their systems were not headquartered in buildings destroyed by the terrorist attack, their systems were still affected because they used systems that depended on the Verizon telecommunications switch hubs that passed through destroyed buildings such as 7 World Trade Center. When the events of September 11 occurred, the firm had separate, independent operating sites in three locations in lower Manhattan, all of which became inaccessible by order of governmental authorities. Following the existing business continuity plan, the firm was able to transfer some settlement operations to a contingency site outside the restricted zone, and was able to rely upon remote data centers and telecommunications facilities established in other states and command centers geographically disbursed in the Uniter States, Europe, and Asia.

Later, the Securities and Exchange Commission published post-September 11 guidelines for all financial institutions specifying three objectives:

1. Rapid recovery and timely resumption of critical operations following a wide-scale disruption
2. Rapid recovery and timely resumption of critical operations following the loss or inaccessibility of staff in at least one major operating location
3. A high level of confidence, through ongoing use or robust testing, that critical internal and external continuity measures are effective and compatible

The events of September 11 reinforced the firm's belief regarding the importance of geographical dispersion of primary and backup operations sites. The closure of lower Manhattan caused the firm to implement a number of steps to improve its business continuity plans, including establishing additional geographically disbursed operational sites, designed so that each operational, data, or telecommunications site is capable of supporting the functions of others. Moreover, the firm also realized that the reliance upon physical operational sites was not as critical as the housing and protection of data. The firm's plans now include allowing employees to work from home—a benefit of technological advances discussed above—and storing data in a secure location so it will be accessible from a range of locations. The strategies have been modified to give primacy to the standardization and protection of data above protecting operational facilities.

THE FUTURE

Tony Rossini glanced at his watch. It was 2 p.m. Soon he would leave for the airport to pick up his daughter who was returning from college for the holidays. She was a junior majoring in business and in her operations management class she had studied supply chains and had even done a project on how a disaster involving one component of the chain could affect the others. She texted Tony, informing him of the A she had received on her presentation, as well as gently reminding him of the risks that were probably hidden within *his* supply chain. "Tell me about it," Tony texted back. The blank sheet was still before him. He had ten minutes to write down some thoughts concerning the key issues to be addressed moving forward. Though the economy was beginning to recover from a near-depression, many former colleagues in the financial services industry were either still unemployed or in second careers. Technologies continued to evolve ever more rapidly and Tony wondered how long it would be before his laptop became a relic and everyone communicated over the Internet with future generations of an iPhone or BlackBerry and using social networking sites such as Facebook, LinkedIn, and Twitter. The firm continued to grow, as did new IT requirements, and the specter of increased competition, customer expectations, and government regulations grew larger. He rubbed his forehead and began to jot down some initial thoughts regarding future directions. He would think more about these on his drive to LaGuardia.

13

A COMPARATIVE STUDY OF FINANCIAL AND OPERATIONAL MEASURES IN THE AUTOMOTIVE INDUSTRY

Constantin Blome, Volker M. Groetsch, Michael Henke, and Christopher S. Tang

INTRODUCTION

The current economic crisis has played havoc with many automotive manufacturing companies. As General Motors (GM) filed for bankruptcy, Daimler is facing declining sales, BMW is riding out the current crisis, and Volkswagen (VW) is one of the few companies with sustainable profitable growth (Hawranek 2008). The contrasting fate of different original equipment manufacturers (OEMs) makes one wonder—what are the underlying causes for the failure of some companies, such as GM, and the success of other companies, such as VW?

The contrasting developments of these firms can be explained in part by their different geographic presence—the U.S. market for example, GM's home base, was hit hardest. However, sales alone do not tell the whole story, as the contrasting positions of Daimler and BMW show (Hawranek 2008; VDA 2008). The revenue of an automobile company is driven by sales, which depends on factors such as price, design, functionality, and quality. However, procurement and production costs are central factors that affect the gross margin, which is a key success factor. With a rather low degree of differentiation, one distinguishing factor that affects the survival of an OEM is the characteristics of its supply chain and the survival of its suppliers.

The current economic crisis has had a significant impact on the industry, which puts about 50 percent of the top 30 automotive suppliers in fiscal danger (Wyman 2009). In addition, automotive supply chains are highly integrated, characterized by long-term relationships, highly specialized actors, significant relationship-specific investments and a high interdependency of OEMs and suppliers (Richardson 1993; Asanuma 1989). Thus, supplier bankruptcies are expected to have a significant impact on automotive OEMs, which would give a high level of importance to supply risk management practices.

Recognizing the fact that the question of why GM failed and VW prospered is too broad and too difficult to answer, we redefine the question as: What are the differentiating financial and supply chain operations measures between a high-performing OEM and low-performing OEM from a supply and risk manager's perspective? To understand how companies with different supply risk management systems (SRMS) mitigate the impact of supplier bankruptcies, we collected comparative data on two distinct European automobile manufacturing companies. In addition, we based our further analysis on a study of current practices for supplier risk management, taking supplier insolvencies into special account. Supplier risk management in that sense is part of a comprehensive enterprise and supply risk management system (Henke 2008). The findings include a set of practice-oriented measures, which can be used to enable firms to manage the risks that are present in their complex supply chains (Henke, Weimar, Potzner, and Besl 2009).

BACKGROUND OF CASE COMPANIES

As stated previously, we chose both of our case companies from a group of Europe-based automobile manufacturers. According to the European Automobile Manufacturers' Association (ACEA), both companies have experienced a drop in sales between 10 and 20 percent in the European market since the beginning of the crisis. Thus, we assume a comparable power of the external shock from the market on the company, which increased the comparability of our observations.

To analyze two fundamentally different supply risk management approaches, we chose firms from two different industry segments, implying that they use distinct production setups and thus have different distinct relationships to their suppliers. PrimCar, the first case company, has tailored its product portfolio to the high-price, prestige market segment. In contrast, MassMobile, our second case company, has been focusing its activities mainly on high-quality, low-budget vehicles. With the external impact from the market being comparable, we ensured the impact of supply risk management at each side was accurately identifiable without being subject to a systemic bias of the product or industry segment.

To understand their risk practices, we approached the chief supply risk manager of both companies and arranged a series of on-site and/or telephone interviews. The selected interview partners represented both supply and risk managers, where supply managers were selected from the companies' major purchasing categories.

ANALYSIS OF CASE COMPANIES

Characteristics of the Distinct Supply Risk Management Systems

The SRMS adopted by both companies utilized similar risk management processes. As a first step, both firms collect a variety of information about their suppliers to assess their particular situation. The interval of these assessments generally depended on the importance of the supplier. Strategic suppliers were screened on a weekly basis by both firms. PrimCar kept up this frequency also for nonstrategic suppliers. MassMobile increased the assessment intervals to quarters for nonstrategic suppliers.

The assessment was done on the basis of various types of information. Although each company pursued its individual risk management approach, a set of core information was present at both sites. In total, the overlap of both information systems was more than 50 percent. This common core of information comprised first and foremost financial- or finance-based rating information. However, both case companies had different approaches of obtaining this information. While MassMobile relied heavily on external agents, PrimCar gathered the data from its suppliers itself and used external agents only as a complementing source. Further information considered important was the degree of specialization a supplier had in the automotive industry, its operational performance in the sense of product quality and delivery service levels, the structure of its customer portfolio, and the level of competition in the industry. During our meetings, supply managers of both companies further placed high value on subjective information like market rumors, fluctuation of key personnel or contact persons as well as personal impressions on-site and during meetings.

Next to this common core data, both companies further used individual information to complement their risk assessment. The amount of additional sources used was different between the case companies. For PrimCar, the core information only accounted for 60 percent of the overall assessment data basis. For complementing the core information, supply and risk managers at PrimCar conducted a complete investigation of their suppliers' business, including analyses of their suppliers' business plans, of their financiers and of their supply markets.

MassMobile had the opposite approach and relied primarily on the information, which was introduced as core information above. This information was complemented by explicit spot-light impressions from buyers at the suppliers' production sites, including the utilization levels of the suppliers' equipment, the outbound stock level or the age of the machinery. Figure 13.1 summarizes the information used in both company's supply risk management system.

After collection, the information was processed semiautomatically by both companies in order to create a complete risk profile of each supplier. At both sites, color coding was used to show each supplier's current status. If the system indicated that a supplier needed special attention, contact was made and an in-depth analysis of the current situation of the supplier was performed, followed by an action plan. If a

Bankruptcy risk indicators in use	PrimCar	MassMobile
Financial indicators	✓	✓
Industry diversification	✓	✓
Structure of customer portfolio	✓	✓
Operational performance (production, quality, delivery)	✓	✓
"Ear to the market"	✓	✓
Personal impression from contact with suppliers	✓	✓
Supplier dependency and switching opportunities	✓	✓
Competitive situation of supplier	✓	✓
Fluctuation of (key) personnel	✓	✓
Production utilization		✓
General situation at production site (stocks, assets, etc.)		✓
Quality of business plans and business strategy	✓	
Characteristics of investors & financiers	✓	
Organizational structure and governance	✓	
Problem at subsidiary companies	✓	
Law suits against customers or suppliers of supplier	✓	
Supplier base, network and supply market of supplier	✓	

Figure 13.1 Bankruptcy Risk Indicators.

supplier went bankrupt, measures of crisis management were carried out. At MassMobile, all phases of the risk management process were carried out by the supply manager in charge, supported by a supply risk manager. At PrimCar, the supply manager was in charge of all steps of the risk management process except the last. While he was supported by supply risk management throughout, he handed over the case to a specialized crisis management team, once a supplier filed for bankruptcy.

From these first impressions, we deducted that PrimCar made considerably more effort than MassMobile for managing their supply risks. The company did not only gather a considerably larger amount of data than MassMobile, but it also supervised more suppliers on shorter intervals. Consequently, PrimCar had built up significantly more capacity for managing supply risks than MassMobile—while MassMobile had four employees working fulltime on supply risk management, PrimCar employed two teams. In addition, PrimCar supply managers dedicated 10 percent of their time for supplier risk assessment.

When asked to evaluate their company's SRMS in general, half of PrimCar's supply managers found the system to be effective. However, the other half of the interviewed supply managers indicated a lack of effectiveness, or at least an imbalance between effort and effect. Supply managers at MassMobile were totally supporting the company's SRMS, with one quarter explicitly labeling their system to be very effective, and no critique or negative comments were expressed throughout all MassMobile interviewees. Nevertheless, they agreed that their system was very *lean*. From our perspective, supply and risk managers were actually concerned that MassMobile invested too little in its SRMS, as these comments indicate.

At both firms, supply managers were satisfied with the scope of information their SRMS provided, and criticism was, thus, only scarcely expressed. A clear point for dissatisfaction at both firms was the quality of risk ratings and financial information provided by external agents. Supply managers indicated that this information was regularly outdated and/or inaccurate, and indicated a high potential of improvement in this field.

To summarize, we found the SRMS of both OEMs to have distinct characteristics: PrimCar applied an extensive, slightly excessive SRMS, which emphasized the early detection of supply risks via a complete analysis of a supplier's business situation and surrounding. MassMobile pursued a strictly lean philosophy, which used only the most common sources of information and limited the additional effort for collecting further data. Yet, this lean approach left out strategic aspects of a supplier's business situation, such as the business plans, governance aspects or the characteristics of its financiers.

Consequently, we characterize PrimCar's risk management approach to be proactive because it covers early strategic aspects. In contrast, we perceive MassMobile's risk management approach to be rather reactive, because leading indicators were much less emphasized and risk assessment was highly relying on lagging information. This approach explained the increased emphasis MassMobile placed on *soft*, subjective information for completing their risk assessment. In contrast to that strategic analysis, this information is already present in the company in the form of each supply manager's personal impressions.

Experience with Supplier Bankruptcies

During the interviews, supply managers of both OEMs pointed out that increasing financing and cash management problems were major consequences of the current economic crisis because banks stopped providing easy credit. Further, it was mentioned that the whole industry suffered from a discount on credit ratings, which led to lending money getting more expensive and suppliers becoming frailer. As a consequence, both OEMs experienced about 50 to 60 cases of bankrupt suppliers each between January 2008 and December 2009.

On average, each PrimCar supply manager had to cope with four strategic suppliers filing for bankruptcy during this period, which propelled its total additional expenses beyond 200 Mill Euro. As an additional consequence, operations got unstable at PrimCar, where, in one case, the collapse of a strategic supplier made production stumble. Yet PrimCar risk managers regarded this incident as an exception, as it was the one and only case where production was on hold due to a supplier going bankrupt. PrimCar further managed to keep its product and delivery quality unaffected by supply bankruptcies. Two supply managers at PrimCar, for example, reported that they were able to shift purchasing volume from the bankrupt supplier to their backup supplier, which lead to additional price savings.

One reason why operations were hardly affected by supplier bankruptcies laid in the well-planned preparation of PrimCar. In the vast majority of bankruptcy cases, the risk management team and the supply managers at PrimCar knew in advance that the supplier had severe problems that might lead to insolvency. Yet, although tremendous effort was taken by PrimCar to identify potentially distressed suppliers ahead of time, risk management indicators were only named in 40 percent of all interviews as pointing supply managers towards a problematic supplier. Similarly, 40 percent of all interviewees at PrimCar named requests for changes in contract terms as a strong and reliable indicator for a supplier facing significant problems. If a supplier asked for shorter payment terms, or for advance payments of material or tools, the supply managers knew that the supplier had significant cash problems.

In contrast to these hard facts, more than two thirds of all supply managers indicated that the best kinds of information on upcoming critical problems were soft factors, like alerting changes in the behavior of the supplier. Whenever a supplier started to desperately bid for a new assignment, offering prices close to, or below, total cost, supply managers increased their attention. Or, if the supplier escalated problems far quicker and more seriously than before, supply managers sensed significant problems. If a supplier started to collect old payments of minor amounts from past years, supply managers started to become alert. Another soft aspect found important by 40 percent of PrimCar's supply managers was personnel fluctuation. Whenever the members of the management board, key personnel in general, or especially the sales personnel dealing with the firm changed with increasing frequencies, supply managers suspected a negative outlook for the supplier's close future. Last, at least 30 percent of PrimCar's supply managers indicated further sources of important information on a supplier's business, such as market rumors, hints from banks, comments from the supplier's competitors, or notes from other car manufacturers.

In contrast to PrimCar, each MassMobile supply manager reported, on average, only one strategic supplier going bankrupt, which is reflected in its total additional expenses of less than 50 Mill Euro. Risk managers at MassMobile identified two reasons for this low amount of extra cost. First, they claimed to have an SRMS, which notified the company early enough to build up sufficient safety stock, while supply managers were ramping up backup suppliers. Second, they believed to have a real cooperative relationship with their suppliers. Everybody at MassMobile's supply management department was convinced that their fair contract terms and rates, especially with strategic suppliers, mitigated bankruptcy effectively.

Similar to PrimCar, the majority of MassMobile's supply managers reported no production delay or disruption, or other problems whatsoever, caused by the supplier bankruptcies, except extra effort. Only 25 percent of our MassMobile interviewees indicated an effect on operations in the case of supplier bankruptcy. Yet, they pointed out that safeguarding product quality in cases where production volume was shifted from a bankrupt to a backup supplier, was sometimes an issue. Finally, supply managers at MassMobile also found positive effects of supplier bankruptcy and distress. It was openly admitted that these situations were good opportunities and, thus, systematically used to phase out business with suppliers. MassMobile was not satisfied with or did not want to cooperate with them in the future. Hence, the supply management at MassMobile made use of the current economic crisis in general, and of distress at suppliers in particular in order to optimize their purchasing portfolio.

When it came to recognizing distress with a supplier, MassMobile's supply managers relied heavily on their company's risk management system: More than half of the interviewed supply managers stated that the risk management system warned them in case a supplier was facing significant troubles. Change requests on contract terms were also named by supply managers at MassMobile as a reliable indicator for upcoming supplier bankruptcy. Another, softer, yet important source for them was a visible mismatch of supply and demand. One quarter of our MassMobile interviewees indicated that a supplier who lost important clients or had quality problems would be in danger of bankruptcy soon. Finally, supply managers at MassMobile also valued rumors in the market or information from third parties.

It became clear that supply managers at MassMobile mainly learned about an upcoming bankruptcy from the supplier itself. Most often, a representative of the supplier or even the bankruptcy manager approached the MassMobile buyers with the bad news. Although supply managers stated that in 19 out of 20 bankruptcy cases they were not surprised, but rather informed about the seriousness of the supplier's situation, our observations also show us that supply managers at MassMobile did not learn about a supplier bankruptcy far in advance, so that strategic countermeasures were not applicable.

Interestingly, at PrimCar, where the SRMS was far more advanced and profound, soft subjective indicators were found to be particularly useful when it came to recognizing distressed suppliers. It is also striking that PrimCar, despite its significant effort to proactively manage its supply risks, experienced more than four times higher extra cost than MassMobile with their reactive, lean approach.

Reactions to Supplier Bankruptcies

Following their different risk management philosophies, both companies' approaches in cases of supplier bankruptcy were also quite distinct. At the moment a supplier filed for bankruptcy, a specialized crisis management team took over at PrimCar, leaving the normal supply manager and the risk management team mostly out of the process. The crisis managers had a large portfolio of possible reactions to the supplier bankruptcy at their disposal. It is important to note that the application of these alternatives was especially dependent on the importance of the supplier for PrimCar. If it was a strategic supplier, PrimCar went to considerable effort to support the supplier. First and foremost, they agreed to temporarily change the terms of the relationship, for example shortening payment times, by paying for material or tools in advance or by giving guarantees to second tier suppliers. In special cases, they also agreed to freeze automatic price reductions or even provided funds to the strategic supplier in need.

As PrimCar was pursuing a proactive risk management approach, they also engaged in co-managing their strategic suppliers and provided active support during strategic turnarounds or for finding new investors. Yet, although these cooperative approaches were used at PrimCar, they constituted an exception. As one manager pointed out, "If the supplier expresses an additional need of liquidity, it is an extreme problem, as our payment terms are clear and, in fact, are not subject to negotiation."

Managers only entered into this cooperative procedure if PrimCar was totally dependent on the bankrupt supplier.

In the remaining cases of bankruptcy, and especially if they touched nonstrategic suppliers, PrimCar applied a rather restrictive crisis management approach. After taking measures to cover their supplies, managers at PrimCar ramped up production at backup suppliers and shifted their purchasing volume.

Unlike PrimCar, MassMobile did not split up their risk management activities into risk and crisis management. In line with its lean risk management approach, MassMobile's distressed suppliers were mainly taken care of by supply managers, accompanied by risk managers. Similar to PrimCar, MassMobile's reaction approaches also depended on the importance of the specific supplier. If a supplier was of strategic relevance, MassMobile was very interested in a partnership relationship as was unanimously expressed. With this in mind, supply managers were supportive with strategic suppliers in the case of distress. One supply manager justified the extra cost as follows: "Switching horses is not the single best way." He believed that it is more beneficial to help a strategic supplier in the moment of distress and yield a competitive advantage in the long run by having primary access to key technology, than to save money on the spot and substitute the supplier. Similar to PrimCar, cooperative actions taken by MassMobile suppliers included temporary changes of the contract terms or the provision of additional funds. Yet, unlike PrimCar, aid was only granted financially, while intense strategic supporting actions like management support were not provided.

In the case of a nonstrategic supplier going bankrupt, MassMobile pursued a clear-cut action plan. Supply managers first build up sufficient safety stock to endure a delivery stop. Simultaneously, volume was shifted to backup suppliers, preparing the total substitution of the supplier.

When comparing the different reaction approach of both case companies, three aspects became clear. First, PrimCar was acting much earlier and with more strategic support than MassMobile. Second, once strategic support actions failed and a supplier filed for bankruptcy, PrimCar's reaction attitude was less cooperative than MassMobile's. Third, once actions were taken in this situation, they were much more narrow, clear-cut, and simple at MassMobile than at PrimCar, where alternatives were various and conditional on previous actions of the car maker. Yet, besides all efforts to cooperate and support suppliers, both OEMs still considered supplier bankruptcies as an opportunity to decrease the number of suppliers to a large extent, which is why substituting the supplier still received high ranks at both sides.

CONCLUSION AND LESSONS LEARNED

Our analysis suggested that PrimCar followed a far more extensive supply risk management approach than MassMobile. Both case companies experienced a considerable number of supplier bankruptcies, causing them additional costs. Although the overall effects of the economic crisis on both companies' supply chains were comparable, each case company showed different detection and reaction patterns to cases of distressed suppliers, which followed their individual risk management approaches.

PrimCar pursued a proactive risk management approach and put in significantly more effort than MassMobile with its reactive approach. Risk managers at PrimCar intervened earlier and had measures of strategic support at their disposal.

MassMobile focused on detecting significant distress and applied reactive approaches of temporary support to strategic suppliers. At MassMobile, the decision making was reduced to support/no-support decisions in the moment of crisis. One would suspect that the number of strategic suppliers going bankrupt was far lower at PrimCar than at MassMobile or alternatively that the damage dealt by distressed suppliers was significantly higher at MassMobile. Our observations have shown the opposite. Despite leading indicators and early action-taking, PrimCar experienced more bankruptcies of strategic suppliers and suffered worse from them.

The key lessons learned from our study include:

- Increasing the scope and volume of supply risk information increases the likelihood of preventing risk mitigation by drawing wrong conclusions

- A portfolio of clear-cut reaction alternatives and continuous management of a distressed supplier lead to more effective risk mitigation in the short run
- True cooperative behavior yields more effective risk mitigation than non-cooperative, false, or faked cooperative behavior

REFERENCES

Asanuma, B. 1989. "Manufacturer-Supplier Relationships in Japan and the Concept of Relation-Specific Skill." *Journal of the Japanese and International Economies* 3(1):1-30.

Harwranek, D. "German Auto Industry Facing the Abyss. *Der Spiegel Online,* 25 November 2008, Retrieved on 13 January 2010 from http://www.spiegel.de/international/business/0,1518,druck-592658,00.html.

Henke, M. (2008). "Enterprise and Supply Risk Management." *Supply Chain Risk. A Handbook of Assessment, Management, and Performance.* Eds. George A. Zsidisin and Bob Ritchie. New York. 177-185.

Henke, M., M. Weimar, A. Potzner, and R. Besl. *Supplier Risk Management in der Automobilindustrie.* Wiesbaden, 2009.

Oliver Wyman. 2009. "New Automotive Deal? Management Summary." Oliver Wyman, Munich. Retrieved on 2 January 2010 on http://www.oliverwyman.com/de/pdf-files/ManSum_New_Automotive_Deal.pdf.

Richardson, J. 1993. Parallel Sourcing and Supplier Performance in the Japanese Automobile Industry. *Strategic Management Journal* 14(5):339-350.

VDA. 2008. *Auto Annual Report 2008.* Verband der Automobilindustrie e.V., Frankfurt am Main.

14

A TOOLKIT TO SECURE SUPPLIES FOR EFFECTIVE SUPPLY CHAIN RISK MANAGEMENT IN THE AIRCRAFT CONSTRUCTION INDUSTRY

Olivier Lavastre

PLANECO AND ITS SUPPLY CHAIN

PlaneCo (pseudonym) is one of the two biggest companies in the global aircraft construction industry. Its main business units are development, assembly, testing, certification, sales, and shipments of civilian and military aircraft. PlaneCo employs 56,000 people worldwide, has 306 airlines as clients, and more than 1500 suppliers. PlaneCo achieved 27.45 billion Euros in sales in 2008. The company has built roughly 5500 airplanes over time, and builds around 470 new civilian airplanes each year.

PlaneCo has developed commercial activities in several countries, but its production is concentrated in Europe. There are three final assembly centers: two in their historical markets of Germany and France, and the third in China, a new market. This case focuses on the assembly activities for the electric elements of a plane in the group's principal factory in France.

Quality, cost, timing, and flexibility pressures are among the main factors driving the emergence of supply chain risks. PlaneCo's policy choice to expand outsourcing assembly activities seriously increases these risks. To illustrate, PlaneCo buys and assembles 10 percent of the electric components necessary to produce electrical equipment boxes used in planes. The remaining 90 percent are manufactured by its principal subcontractor industrial partners who provide finished subassemblies and components for the final assembly. The production model reduces investment and spreads risks and benefits of the developing expertise over many partners and therefore, requires increased monitoring of the partners.

This case deals with the buying, supply chain, and quality center for PlaneCo's electric components division. In general, supply chain risk management (SCRM) is focused on the subcontractors who develop products specifically for PlaneCo. These relationships usually last five years, in others words, the length of a component lifecycle, from conception through use in production.

PlaneCo has five privileged subcontractors, those having the biggest buying and supply chain activity roles, but supply chain risk management is practiced with the 38 subcontractors working with the electric components division. A number of monitoring tools and practices, primarily intended to increase supplier involvement in improving logistics and quality performance, have been established to secure the supply chain. PlaneCo has two main supplier requirements: supplier implication and living up to the logistical and quality performance defined by PlaneCo.

An Overview of the Supply Chain Risk Management Tools

PlaneCo has deployed its supply chain risk management based on four tools. They include a Supplier Risk Register tool, Supplier Control Review tool, Consigned Vendor Managed Inventory tool, and No Conformity Costs tool. These tools represent the four typical SCRM methodological steps: risk identification, risk assessment, decision and implementation solutions, and risk monitoring and control. PlaneCo's choice of tools enables them in:

1. *Choosing* lowest risk suppliers, according to a calculated ranking based on supply chain risks over the course of the relationship between PlaneCo and the supplier
2. *Verifying* supplier activities, confirming that suppliers are approved and continually live up to company specifications and requirements
3. *Securing* operational product flows to have nondisrupted subassemblies flow and minimized safety stocks
4. *Involving* suppliers in managing product flows in case of a problem via contractual allocation of costs to suppliers due to quality nonconformity and/or poor logistic performance

TOOL 1: *CHOOSING* THE LOWEST RISK SUPPLIER

A strategic project was developed two years ago to protect procurement of goods and services against foreseeable events that would have detrimental impact on product safety. This project was called *Procured Products and Services Risk Management*. This process uses multitrade teams including purchasing, supply chain and quality, as well as engineering to evaluate the inherent risk of a supplier.

To select an industrial partner, PlaneCo takes into account not only the risks associated with this partner, but also the risk management process used by the partner. This proactive attitude is employed throughout a product's life cycle. The desired result of applying this tool is to reduce frequency and consequences of risk realization by continually monitoring risk via frequent fixed supplier reviews and audits over the product life cycle. Stages of the Supplier Risk Registration process are illustrated in Table 14.1.

Table 14.1 Three stages of Supplier Risk Registration and the associated SCRM actions

	Actions for conception and industrialization of products	Specific SCRM actions
Stage 1: Supplier process selection	1. Suppliers are identified for providing a new product.	
	2. Suppliers apply for the pretender.	
	3. Supplier pre-tender applications completed.	A. Pre-tender responses are analyzed and risks identified
	4. Potential supplier list is edited.	B. Supplier factories are audited. Identified risks are added to the supplier's Risk Register to be used as selection criterion.
	5. The supplier is selected and the contract is signed.	
Stage 2: Engineering product program	6. Products are developed and technical skills are specified.	C. Risks are identified and managed through the Engineering product program.
Stage 3: Industrialization of mature products	7. First product quality inspection completed.	D. The review of the first quality inspection is analyzed. The identified risks are added to the supplier's Risk Register and are minimized by management.
	8. PlaneCo places its first orders and the supplier industrializes and delivers its products.	E. Key procurement business reviews are done and planed, with a focus on risk analysis concerning: finance, commercial, quality, industrialization, engineering, delivery, customer support, and supplier risk management.

Initially, supply security is based on provider identification and management of risk: Can we entrust our business supply to a particular supplier? Is this supplier riskier than others? What are the risks? If we choose a given supplier, is risk prevention possible?

The three main questions associated with these different stages are:

1. How can risks associated with suppliers in our supply chain be identified?

   An exhaustive list of potential risks must be established, such as through benchmarking other divisions of the firm, by brainstorming during meetings, by interviewing experts, and by analyzing past incident reports. This list can potentially become extremely long, and therefore focusing only on *real* risks, frequent risks, and most critical risks becomes important.

2. How can we evaluate and rank these risks?

   The preceding questions resulted in a list of more than one hundred risks, some of which may be difficult to manage. Risk classification must be undertaken to determine which risks the team will concentrate on. A four item numeric risk evaluation scale has been developed, taking into account the probability of loss due to an event and the significance of that loss. The relative importance of a risk is the combination of these two dimensions. The scale consists of:

   1: Nonrisky situation; providers with prior experience *best practices* used; methods are satisfactory to the company
   4: Potentially risky situation that needs to be monitored; the supplier must prove themselves by improving the process
   7: Risky situation; unsatisfactory supplier methods are not effective and must be improved
   10: A very risky and unacceptable situation; necessitating planned actions to establish immediate emergency involvement by members of the center

   To quantify the risk the team organizes brainstorming meetings with experts. After discussion and reaching a consensus, a value is attributed for each aspect of each risk.

3. How do we choose the risks to mitigate?

   Using the scale and ranking, the risks are classified. From this ranking 12 risk groups have been identified by the buying, supply chain and quality center as requiring management. They are detailed in Table 14.2.

For each risk, an identification checklist has been created to enable quick and reliable problem diagnosis. Each checklist combines information concerning the source of each risk and its consequences. These circumstances have been defined to simplify the provider audit and to facilitate evaluation of a situation. The described situations are those most frequently encountered, historically, and during supplier audits. The checklist details are shown in Table 14.3.

Table 14.2 The 12 groups of supply chain risks chosen for management

1. Provider capacity management
2. Management of suppliers and subcontractors
3. Production management system
4. Major events (ERP change, moving factory or other critical event)
5. Supplier location
6. Root cause analysis for problems
7. Risk analysis methodology
8. Communication and responsiveness
9. Monetary and currency change risks
10. Dependence risks for the supplier
11. Financial risk (supplier financial health)
12. Risks associated with agreements and capacity sourcing

Using the scale, the manager evaluates each risk and synthesizes the analysis in a table. This is illustrated in Table 14.4.

By allotting one column per supplier, the manager can compare suppliers while taking into account their risks. This document can determine provider criticality, and moreover it can help managers to define short-, medium-, and long-term actions plans to put in place for minimising risks and for securing the supply chain.

Similar to a *Failure Mode, Effects, and Criticality Analysis*, a risk and supplier prioritization is established to identify those risks and which suppliers require attention. A quarterly review is conducted during a buying, supply chain, and quality center meeting to obtain feedback about risk and the prevention and management techniques used during the previous quarters.

Three questions concerning the Supplier Risk Register are examined:

1. What real impact does the Supplier Risk Register have on supply chain risk management?

    The Supplier Risk Register is used before and during the supplier selection process and contract signature. This process, however, relates to long-term projects spanning the entire duration of the contractual commitments that generally last around five years. It therefore has no immediate impact on current suppliers. Findings or outcomes resulting from the Risk Register will not affect a supplier's current business with PlaneCo by resulting in penalties or loss of market share.

    The supplier risk identification is undertaken with the sole objective of decreasing supplier risks and to secure supplies by putting in place corrective actions. This is the first link in the process of controlling risks. Once suppliers' risks are documented, it is essential that the manager in charge of the supplier, in collaboration with a supplier project team, think of creating

Table 14.3 The details of the Supplier Risk Register checklist

1. Capacity management provider	1. Satisfactory method: proven ability over a period of 3 years
	4. Ability needs to be demonstrated
	7. Capacity done but not supported by a robust method
	10. No methods, unproven ability
2. Management of suppliers and subcontractors	1. Risk analysis suppliers: methodology and application satisfactory (the suppliers are evaluated each month by using indicators, action plans, audits, or other methodologies)
	4. Actions in place with providers but not supported by a risk analysis methodology
	7. Risk analysis established but untreated and not followed
	10. No analysis of risk supplier, no rating and no tracking of suppliers
3. Management production system	1. Production management system in place, including the actions planning in short, medium and long term (S&OP, MPS, and MRP)
	4. Production management system in place, but the actions planning in short, medium and long term is not robust and unsatisfactory
	7. No production management system but an activities planning in short term exists
	10. No production management system exists and no activities are planned
4. Major events (ERP change, moving factory or other critical event)	1. No major events are expected
	4. Major event is expected but under control (action plan, risk analysis, defined schedule)
	7. Major event is expected but not under control (action plan, analysis risk, schedule is nonexistent, incomplete or partially defined)
	10. Major event is not communicated or disclosed and without detailed and accurate information
5. Supplier location	1. Production in Europe or North Africa and under management control
	4. Production in Asia or the United States and under management control
	7. Production in Europe or North Africa and no management control
	10. Production in Asia or the United States and no management control

6. Root cause analysis (RCA) for problems	1. RCA systematic: corrective and/or preventive actions implemented
	4. RCA systematic: but action plans are not robust
	7. No systematic RCA and/or action plans are not systematic
	10. No RCA
7. Risk analysis method	1. Formalized process: systematic risk analysis with frequent update
	4. Formalized process: risk analysis, but without update
	7. Risk analysis: no formalized approaches or regular updates
	10. No analysis of risk products or processes
8. Communication and responsiveness	1. Business organization known: proactive communication
	4. Business organization known: focal points are identified
	7. Business organization known: no focal points identified
	10. Business organization known: no proactive communication
9. Monetary and currency change risks	1. Supplier delivers from a country where the currency is the dollar and the supplier uses dollar
	4. Supplier is not located in a country where the currency is the dollar but the supplier uses the dollar
	7. Supplier is not located in a country where the currency is the dollar; the supplier uses the euro but it deploys an action plan to change to the dollar
	10. The supplier uses euro without an action plan to change to the dollar
10. Dependence risks for the supplier	1. The supplier turnover with PlaneCo is between 10 and 30% of its total turnover
	4. The supplier turnover with PlaneCo is between 30 and 50% of its total turnover
	7. The supplier turnover with PlaneCo is a small fraction of its total turnover
	10: The supplier turnover with PlaneCo exceeds 50% of its total turnover
11. Financial risks (provider financial health)	1. No financial risk identified
	4. The financial risks identified are managed or acceptable
	7. The financial risks identified are not acceptable but are managed
	10. The identified risks are unacceptable and are not managed
12. Risks associated with agreements and capacity sourcing	1. Multiple sourcing with long term agreements
	4. Single sourcing with long term agreements
	7. Multiple sourcing without long term agreements
	10. Single sourcing without long term agreements

Table 14.4 The use of the Supplier Risk Register checklist

Registration date		DD/MM/YYYY	DD/MM/YYYY		
Supplier name		Supplier A	Supplier B		
Quality and supply chain risks	Provider capacity management	1	4		
	Management of suppliers and subcontractors	1	4		
	Production management system	4	7		
	Major events (ERP change, moving factory or other critical event)	4	10		
	Supplier location	4	1		
	Root causes analysis for problems	4	4		
	Analysis method risk	1	7		
	Communication and responsiveness	1	4		
Purchasing risks	Monetary and currency change risks	4	7		
	Dependence risks for the supplier	7	10		
	Financial risks	1	1		
	Risks associated with long term agreements and with mono sourcing	10	1		
TOTAL	Risk level	42	60		

and implementing plans to reduce these risks. Otherwise, the Supplier Risk Register tool will not help.

2. Is there an optimal timing for Supplier Risk Register meetings?

The results of the Supplier Risk Register and the associated action plans are analyzed during quarterly meetings. But, this three-month cycle is not always long enough for the establishment and implementation of corrective actions, especially if they involve organizational changes, additional resources, or the introduction of new processes for a supplier.

For some suppliers, it is possible that the risk register will remain identical for two or three meetings. In this case, there is a longer timeframe for the project, and the meeting frequency seems inappropriately rapid for deployment of efficient preventive/corrective actions. Another disadvantage of closely spaced meetings in this particular example is the possibility that buying, supply chain, and quality center members will become disinterested if the meetings are inappropriately spaced because they will have an impression that the project is not progressing. In this case, the Risk Register only needs to be updated every six months, thus providing time for the tools to take effect, and for results of these efforts to be seen. This also provides greater motivation for the team members as they see tangible results of their labor.

3. What is the method for choosing the best criteria for the checklist?

As with any multicriterion tool, the Supplier Risk Register asks questions about the appropriateness of the criteria. The first list is initially created, but changes over time. Therefore, it is necessary to regularly update the criteria and the groups of supply chain risks that are chosen for action, those that need analysis and represent the current main problem(s).

All current problems do not need to be taken into account in the Supplier Risk Register because they can also be considered in the supplier selection phase by means of various on site surveys and audits. Likewise, they may not be followed-up after selection, as for example, environmental, design, engineering, and health and safety issues which are often dealt with in-house by suppliers.

TOOL 2: *MONITORING* AND *VERIFYING* SUPPLIER ACTIVITIES

Once the Supplier Risk Register is produced, a *Supplier Control Review* (SCR) tool is launched under the supervision of the providers. The SCR is an information base where all activity checks carried out on the supplier, such as certifications, in-factory audits, quality evaluations, or capacity production controls are listed. The SCR is also a monitoring tool that helps systematize and automate control of suppliers. This tool can provide leverage for problem identification, resulting ultimately in development and realization of preventive or corrective security activities as well.

The aim of the SCR is to demonstrate that all providers are approved, are continuously under scrutiny, and that they satisfy the exigencies of the firm on an ongoing basis. For this company, control is established at the start of the relationship when the contract is signed, and must be maintained throughout the relationship during the product life cycle.

The SCR is a set of planned reviews, where all information relating to suppliers (criticality and risk, performance, status of certification) are analyzed to determine if corrective actions are necessary. Corrective actions can be long- or short-term, and can concern the provider/supplier relationship, the supplier itself and/or PlaneCo's supplier evaluation process. These actions can include, for example, an evaluation to check the supplier's industrial process management capability, an external certification such as ISO, an increase in the SCR frequency, or updating the Supplier Risk Register.

With the Supplier Control Review, part of the control is outsourced to an external partner. Indeed, an additional level is added to supply chain risk management: the active participation of fourth party logistics providers in securing supplies. They are responsible for coordinating the different partners in the supply chain and their task is to complete the SCR for all their first-tier suppliers.

The logistics provider agrees to give the buying, supply chain, and quality center all information concerning quality management, product traceability, and all alerts in case of any changes in supplier organization or processes. The logistics provider also agrees to measure and manage performance of its suppliers via different indicators. In case of failure, it will be obliged to analyze the problem and develop action plans.

This tool presents a few key advantages for PlaneCo and especially for the buying, supply chain, and quality center:

1. Decreasing the number of stakeholders (logistic providers as sole interface), thereby simplifying supply chain management
2. Avoiding evaluation and monitoring of suppliers; this activity is undertaken by the logistic providers
3. Contractually binding partners to respect exigencies; the firm secures its supply and gives responsibility to logistics providers for supplier monitoring

The periodicity of SCR is dependent on the criticality of the supplier. *Criticality* is measured and defined by the Supplier Risk Register. For suppliers defined as *non-risky*, the periodicity is three years. But, for suppliers defined as *risky*, single source suppliers, or suppliers that have to take actions set by the Risk Register, the SCR needs to be biannual, according to the level of criticality.

In this particular case, the databases have been harmonized by a newly created, centralized information system to facilitate the supplier approval process and thereby information exchange between partners. This tool was developed by extracting information from the SAP ERP system, performing a *data cleaning* and an alignment in all the SAP systems of all European subsidiaries. This system became the new frame of reference for managing suppliers. The users could report directly on a supplier's page after a visit, post comments after an incident, or give recommendations to improve supplier performance and control.

Further, the SCR spreadsheet provided the current state of supplier control, upcoming actions for deployment, and timing for the next Supplier Control Review. Two questions arise concerning the Supplier Control Review:

1. Is there an ideal format for the spreadsheet?

   The spreadsheet is an Excel file with complex and large macros, and as such, cannot be sent to users via email because it would block their inboxes. The size of this file, greater than 10 octets, is a first constraint for a tool that must be easy to use. The second constraint is the time required to select and modify supplier information. Due to the many macros, selecting a supplier or performing any operation, such as changing a character, or adding a line, takes about a minute, which over the long haul could become burdensome. Technical challenges are not insurmountable and are solved step by step, but member motivation must be attended to and maintained.

2. Do fourth party logistics providers do their job?

    The use of SCR requires significant work in gathering information from suppliers. This work is all the more difficult when fourth party logistics providers do not share collaborative databases with their suppliers. The buying, supply chain and quality center needs to demonstrate the value of shared information for all concerned parties: the logistic providers, the suppliers, and PlaneCo.

TOOL 3: *SECURING* OPERATIONAL PRODUCT FLOWS

One of PlaneCo's goals with supply chain risk management is to secure material flow between its suppliers and its final assembly center. Securing flow will be achieved during the procurement phase with *Consigned Vendor Managed Inventory* (CVMI). This is a collaborative solution for inventory management that is part of PlaneCo's SCRM. It maintains minimum inventory in realtime, thus increasing available financial liquidity.

Two traditional methods exist for external stock management: Vendor Managed Inventory (VMI) and CoManaged Inventory (CMI). With VMI suppliers are responsible for maintaining and guaranteeing client in-house stock levels. Responsibility can be total as with VMI, or partial as with CMI, in which case, suppliers deliver stocks only with customer permission. Both variations imply information exchanges, a certain level of trust between logistic and industrial partners, a mature supply chain, and investment. Implementation is not mandatory, but does result in increased efficiency and enhanced supply chain responsiveness. These systems demand long-term partnerships and continuity.

The main difference between VMI and CVMI concerns stock property transfer. With CVMI, stocks are located with the client, but belong to the supplier. The client becomes owner of the stock when merchandise is removed from the reserve.

CVMI is not universally used. It primarily concerns products with high volume consumption and turnover. It also concerns high-priced products to allow for short-term savings by reducing stock value. CVMI deployment is a three-step process:

1. The first step (*pilot phase*) lasts at least 12 weeks, during which time the supplier tests and learns the processes and tools used for CVMI.
2. The second step (*extended pilot phase*) continues for another 12 weeks, during which time the supplier needs to show mastery and command of this sort of inventory management by developing integrated information systems. In general, these two first steps are deployed using a test panel of five components, with logistic and quality performance measures in place, but without penalties.
3. The last step (*deployment phase*) is the gradual expansion of the CVMI to all the eligible component references between PlaneCo and its suppliers.

CVMI creates four principal advantages for PlaneCo:

- Financial: PlaneCo retains its available cash because payment to the supplier is delayed until merchandise is used. The downside of this method is that the customer must pay for warehousing and inventory management.
- Logistics: With stocks secured, the customer achieves flow management security.
- Cost reduction.
- Reduced delivery delays.

CVMI creates numerous advantages for the suppliers as well:

- Improved order-fill ratio: Consequently, the supplier will have a stronger position in purchasing negotiations and will enjoy a good reputation.
- Full visibility of PlaneCo's requirements as compared to classic inventory controls, i.e., VMI.
- Reduced in-house stocks: Supplier risk is reduced by making stocks available at the customer site, rather than relying on forecasts calculating safety stocks. (This can be further aggravated by the risk of false forecasts, as with the *Bullwhip effect*.)
- Improved resource planning via an IT tool that publishes daily and weekly stock forecasts based either on past consumption, or on dependent requirement planning.
- Optimized transportation empowering the provider to manage its replenishments. This solution allows for shipment mutualization and reduced emergency transport and its associated cost.
- Computerization, automation, and acceleration of the interface between PlaneCo's ERP and the supplier's ERP to secure data exchanges.
- Levelling/smoothing of production, anticipation or delay fluctuations owing to PlaneCo's improved forecasting and tracking of actual consumption.

In addition to securing material flows, CVMI reduces stock levels and significantly improves supply chain management in the following ways:

- Productivity in supply management and planning: PlaneCo and its suppliers spend less time fixing order information errors.
- Better quality data: Errors in data entry are reduced through EDI (electronic data interchange). For example, when a supplier provides a component, it sends an electronic delivery order featuring a barcode by EDI. This indicates volume, timing and transport details concerning the merchandise delivery. Upon reception, the handlers simply scan the barcode, and confirm the quantity and date of merchandise receipt. The speed and quality of data exchange is improved.
- Enhances provider service to customers. Both parties have an interest in providing the best possible service to end customers. This is realized by having the right item in stock when the end customer needs it, thus benefiting both partners.

- Greater flexibility, increased financial liquidity, and rapid capacity to provide needed stock.
- Better relationships with suppliers: By working together and sharing information, the partners are better prepared to meet demands.

CVMI is an approach that enhances SCRM efficiency via faster information transmission, greater sharing of information, improved forecast and planning visibility, enhanced reactivity, and overall performance improvement.

Despite the advantages, there are certain problems associated with CVMI. The first concerns the supplier's ability to maintain traceability of its components. The supplier does lose control and monitoring of its goods in consignment stock. Further, there is no guarantee that FIFO (first in, first out) is adhered to, which can prove critical when products have expiration dates.

The second involves the investments necessary to setup CVMI. It is a solution that requires heavy supplier investment, particularly in terms of workload. During the first step (*pilot stage*), it is necessary for the supplier to have full-time resources to handle the logistics required by the specific solution and to establish a system for monitoring inventory in the PlaneCo warehouse. To this end, the supplier can establish a threshold for automatic replenishment. However, some suppliers prefer to establish a system of weekly deliveries with varying volumes depending on PlaneCo's consumption and forecasts to optimize the stock in PlaneCo's in-house storage facility. The required investment is significant. To automate the solution, the supplier must implement software (sold by PlaneCo) that transfers data from PlaneCo's ERP to the supplier's information system. The software, however, does not fully respond to the problem and the supplier needs to develop the link between the new file and its own system. Therefore, without a computer gateway to make the link between PlaneCo's ERP and a supplier's IS, deployment of consigned VMI cannot be accomplished. The cost of such systems can be heavy to bear for small and medium-sized companies.

The third problem concerns changes in the billing process. Under the new system, billing is no longer done for several parcels at their reception, but rather for each product at the moment it is taken from the inventory when a specific request is sent. Thus, a bill is issued every time the customer withdraws a product. It often happens that the cost of issuing the invoice is greater than the price of the product itself. At the request of providers, the accounting department has developed an automated billing solution that groups samples, relying on the suppliers' accounting to take from the remaining CVMI stock every Monday. This solution simplifies the task and decreases administrative costs.

TOOL 4: *INVOLVING* THE SUPPLIER

Finally, to increase supplier involvement in the supply chain, secure supplies and enhance overall performance, PlaneCo developed a system to contractually allocate costs to suppliers in case of nonquality and poor logistics performance. This program is called *No Conformity Costs (NCC)*. Its two goals are to hold suppliers responsible for the quality of their services, namely logistical performance and quality, and to make the suppliers responsible for the financial effects of poor quality and late deliveries.

Purchase contracts are negotiated by PlaneCo's central administration, thus at a high and general level. But, historically they have not contained details concerning application of supplier penalties. For example, there were no financial specifics for quality problems, other than repairs on aircraft, that were based on real costs. There are standard penalties concerning quality and logistics, both supplier activities, but they are not applied in a homogeneous manner due to managerial discretion. In addition the penalty amounts were too low to be truly dissuasive and as a result, suppliers were not strongly encouraged to improve their performance. Therefore, it was decided to develop a new method of calculating penalties, and to find ways to implement them.

To obtain greater supplier implication and a higher level of logistic and quality performance, the buying, supply chain, and quality center revised the system for charging costs to the supplier for nonquality and poor logistics performance, known as NCC. Under the revised system, suppliers that do not meet the quality and supply objectives defined in their contracts pay PlaneCo financial penalties. The NCC process is defined in three stages:

Stage One: Add a section outlining penalties related to supplier logistics and quality activities to current contracts after an analysis of each contract.

Stage Two: Map supplier performance over the past year to estimate a total monetary amount to be imputed to suppliers.

Stage Three: Plan frequent recurring meetings to review supplier performance.

Penalties due to nonconforming activities are first calculated by taking into account:

- The gravity of the consequences of a problem. Two widely used indicators in the monthly performance reports are the indications given in the quality report written by the PlaneCo Quality Service division and the number of defects in parts per million.
- The evolution of supplier performance. The calculation of penalty amounts increases proportionally to the decrease in performance. This indexation creates an efficient lever to help suppliers feel more responsible for the potential severity of poor, long-term logistics and quality actions.

The buying, supply chain, and quality center, jointly with the purchasing department, decided to cap the total potential penalty at 3 percent of supplier turnover by quarter, and introduce the possibility of erasing the penalties. The goal is to increase supplier performance, but not to penalize them excessively or place them in financial difficulty. Thus, a supplier whose performance has not met the requirements for a given quarter will be granted a period of 3 months to achieve the objectives. During this period, the penalties of the previous quarter will be suspended. If for quarter $N + 1$, the supplier achieves its objectives, the penalties of quarter N will be canceled; otherwise, the penalties must be paid. Three questions associated with NCC systems can arise:

1. Is it possible to negotiate the penalties?

    The buyers have now amended the NCC program in the purchase agreements. These new contracts are now used and were presented to suppliers in connection with the tender of the new PlaneCo plane. Therefore, the signing of this program is mandatory for the new PlaneCo contract. However, each supplier tries to negotiate specific terms and attempts to obtain from the purchaser a revaluation of the formula. For example, one supplier requested a new definition of objectives and a penalty cap of less than 3 percent.

2. Who is responsible in case of a component shortage or a backorder situation?

    Poor logistics performance is not always due to mismanagement of supplies. Sometimes PlaneCo unexpectedly places an order, or in the case of CVMI, consumes a consignment stock beyond the forecast quantities. In these cases, there is no contractually agreed upon method to differentiate between delay due exclusively to the supplier or due to unforeseen PlaneCo utilization of stocks.

3. Can opportunistic behavior on the part of suppliers lead to rising component prices?

    A shift in product pricing can be observed in the case of companies putting in place a supplier penalty program. For the supplier, there is transparency concerning the method of penalty calculation. The supplier, in turn, estimates their prices based on its past performance (and incurred penalties). It is likely that the supplier uses this figure as a base for calculating its initial prices by pretending there has been an increase in raw materials or in other cost centers. Buyers should therefore identify and call out this practice in future bids using their knowledge of market prices to detect these disguised cost increases.

CONCLUSION

Supply chain risk management has assumed considerable importance across most industries in recent years. In this case study, securing supplier component flow to PlaneCo is the primary objective in supply chain risk management. PlaneCo has developed several SCRM tools to manage risks associated with this flow:

- The Supplier Risk Register identifies and updates current risks, aiding in the choice and surveillance of suppliers
- The SCR monitors suppliers' activities and performance

- Enlarging the use of CMVI improves supplier performance, secures flows and optimizes stocks
- The NCC program maintains and rewards supplier motivation and implication in achieving performance goals in terms of logistics, quality, and CVMI.

In theory, these tools appear simple to set up and use. But in practice, they are complex, especially in terms of supply chain management and relationships with industrial partners. In light of the complex issues surrounding the use of these tools, certain questions need to be solved to enable their deployment in other situations and between other customers and suppliers such as: analyzing the influence of power in these relationships and whether these tools can be deployed between all partners. Furthermore, an assessment of what components can be managed by using these tools would provide useful insights. In addition, it is imperative to understand the real advantage of using SCRM and what improvements can be made to enhance the effectiveness and efficiency of SCRM tools.

15

USING INFORMATION TECHNOLOGY TO MITIGATE SUPPLY NETWORK RISK

M. Douglas Voss and Omar Keith Helferich

This case is based upon interviews with representatives of jadian enterprises (jadian), and Supply Chain Sustainability, as well as publicly and non-publicly available information provided by the firms. The authors would like to extend their appreciation to the employees of jadian and Supply Chain Sustainability for their cooperation in producing this work. Although both authors are partners in Supply Chain Sustainability, the purpose of this chapter is to provide insights to a process for identifying, assessing, and measuring supplier risk.

INTRODUCTION

The importance of supply chain management came to light partially due to the successful implementation of its principles by firms such as Wal-mart, Dell, and Toyota. Wal-mart maintains its position as a low-cost leader in the retail segment through globalization of its supply base to acquire less expensive goods while effectively and efficiently managing logistics processes such as transportation and inventory management. Dell has recently fallen on hard times, but its use of the response-based business model and postponement allowed them to reduce finished goods inventory and allowed consumers to purchase products that better fit their needs. Toyota's success is due in part to its use of lean principles to reduce costs while simultaneously improving quality. Other supply chain strategies, such as supply base rationalization, are ubiquitously applied by a variety of firms.

Each of these strategies has its benefits. However, as with many other supply chain principles, they also involve trade-offs. For example, the response-based business model seeks to allow demand to *pull* product through the supply chain, thereby overcoming the excess finished goods inventory and other problems posed by the forecast driven anticipatory business model. The response-based business model allows the firm to only produce what is demanded by its customers. This reduces dwell time (the amount of time supply chain assets sit idle, not contributing to value creation) and requires increased visibility of supply chain assets and closer supplier relationships.

The response-based business model also has its pitfalls. Similar to the application of lean principles, the response-based business model reduces supply chain inventory buffers, exacerbating the effects of supply disruptions. This increases the importance of monitoring suppliers and sharing information both internally and externally to ensure supply continuity and prevent disruptions before they occur.

Globalization increases the number of parties involved in a given supply chain. Each node in a supply chain has a given probability of failure (e.g., financial, quality, or security failure) at any given time. As the number of nodes in a given supply chain increase, these failure probabilities are compounded, and the probability of failure at some point in the supply chain rises. Further, as firms rationalize their supply base, they become more dependent on each remaining supplier.

Dependence may be the key theme in the preceding discussion. As firms implement supply chain strategies they become more dependent upon their suppliers and their risk of supply disruption increases. Firms must find a way to incrementally improve supply chain strategies without adding counter-productive inventory and mitigate disruption risk through the exchange of information both internally and externally.

One method of accomplishing this goal is through the implementation of supply chain assessment and monitoring technology. Appropriate technology should allow the purchasing firm to calculate the consequences posed by the failure of any given supplier then allocate monitoring resources to those suppliers with the greatest *a priori* probability of failure and the greatest potential to negatively affect performance. The confluence of consequence severity and probability of failure defines the risk posed by any given supplier.

Methods of monitoring suppliers may include self-assessment benchmarking of financial metrics or third-party audits of production and supply network facilities to ensure sustainable business practices and quality compliance, among others. Information gathered should feed back into risk algorithms to adjust suppliers' failure probability. Information should also be shared vertically within the purchasing firm and horizontally with suppliers to proactively prevent and mitigate failure and subsequent supply chain disruption. The use of such technology simultaneously increases coordination efficiency and effectiveness both internally and externally.

This chapter profiles two Michigan (USA) based firms—jadian and Supply Chain Sustainability—and illustrates how a web-based software tool called CommonView© can be used to mitigate supply network risk by monitoring suppliers and exchanging information both internally and externally. Information used in this case is based on interviews with jadian and Supply Chain Sustainability executives as well as publicly and non-publicly available information provided by the firms. Following an overview of jadian and Supply Chain Sustainability, CommonView is described and coupled with a detailed discussion of how supplier risk is incorporated into the tool with a real-world application of a supplier risk calculation. Next, a template for technology implementation is provided. The chapter concludes with benefits of implementation. Caveats are discussed throughout the chapter.

JADIAN AND SUPPLY CHAIN SUSTAINABILITY CORPORATE OVERVIEWS

The jadian organization is a Lansing, MI, global software and services company that provides complete solutions for managing compliance, audits, inspections, work orders, licenses/certificates/permits, and enforcement activities. Its solutions are being used 24 hours a day, seven days a week and process over a million audits per year with certifications issued in over 49 countries in multiple languages. Jadian's customers include a wide variety of private industry companies and government agencies, including public health agencies, audit and inspection companies, road transportation authorities, national accreditation bodies, and federal agencies. Their software is used for inspection and audits of such high profile facilities as The Indianapolis 500 Speedway and the Burj Khalifa, which is the tallest building in the world at 2684 feet.

The concept for jadian was developed in the mid-1980s by Jerry Norris, an auditor and business process consultant who envisioned a way to streamline field audit and report writing tasks related to ISO certification. This vision has grown to incorporate all aspects of compliance management. Today, jadian is a privately-held corporation offering multiple software solutions to its rapidly growing customer base. It provides all of the services critical for a successful implementation, including consulting, software configuration and customization, data migration, systems integration, hosting services, and ongoing support.

Jadian partners with select firms that provide specific domain knowledge and assist in the sales and software implementation processes. For many supply chain and supply chain risk related projects, jadian partners with Supply Chain Sustainability. Supply Chain Sustainability is an Okemos, MI, limited liability corporation comprised of a core group of professionals with experience in supply chain management, benchmarking, security, disaster management, and environmental issues. Its focus is to utilize knowledge of the above domains to improve client performance through the implementation of risk-based management processes and information technology tools.

The remainder of this case draws upon information gleaned from these two firms to detail how technology can be used to monitor global supply chains. It is important to note that this chapter does not focus on the mitigation of any one risk. Tools such as CommonView are adaptable for the assessment and monitoring of multiple domains separately or simultaneously. This case is intended to illustrate how information technology can be used to mitigate a firm's supply related *risk of choice* through assessment, monitoring, and information exchange.

RISK MITIGATION: THE ROLE OF COMMONVIEW

As previously mentioned, many supply chain relationships and strategies are based upon acknowledged dependence. Acknowledged dependence implies that the performance of one supply chain partner is heavily contingent upon the performance of another. For example, a purchasing firm is dependent upon its suppliers to reliably deliver quality inventory. A supplier's efforts to accomplish these goals may be hampered by intentional or unintentional product defects, financial hardships, or security issues. The effects of intentional/unintentional product defects has been widely publicized in the consumer goods industry with recent recalls of toys with excessive lead content, pet food containing unauthorized and harmful ingredients, and peanut butter tainted with salmonella.

Rightly or wrongly, the purchasing firm is often held liable for problems caused by supplier mistakes. Purchasing firms must take proactive steps to mitigate this risk through auditing and assessing suppliers, then sharing results both internally and externally. A number of issues complicate the matter. First, a large purchasing firm may have thousands of suppliers that sell diverse products, which leads to a diverse set of risk profiles. Given limitations on audit and assessment resources, it is impractical and foolish to devote the same resources to all suppliers. Therefore, it is necessary to determine the risk of failure for each supplier and allocate more resources to those suppliers at greater risk of failure. Second, given the voluminous amount of data generated from audits and assessments, there exists a need to standardize and prioritize the results, (e.g., nonconformances, product test failures) and make them available to relevant internal and external parties quickly and in an actionable format so that issues can be proactively addressed.

This is where information technology tools such as CommonView are useful. CommonView is a web-based software solution produced by jadian that consolidates compliance data from multiple systems into a manageable online format. It provides a centralized location for executives and managers to view multisite and supply chain performance in the areas of inspections, nonconformances and corrective actions, product samples and test results, second and third party certifications, security, and other domains of interest. The system automatically calculates supplier risk scores based on business rules. These risk scores are then used to drive risk mitigation activities and focus resources on higher risk sites and critical suppliers. Risk scores can be used to determine inspection frequencies, sampling and test plans, and other requirements.

Defining risk is often one of the more challenging aspects of implementing tools such as CommonView, which this chapter will refer to as supply chain risk monitoring software (SCRMS). The first step to defining the risk of a certain outcome, such as a supplier security failure, is to determine the probability and the outcome severity of that event. For example, a security failure may take the form of a case of product stolen from a supplier's 53' trailer. This is a high probability event that likely occurs relatively frequently. However, the severity of the outcome related to this event is likely negligible. Conversely, a security failure may take the form of a disgruntled supplier employee contaminating food product with a substance that is dangerous or fatal to those who consume it. This is likely to be a relatively low probability event, but one that has a severe outcome, should it occur. Each supplier's probability of failure and failure outcome severity would be fed into an SCRMS solution to calculate the supplier's risk profile, as illustrated in Figure 15.1.

The *outcome severity* of a security problem related to a given supplier may be relatively static. While some suppliers supply multiple products, others only supply a single input and the outcome severity of that input does not change. However, the *probability* of a security problem related to a given supplier is likely to be more dynamic.

For example, take the case of a fast food establishment that purchases chicken breasts from a poultry processor based in the Southeast United States. A security issue related to the poultry processor's product could have severe effects (i.e., customer morbidity or

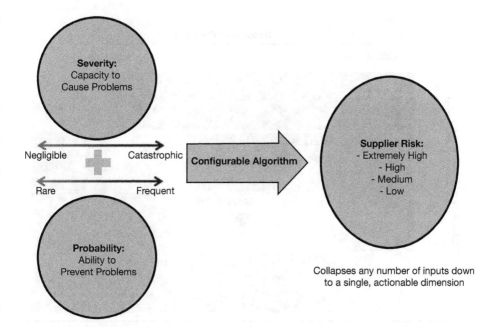

Figure 15.1 SCRMS solution example.

mortality). However, the fact that this poultry processor has had few security issues in the past, led the fast food establishment to consider them a relatively low risk supplier.

Over the course of a month, the fast food establishment began receiving complaints from customers that their chicken breasts contained small, black pieces of plant-like material. The fast food establishment's employees can feed these customer complaints into a SCRMS solution. These systems automatically calculate supplier risk based on the fast food establishment's business rules. In this case, the supplier's risk profile was changed from a medium risk supplier to a high risk supplier due to the customer complaints. Figure 15.2 illustrates this change in relation to the risk profiles of the rest of the fast food establishment's suppliers. The size of the black circles in Figure 15.2 represent the number of suppliers that occupy a given risk category. As the number of suppliers in a given risk category increases, so does the size of the circle in that category.

This change in the supplier's risk category triggered emails, short message service (SMS) messages, and other alerts to relevant parties that a problem with the supplier may exist. The fast food establishment then quickly contacted the supplier and informed them of the nonconformance and that an audit of their production procedures would occur. This audit uncovered several potential security problems and determined that the root cause of the chicken breast contamination was an employee dumping smokeless tobacco into product as it travelled through the production process. While the presence of smokeless tobacco did not pose a severe health risk to consumers, it did indicate a security issue on the part of the supplier.

A strong SCRMS solution would also make risk mitigation activities transparent. The system tracks root cause and corrective action plans submitted by nonconforming

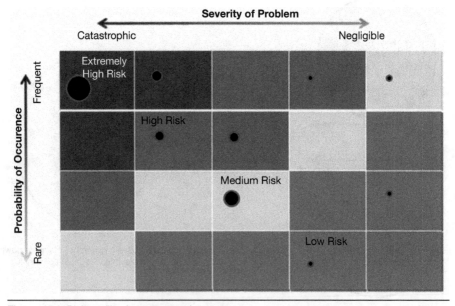

Figure 15.2 Risk profile change example.

sites or suppliers. The poultry supplier mentioned previously would be required to submit a plan to correct the security issue, possibly beginning with firing the offending employee then proceeding to ban personal items and tobacco from the production line. Executives can then easily assess what the poultry supplier is doing to become compliant, whether the supplier should be put on probation or disqualified, and how quickly vulnerabilities are recognized and addressed.

All SCRMS information is available online, in the form of an easy-to-read performance scorecard. Aggregating information from all suppliers allows executives and managers the ability to easily identify their best and worst-performing suppliers, the most common nonconformances, plans to achieve conformance, and other issues.

THE RISK-BASED SUPPLY CHAIN MONITORING PROCESS

While the above fast food restaurant case illustrated one possible use of an SCRMS solution, it would be helpful to detail the separate activities that compose the implementation and use of such technology. The process advocated by jadian and Supply Chain Sustainability is illustrated in Figure 15.3.

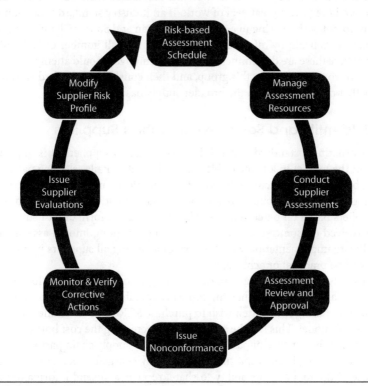

Figure 15.3 Supply chain monitoring process.

Step 1: Define Risk Based Supply Chain Standards

The first step firms should take to monitor supply chain risk is to define the standards on which they will measure their suppliers. This could take the form of any of the ISO standards, the Business and Institutional Furniture Manufacturer's Association (BIFMA) standard for environmental sustainability in the furniture industry, Customs-Trade Partnership Against Terrorism (C-TPAT) standards, and Food Safety and Inspection Service (FSIS) guidelines for the food industry, as examples. This step is obviously driven by the domain of concern, such as quality, environmental sustainability, and security. Firms often find that a number of standards exist for any given domain, which causes confusion as to which standard is the best for their particular application. It is also possible that firms lack sufficient and specific domain knowledge to even begin the process. To remedy this confusion, many firms consult industry groups for advice or may employ third parties to construct a standard that specifically applies to their operations.

Supply Chain Sustainability executives recounted an instance involving a major consumer products manufacturer with multiple production facilities across North America. This firm had recently merged with another large firm. The two merging parties had vastly different or non-existent standards. In this instance, the construction of a shared, mutually agreeable standard that suited their needs was a difficult task that would require a great deal of work. If an industry standard is not applicable, and firms do not wish to bring in a third party, Jadian and Supply Chain Sustainability advise that firms begin by informally determining a small number of *best* and *worst* suppliers. Once these are determined, firm representatives should attempt to ascertain the best and worst practices of this group, and then construct a standard around these practices that can be applied to the broader supply base.

Step 2: Identify and Select Participating Suppliers

After constructing a standard that will be used to assess suppliers, it is important to implement the project in a manageable way. This likely entails selecting participating suppliers based on some factor of import. For example, firms often decide to begin by assessing their *Top 100* suppliers based on purchase spend. Firms may also segment their suppliers based on perceived risk. This may take the form of past supplier incidents, perceived outcome severity, or both. Going headlong into an assessment and audit software implementation with the goal of assessing all suppliers immediately is not likely to be practical or achievable.

Firms must also be pragmatic in determining who is going to pay for the chosen software package. While an ownership model is available from many software service providers, purchasing firms often wish to purchase SCRMS tools on the Software as a Service (SaaS) model. This has the advantage of decreasing the cost borne by the purchasing firm at the expense of passing this cost off to supply chain partners. Utilizing the SaaS model, supply chain partners are typically charged a recurring monthly fee for the use of the tool and the ability to share, receive, and send information related to assessments, nonconformances, and efforts to rectify any nonconformances. If the purchasing firm has the channel power to impose this fee on its suppliers, or if suppliers are able to see the benefits of software implementation, this may not be an issue. However, the purchasing firm must be prepared for the unwillingness of some suppliers to participate. The purchasing firm may wish to engage unwilling suppliers in meetings to discuss the advantages and disadvantages of implementation. If these meetings are not successful, the purchasing firm may discontinue doing business with a noncompliant supplier or impose some other penalty.

Step 3: Supplier Assessment Tools

Supplier assessment tools can take many forms and this stage could be interpreted as, "Who inputs the information into the software, and how?" According to jadian and Supply Chain Sustainability, the options range from the relatively simple and easy to the complex and difficult. In the case of the fast food establishment with contaminated chicken, CommonView could be used as a method to collect customer complaints. In this case, employees at the retail level would log-on to CommonView and fill out a relatively simple customer complaint form. More applicable to the supplier audit theme is the case of a team of internal or external auditors traveling to a supplier's facility to determine compliance to a standard of interest. In this case, the auditors may employ handheld electronic devices allowing them to complete standardized questions. Results of this would be automatically uploaded to tools such as CommonView. Another option would be the use of *paper and pencil* during the actual audit with auditors logging-on to the software tool later to input results.

A more complex option is to integrate tools such as CommonView with existing software. In this instance the tool would *sit on top of* existing software, collect information, and use that information to determine supplier risk. This allows the firm to leverage existing legacy systems. For example, a purchasing firm may employ a quality system that tracks out-of-spec product delivered from its suppliers. The same firm may employ a transportation management system (TMS) that tracks over, short, and damaged (OS&D) deliveries from suppliers. If the purchasing firm believes that product quality problems and OS&D are indicators of a lack of security control on the part of its supply base, tools such as CommonView may be integrated with the quality system and TMS, and these two systems would feed the number and type of quality and logistics nonconformances into the risk model. In this sense, CommonView would serve as a quasienterprise resource planning system that aggregates risk related information from multiple legacy systems to calculate a supplier's risk score.

Step 4: Defined Certification and Audit Cycle

The certification and audit cycle is the process of formally scheduling assessments, managing assessment resources, conducting assessments, issuing nonconformances, correcting nonconformances, evaluating suppliers, modifying suppliers' risk profiles, and restarting the process. Scheduling assessments, managing assessment resources, and conducting assessments are, at face value, most applicable to the formal acts of scheduling times to audit a supplier's facility, determining the manpower and manpower qualifications available to conduct the audit, and formally conducting the audit. SCRMS solutions often possess the ability to schedule the formal audit and also track the resources available to conduct audits. Jadian and Supply Chain Sustainability report that purchasing firms with a large number of suppliers often find it difficult to:

1. Schedule audits at times amenable to both the supplier and the audit team
2. Remember to schedule assessments at regular intervals so suppliers are not audited too frequently
3. Schedule unannounced audits with an audit team but without the knowledge of the supplier

Further, auditing supplier performance on a particular domain of interest (e.g., security) often requires specific domain knowledge. For firms wishing to audit a large number of suppliers on a large number of domains of interest, the capability to collaboratively schedule audits and determine whether auditors possessing requisite knowledge are available is particularly valuable.

By following the audit and input of information into the software, tools such as CommonView issue nonconformance reports to suppliers and alert relevant parties inside the purchasing firm of these nonconformances. CommonView specifically offers customized dashboards for suppliers, purchasing managers, and executives that detail information most relevant to their tasks. For instance, the supplier would be most concerned with any nonconformances found during the course of the audit. The purchasing manager would not only be concerned with the nonconformances, but also the supplier's plans to correct the nonconformances as well as the performance of the other suppliers under his or her purview. An executive in the purchasing firm may wish to detail the performance or risk profile of all the firm's suppliers and the purchasing managers' progress in ensuring suppliers correct nonconformances. After noncompliances are corrected, and the risk profiles of each and all suppliers are modified, the process begins again with scheduling further audits and assessments.

SUMMARY OF BENEFITS AND CONCLUSION

Supply chain risk has simultaneously become more difficult and important to mitigate as firms employ the supply chain strategies mentioned at the beginning of this case. Despite supply base rationalization efforts, many firms utilize thousands of suppliers. Purchasing firms are faced with the need to ensure product safety, security, and quality, while simultaneously determining if suppliers provide appropriate working conditions for their employees. Further, Wal-mart has recently set a goal of determining the carbon footprint of each product they sell and will begin requiring suppliers to assess the environmental sustainability of their supply chains. Assessing suppliers on any or all of these domains is a daunting task requiring appropriate information technology and processes. Tools such as CommonView may hold the key. The benefits of implementing such software include:

- Ability to monitor supplier performance on any risk related domain of interest
- Online, anytime, anywhere access to supplier risk related performance information
- Ability to integrate information from disparate legacy systems to collect, synthesize, and analyze supplier risk related performance
- Customized, dynamic risk model that automatically calculates the risk of any given supplier and alerts relevant personnel if a supplier moves from a lower to a higher risk category
- Reduced response time to risk related incidents through alerts in the form of customized SMS messages, emails, and other methods ensuring potential and actual risk related issues are not buried in paperwork and corrective actions are taken expediently
- Ability to analyze risk related metrics by type, supplier, location, time, or any other variable collected by the software in the form of graphs, charts, or other chosen output methods affording the ability to track root causes
- Access to customized dashboards for suppliers, purchasing agents, appropriate domain staff, and executives
- Reduction in risk related incidents
- Reduced costs related to risk related incidents and, in some instances, increased customer service resulting in enhanced revenues and other, less tangible improvements, such as improving public relations

The first step firms must take in implementing supply base assessment and monitoring tools is likely to be overcoming the myopic *What we don't know can't hurt us* mindset. While supply chain assessment and monitoring will likely uncover difficult issues, it benefits all parties involved to rectify these problems before they affect the end consumer. If recent history has taught us anything, it is that a purchasing firm is held responsible for the actions of its suppliers. Perhaps now is the time to reach back one, two, or even three tiers and determine whether suppliers are living up to your firm's standards.

16

PRACTICAL APPROACHES TO SUPPLY CHAIN CONTINUITY: NEW CHALLENGES AND TIMELESS PRINCIPLES

Cliff Thomas

Today's hypercompetitive economy is changing the nature of how business gets done. It is also changing the way that business does *not* get done, that is to say, the way that organizations experience debilitating disruptions. Techniques used to prepare for, and respond to, disruptions caused by supplier failures must evolve as well. Though the challenges are new, the solutions are grounded in time-tested principles.

A review of recent business disruptions helps to illustrate the challenges associated with supply chain continuity; these examples will shed light on practical approaches for coping with the risk landscape. Before delving into supply chain continuity, it is important to establish an understanding of business continuity.

BUSINESS CONTINUITY DEFINED?

Business continuity is a term that really ought to be self-defining. After all, the practice has been with us under that moniker for about two decades, and far longer under the more general category of contingency planning. Unfortunately, it has not proven to be self-defining, and even where standards exist, they remain subject to a wide range of interpretation. Such inconsistencies result in wildly different approaches to implementation and management.

To set a baseline for this analysis, the following working definition is suggested: *Business continuity involves the planning and resource utilization required to recover critical functions following a business disruption.* The definition warrants elaboration in two areas. First is the need to clarify the term *disruption*. Simply put, a disruption is an event that prevents an organization from carrying out important activities: selling, manufacturing, delivering, maintaining its product or service, and such. In this context, disruptions are debilitating, not mere nuisances. Minor disruptions, such as short-term power outages or temporary building closures, are usually not the primary emphasis of a business continuity program. Significant disruptions result from any number of scenarios: natural disasters, building fires, technology failures, public health epidemics, and others. Descriptive words like *emergency, disaster, catastrophe,* and *crisis* come to mind when thinking about business continuity planning scenarios.

Second, the idea of recovering *critical* functions, as opposed to *all* functions, is an important aspect of business continuity. An organization is ill advised to attempt the recovery of all business activities immediately following a significant disruption. A highly disruptive event will force a triage-like prioritization of recovery activities. An organization will likely flounder in its response to crises if there is a lack of a clear sense of priorities. Addressing these priorities before the disruption occurs is helpful, if not essential, and will have direct implications on how the organization deals with supply chain continuity.

ELEMENTS OF A BUSINESS CONTINUITY PROGRAM

A well-implemented business continuity program requires significant leadership commitment and dedication of resources across an enterprise. Although simplistic from a conceptual standpoint, the real-world implementation of business continuity often becomes a highly complex activity. As such, one cannot capture the practical challenges by boiling the process down to a few steps. Nevertheless, in order to set the stage for examining supply chain continuity challenges, that is exactly what must be done:

1. Prioritize business activities based on pain that will be felt if they are *not* performed. Usually the pain comes in the form of lost revenue, production delays, customer service impacts, noncompliance with regulations, legal liability, operational infrastructure failure, and damage to brand reputation.

2. Identify and mitigate the threats that can cause the pain. More or less, traditional business continuity planning has focused on a standard menu of threat categories: exposure to natural disasters (e.g., tornadoes, earthquakes, floods, and the like) and specific man-made disasters (e.g., building

fires, power failures, telecommunications failures, and others). Later, we will discuss the changing nature of business threats.

3. Develop recovery procedures for critical functions. These procedures cover a range of contingencies: communications, alternate work locations, employee roles and responsibilities, technology disaster recovery, supplier failures, and others. These procedures become the *playbook* used to guide recovery activities.

4. Validate the business continuity program effectiveness through ongoing review, updates, training, and testing of procedures and capabilities.

SUPPLY CHAIN CONTINUITY INTRODUCED

While work functions can be transferred to a supplier, the purchasing organization retains much of the risk associated with a supplier failure. In essence, organizations depend on their suppliers to be resilient, to engage in proper threat assessments, to implement risk-mitigation controls, to develop recovery procedures, and to deliver their products and services even amidst crisis situations. Managing supply chain continuity involves proactive supplier selection criteria, oversight and validation of supplier recovery capabilities, and the employment of contingencies when suppliers fail to deliver.

In a perfect world, organizations would simply impose *all* of their internal risk mitigation and recovery planning standards on their tier 1 suppliers, and would mandate that they impose the same standards on tier 2 suppliers and further down the supply chain. From a practical standpoint, this is not a feasible option for either party. How would a large manufacturer effectively impose its recovery standards upon thousands of suppliers, and then enforce compliance? It could not. How could suppliers simultaneously meet unique recovery standards set by each of their many customers? They could not. Even where recognized continuity and preparedness standards exist, methods of implementation can cover a wide spectrum. At a minimum, even when rigorous standards have been established, the need for supplier oversight remains.

Let us continue to introduce the need for supply chain continuity through examples of real-world supplier disruptions:

- Land Rover, 2001. Managing Director Bob Dover eloquently summed up Land Rover's problem with a single-source parts supplier: "I want to be 'Land Rover, the car company', not 'Land Rover, the bank responsible for my suppliers' problems.'" Each year, Ford Motor Company's Land Rover division received about 70,000 Discovery chassis from sole supplier UPF-Thompson, a company experiencing debt-related financial problems in 2001. Lacking the fiscal means to continue production operations, UPF-Thompson unexpectedly stopped supplying chassis, demanding that Land Rover inject up to $65 million into the chassis manufacturer's coffers to keep it afloat. Aside from a stoppage in manufacturing, the ensuing stalemate presented Land Rover with the prospect of laying off 1400 assembly plant workers; the jobs of 10,000 workers in Land Rover's larger supply chain were also at risk. The courts settled the dispute, requiring Land Rover to pay off UPF's debts in order to keep the chassis manufacturer solvent and operational. Shortly after, auto parts company GKN acquired the ailing UPF-Thompson.

- Toyota Motor Corporation, 2007. Toyota experienced a severe disruption to its Japanese manufacturing operations after a magnitude 6.8 earthquake caused catastrophic damage to Riken, Toyota's single source supplier of piston rings and transmission seals. Because Riken was unable to deliver parts, activities at all 12 of Toyota's Japanese manufacturing plants were effectively halted for three days. Aside from operational costs, the event delayed the manufacturing and delivery of 55,000 automobiles.

- MDS Nordion, 2009. The Toronto-based pharmaceutical, research, and analytical instruments provider experienced a month-long production disruption when its isotope supplier experienced a heavy water leak in a reactor vessel, rendering the company unable to produce and deliver its specialty isotope materials.

Costs can be heavy when a supplier fails to deliver: lost revenue, lost jobs, damaged brand reputation, costly lawsuits, and others. So what should organizations do? Volumes have been written on techniques for coping with supply chain continuity. This chapter will introduce some of those that are commonly used across industries:

- Minimize single-source supplier relationships to provide flexibility and redundancy during disruptions
- Create geographic diversity among suppliers to prevent a single threat from impacting multiple suppliers
- Maintain an emergency stock of highly critical parts and/or supplies
- To minimize unexpected disruptions, monitor suppliers by reviewing *health indicators*, such as financial statements, continuity plans, SAS70 reviews, and audits
- Validate suppliers' recoverability by requiring their participation in recovery tests and simulations
- Maximize the potential that services will be provided during a crisis through evaluation of service level agreements
- Develop sound procedures to ensure that communications with suppliers continue during a crisis; miscommunication could make the situation even worse

The list is straightforward; do these things and you'll be in pretty good shape from a supplier continuity standpoint. What is not straightforward is their implementation. Often, a single-source supplier is the most viable option for a critical part or service. Such was the case with Toyota's piston-ring supplier and MDS Nordion's isotope supplier. Furthermore, cost pressures might not allow for emergency stocks. Needless to say, Land Rover would not have been enthusiastic about the prospect of storing thousands of spare chassis *just in case*. Even the act of monitoring suppliers' operational and financial health requires the dedication of a great deal of resources; there are no easy answers here.

Ultimately, despite having a checklist of good practices, the art of supply chain continuity management lies in its implementation: Which measures will be employed, and which will not? How will they be employed? At what point will suppliers be deemed too risky? What level of risk is an organization willing to tolerate? How will potential losses be quantified given theoretical supplier disruption scenarios? The challenges don't stop there, as new threats are on the horizon.

THE NEXT GENERATION OF THREATS—INFORMATION SECURITY AND GLOBALIZATION

The changing business landscape can be defined by a number of trends, but this chapter will focus on two that rise to the top of the list: the emergence of information security threats and the global footprint of the supply chain.

Information Security: It is no secret that information technologies are firmly entrenched in virtually all business operations. Computers perform a wide range of functions faster and more efficiently than ever before. As a bonus, technology can often be outsourced for even more cost savings. But the benefits can involve additional risks in the form of data theft, fraud, and other cyber-crimes. An argument can be made that in technology-dependent industries, supplier information security breaches have the potential to cause greater harm that would other types of supplier disruption.

Globalization: Even in the age of telecommunications, there is a great deal to be said for maintaining a direct personal relationship with suppliers. The more that an organization knows about its suppliers, the better it will understand its suppliers' risks, mitigating controls, and response measures. Closer personal relationships usually result in a greater level of trust and confidence. But today, relationships become more difficult to maintain when just one supplier might be located in California, Bangalore, Beijing, and Mexico City. As we go down to lower tiers in the supply chain, the relationships naturally weaken. At some point, an organization can lose visibility into who and where its lower-tier suppliers are. In the absence of other measures, an organization can find itself operating on blind trust.

The following case studies illustrate difficulties associated with managing these emerging threats to the supply chain.

PAYMENT CARD INDUSTRY CASE STUDY—THE HEARTLAND BREACH

In a way, money is no longer made of paper—it is plastic. Payment cards are so convenient that many of us no longer carry any cash. Just look in your purse, wallet, or mailbox for a quick understanding of who the big names are in the payment card industry: Visa, MasterCard, American Express, Discover, Citi, Capital One, Chase, and others. In all, there are about 500 companies in the payment card industry (PCI). As one might guess, credit cards account for a significant portion of the PCI, but the industry also includes debit cards, prepaid cards, ATM cards, store-specific credit cards, and other variations on the theme.

How reliant are we as individuals—not to mention the economy at large—on the payment card industry? In terms of just credit cards, about 144 million Americans carry general-purpose credit cards; the average family in the U.S. has eight of them. In terms of impacts on the U.S. economy, the credit card industry alone accounts for an annual revenue of about $10 billion; cardholders conduct more than 30 billion credit and debit card transactions each year. In countries around the world, the PCI is a ubiquitous aspect of personal life and business transactions: The PCI provides an essential fuel to the global economic engine.

Payment card transactions do not involve just the card provider (e.g., Master-Card) and the merchant (e.g., Walmart). The payment card industry and individual merchants rely on card issuers, usually banks, to get cards into consumer's hands. Merchants, banks, and the PCI also rely on intermediary *payment processors* to manage some of the heavy lifting by processing transactions and dealing with disputes. Usually, the role of the payment processor is transparent to the end consumer. Examples of U.S. payment processors include companies that are unfamiliar to most consumers: Fifth Third Bank, Heartland Payment Systems, and Nova Information Systems. Though operating behind the scenes, payment processors are an integral component of the card transactions (see Figure 16.1).

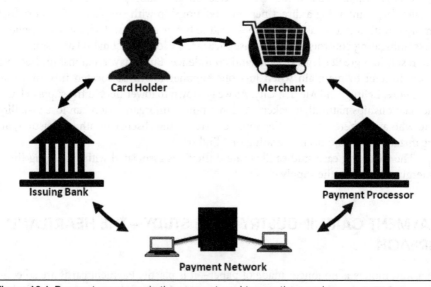

Figure 16.1 Payment processes in the payment card transactions cycle.

The story of the Heartland Data Breach is on par with those concocted by Hollywood scriptwriters, shedding light on a growing cyber-threat to merchants, financial institutions, their suppliers, and their customers. Heartland is one of the largest credit card payment processors in the United States, processing card transactions for merchants at more than 250,000 locations, and processing as many as 100 million transactions each month. In 2009, Heartland Payment Systems disclosed that it was the victim of the largest criminal breach of credit card data in history.

The perpetration of the Heartland Data Breach involved a man by the name of Albert Gonzalez. An interesting figure, Mr. Gonzalez' interest in computers began at the age of 8, and by the age of 9 he was known to remove viruses from friends' computers. By the age of 17, he had penetrated computer systems operated by the government of India. At this point, he had limited his mischief to causing nuisances such as leaving derogatory messages on the secure network. Even though he wasn't amassing a fortune from his exploits, his hacking expertise was well established.

In time, Gonzalez became more involved in crimes related to credit card theft and fraud. Law enforcement indicted Gonzalez for his role in a group of hackers known as the *Shadowcrew*, which had trafficked as many as 1.5 million stolen ATM and credit cards numbers. In 2003, Gonzalez dodged prison time for his Shadowcrew activities by agreeing to provide evidence against other members. In 2007, after government interest in Shadowcrew had subsided, Gonzalez was charged with crimes related to credit and debit card thefts against TJ Maxx, Boston Market, OfficeMax, Sports Authority, and others—charges to which he would later plead guilty.

Despite the pending charges, his criminal activity continued. In late 2009, Gonzalez' lawyer filed papers indicating that he would plead guilty to charges connected to what came to be known as the Heartland Data Breach. After an extensive internal security investigation, Heartland revealed a breach of its processing systems, exposing approximately 130 million payment cards to potential fraud. The breach was executed by penetrating Heartland's network and planting malicious software capable of stealing payment card data. This data was to be sold to other criminal enterprises that would exploit the compromised accounts.

The issues related to this disruption were atypical from those normally associated with supplier continuity. There were no hurricanes, fires, floods, major power outages, financial crises, labor strikes, or shipping delays. Nevertheless, external parties' ability to gain access to sensitive data disrupted normal business at thousands of banks and merchant locations, and prevented over one million consumers from using their compromised payment cards to make purchases and conduct other transactions (McGlasson, 2009).

While the economic impacts of this sort of disruption have not been fully quantified, we can be sure that they were not insignificant. Because of the unprecedented nature of this type of disruption, the effects on merchants that are dependent on payment processors are not yet well understood. Some of the more significant impacts of the Heartland Data Breach included the following:

- Banks and credit unions incurred the costs required to notify all customers of the breach, respond to customer inquiries, and reissue cards—this is not a small task when hundreds of thousands, or even millions, of cardholders are concerned

- Credit and debit card companies imposed multimillion dollar fines on Heartland
- Financial institutions and consumers filed numerous class action lawsuits against Heartland
- Some e-commerce retailers claimed that by issuing new cards, some services that have an *auto-renewal* feature were rendered useless, resulting in the loss of business

The magnitude of the potential threats associated with payment cards has not gone unnoticed by the industry itself. Even prior to the Heartland data breach, the payment card industry had created the Payment Card Industry Data Security Standards. These standards set objectives and requirements related to data protection, network security, vulnerability management, security testing, and security oversight. Payment card companies such as Visa and American Express require that payment card processors become certified in the security standards. But the standards are not perfect; Heartland was certified as being compliant with these standards when the breach occurred.

DATA SECURITY CASE STUDY—COMMUNITY CREDIT UNION

The focus of this study is a Utah-based credit union that maintains six branches serving approximately 26,000 members. Its services are typical for credit unions: branch banking, internet home banking, automated telephone banking, and ATMs.

From an operational and staffing standpoint, community financial institutions generally can be characterized as lean. Unlike regional and global financial institutions, staff sizes are typically small, and responsibilities for risk and compliance could be assigned to a single person having several other responsibilities. Consequently, managing the numerous regulatory requirements associated with banking risk tends to present a significant challenge.

With respect to the management of business continuity and supply chain risk, all financial institutions in the United States are required to comply with standards established by the Federal Financial Institution Examination Council (FFIEC). In banks, standards are enforced by the Federal Deposit Insurance Corporation (FDIC) and in credit unions, by the National Credit Union Association (NCUA). FFIEC standards are known to be quite rigorous if followed in both letter and spirit. Furthermore, FFIEC standards extend to some contractors and subcontractors, as warranted by their access to sensitive files and data.

In the banking industry, supplier oversight is of particular concern because of the extent to which the automated systems are managed by external suppliers, firms to whom sensitive customer data is entrusted. Financial institutions often engage third party *core processors* and other services that provide the computing power required to service the institution's many accounts, services and transactions. Indeed, it is not uncommon for financial institutions to outsource most of their technology-dependent banking functions to third parties, so virtually all of the institutions' sensitive customer data is in the hands of its supply chain.

Now back to Utah. In 2008, one of the credit union's tier-1 contractors, Open Solutions, hired consulting firm Lee & Morris Enterprises to repair and maintain the credit union's data processing systems. In 2009, the controlling partner at Lee & Morris was arrested and charged with bank fraud for siphoning more than $1 million from the credit union over a 10-month period. Charges alleged that the individual used passwords, provided specifically to perform consulting functions, to access the credit union's accounts and to conduct fraudulent electronic funds transfers. Law enforcement investigations alleged that the funds were used for multiple mortgage payments, vehicle loans, bank loans, credit cards, and possibly other creditors. This amount of debt should have been raised as a red flag during background investigations, if they were conducted.

Cyber-threats are particularly nefarious as their impacts are less tangible than with other scenarios. When a truckload of parts doesn't arrive, the problem is obvious. When the failure is in the form of stolen electrons, the situation can be much less noticeable. Apparently, the credit union was unaware of the theft, as court documents reveal that the fraud would have gone undetected if Morris' partner had not reported the issues to the credit union after having detected irregularities in the company's accounts.

GLOBALIZATION CASE STUDY—MENU FOODS

"Sometimes even well respected manufacturers, like Menu, suffer problems caused by others."

—Paul K. Henderson, CEO, Menu Foods

Based near Toronto, Canada, Menu Foods is the largest maker of wet dog and cat food in North America, selling over 90 brands of pet food products to supermarkets and large retailers. Menu Foods distributes its products through large retail chains such as PetSmart, Safeway, and Walmart. Each year, Menu Foods produces more than 1.1 billion containers of pet food (U.S. House of Representatives, 2007).

Wet pet foods commonly contain vegetable proteins in the form of wheat gluten. Pet food producers like Menu Foods often purchase wheat gluten from export brokers and wholesalers. While the brokers and wholesalers might be located in the United States, most wheat gluten is actually produced in Europe or Asia. In the case of Menu Foods, the wheat gluten was purchased through ChemNutra, a U.S.-based supplier of ingredients to multiple industries: pharmaceuticals, food, and animal feed. ChemNutra did not produce the wheat gluten, but purchased it from China-based Xuzhou Anying Biologic Technology Development Co.

In March 2007, the U.S. Food and Drug Administration learned that several pet food brands, to include some produced by Menu Foods, were sickening and killing dogs and cats. The presence of the chemical melamine in the wheat gluten was causing kidney failure in these animals. (In the United States, melamine is not approved for use in human or animal food production; it is most often used to create cleaners, inks, glues, and plastics. According to the U.S. Food and Drug Administration, it is very unusual to find melamine in wheat gluten.) Melamine was not found in wheat gluten that Menu Foods obtained from suppliers other than ChemNutra.

Predictably, pet owners did not respond well when the public became aware of the contamination crisis. Massive pet food recalls were initiated, brand names were damaged, stocks lost value, and lawsuits were filed. The results of the contaminated pet food rippled through all areas of Menu Foods' business:

- Menu Foods recalled over 60 million containers of pet food. Among all brands of wet pet foods, more than 5300 products were recalled
- Menu Foods stock price dropped about 45 percent after the recall was announced, and has not yet recovered (see Figure 16.2)
- Menu Foods web site crashed due to the volume of traffic following the recall, further raising pet owner concerns
- Proctor and Gamble cancelled contracts with Menu Foods
- Menu and other pet food producers were the subject of intense media coverage and public outrage
- While pet owners filed suit against Menu Foods, Menu filed suit against ChemNutra
- Menu Foods discontinued all business with ChemNutra after the incident began
- The U.S. Food and Drug Administration barred all shipments from Xuzhou

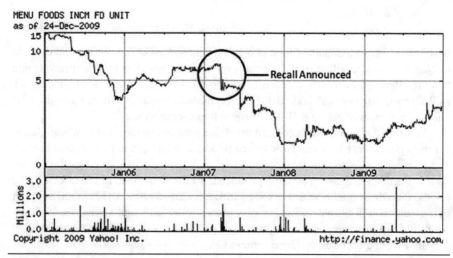

Figure 16.2 Impact on Menu Foods stock price following pet food recall announcement.

Menu estimated its total cost resulting from the wheat gluten contamination at $45-55M.

Ironic, from the standpoint of supplier continuity, Menu Foods began purchasing wheat gluten from ChemNutra because existing suppliers were showing signs that they might not be able to meet Menu's demand. So, Menu was doing the right thing by proactively expanding its supplier base when existing suppliers' production levels were stretched. Without a doubt, Menu Foods regretted its decision, particularly as its very first order from ChemNutra contained the melamine-contaminated wheat gluten.

According to CEO Paul Henderson, in dealing with ChemNutra, Menu Foods had taken the required precautionary measures to ensure that the product met Menu's specifications. ChemNutra agreed to the terms, and Menu Foods *relied on those promises*. As a result of this crisis, some pet food producers reacted by building their own manufacturing plants and engaging in greater oversight of imported ingredients (Bankston, 2009).

PRACTICAL SUPPLY CHAIN CONTINUITY APPROACHES

> *"If he reinforces everywhere, he will everywhere be weak."*
> Sun Tzu, *The Art of War*, 6th Century BCE

Ultimately, supply chain continuity is all about decision making that balances the risk of disruption-related losses with the cost of mitigating that risk: What do we buy and what do we make ourselves? What do we carry in inventory and what will be delivered *just in time*? What should be single-sourced? How much oversight will we apply to our suppliers? How do we ensure that sensitive data is properly protected? Without a doubt, this responsibility is becoming more challenging as new supply chain threats emerge. So what is to be done?

As a business continuity practitioner, one quickly learns not to make too many assumptions about organizational decision making unless one is in the room at the time and has access to the relevant facts. Based on the many variables that come into play, decisions leading up to bad outcomes can sometimes be fully justified and rational. Consider Toyota's piston-ring problem. Part of Toyota's overall success as a car manufacturer has been rooted in its ability to operate leaner than its competitors. Would Toyota have been prudent to sacrifice some of that competitive advantage to decrease its risk? That is a business decision with no clear-cut answer.

However, an evaluation as to whether certain principles have been followed can provide useful insights regarding the soundness of supply chain continuity management. Some of the principle-based approaches that are universally applicable to supply chain continuity are discussed in the following paragraphs.

Prioritize Well

Establishing business priorities sets the foundation for virtually all supply chain continuity activities. If an organization can effectively categorize its business functions into levels of criticality, it can extend those priorities to the suppliers who support those functions. A higher criticality rating warrants a more rigorous contracting process and level of supplier oversight. It makes no sense that an organization would apply identical standards to high-criticality/high-risk suppliers as it would to the rest of the field.

Establish Supplier Continuity Standards

By prioritizing well, the organization will be able to assign consistent standards that are commensurate with the level of supplier risk and criticality. Examples of supplier continuity management standards might resemble the following:

- *Highly Critical.* Rigorous oversight in the form of on-site audits, financial statements reviews, participation in disaster recovery testing, and such. Further, these suppliers may be required to impose the same level of oversight to its suppliers.
- *Moderately Critical.* A modicum of insight into supplier risk and recoverability: evidence of recoverability, risk mitigation and executive-level acknowledgement that the requisite preparedness standards have been met.
- *Non-Critical.* Few, if any, continuity-related requirements apply.

Rather than developing unique standards, organizations can adopt those that have already been developed. Examples of such standards include:

- National Fire Protection Association 1600: Standard of Disaster/Emergency Management and Business Continuity Programs
- BS 25999: Business Continuity Management
- *Federal Financial Institution Examination Council IT Examination Handbook: Business Continuity Planning* (standards are not limited to information technologies)

Incorporate Continuity Measures into the Procurement Process

It is far better to verify that a supplier is resilient before a contract is signed rather than after. During the supplier selection process, organizations should not overlook the opportunity to request evidence of recoverability and threat mitigation. Perhaps Menu Foods would have benefited from a more rigorous review of its tier 1 supplier's purchasing practices. Such contracting practices are becoming more common, but often, the process lives exclusively in the department responsible for procurement, particularly in small- to medium-sized companies. Involving others that interface with the suppliers in the evaluation process will not only provide a better sense of supplier risk and recoverability, but it gives the organization more insight into measures that it can take internally to deal with a supplier failure.

Consider Supplier Access to Sensitive Data

As illustrated by the Heartland Data Breach and the community credit union fraud examples, supplier access to sensitive data presents potentially catastrophic risk scenarios. Purchasing organizations should ensure that suppliers are properly safeguarding data, training employees on data loss prevention, conducting background investigations on employees and subcontractors that will have access to data, conducting information security audits, and the like.

Strive for Simplicity

Even practical approaches to maintain supplier continuity will involve a degree of complexity. With respect to supply chain continuity, businesses benefit by using practical solutions to solve problems—if the organization can understand the solution, it is more likely to garner support for it and realize success. Complex solutions that rely on *black box* decision-support algorithms, say, might be disregarded when the underlying reasoning is not clear.

LOOKING AHEAD

Without a doubt, managing supply chain continuity comes at a cost. But as demonstrated by case studies, the potential for loss provides a compelling argument for its serious consideration. Indeed, the question is not so much *whether* to manage that risk, but *how* to manage it. Organizations will benefit by first establishing internal business continuity capabilities, and then aligning supply chain continuity requirements with those priorities. By applying a few basic principles to supply chain continuity management, organizations will place themselves on solid footing as threats to suppliers continue to evolve.

REFERENCES

Bankston, C., (ed.). *Great Events from History: Modern Scandals, FDA Recalls Deadly Pet Food*. Hackensack: Salem Press, 2009.

Leong, G. 8 April 2009. "Provo man accused of $1M credit-union fraud", *Utah News*, April 8, 2009.

McGlasson, L. (ed.). 23 Feb. 2009. "Heartland Data Breach: 500;pl Institutions Affected," *BankInfoSecurity*, www.bankinfosecurity.com

U.S. House of Representatives Committee on Energy and Commerce Subcommittee on Oversight and Investigations, Written Statement of Paul K. Henderson Chief Executive Officer, Menu Foods Income Fund, April 24, 2007.

17

STRATEGIC SUPPLY MANAGEMENT: THE LITMUS TEST FOR RISK MANAGEMENT IN A THREE ECHELON SUPPLY CHAIN

Reham Eltantawy and Larry C. Giunipero

The purpose of this case is to illustrate the significance of strategic supply management in mitigating supply chain risk. Supply chain risks can have a significant negative impact on organizations. The consequences include not only financial losses, but also interruption to operations, reduction in product quality, loss of goodwill with customers and suppliers, and delivery delays. These all eventually have negative financial repercussions to firms and their respective supply chains.

The supply chain is conceptualized as a network of companies straddling from suppliers to end-users (Gundlach et al. 2006). In today's global environment, supply chains have further lengthened and grown more complex. With this increased complexity, the ability to successfully manage risk has become ever more challenging to many firms. However, supply risk management applications and tools rarely meet their expected results. Recently, researchers attributed the unmet expectations from supply risk management applications to the oversimplification of its implementations, which largely rely on dyadic buyer-supplier analyses (Frankel et al. 2008). The dyadic focus can inhibit the ability of each firm to gain knowledge about other chain members with which it does not have direct business relationships, and therefore cannot effectively manage those pertinent risks. The decisions of these indirect partners, such as suppliers' suppliers and customers' customers, ultimately impacts the performance of the focal firm. This mandate has led industry leaders to tackle this challenge through the adoption of appropriate risk management techniques and improvement methodologies that externalize the analyses beyond simple dyadic relationships to delve deeper into the activities of suppliers at different tiers in the supply chain.

It is increasingly being recognized that strategic supply management means visualizing a bigger picture beyond the first tier of the supply chain. This new vision entails looking further down the supply chain tiers and also forward to customers. Prior applications evidenced that strategic supply management has a positive correlation with purchasing risk taking (Giunipero et al. 2006). Supply management risk-taking activities may occur more often as purchasing managers increase their knowledge base of the entire supply chain. Today's executives and practitioners presume that businesses could only cope with environmental complexity by expanding the purchasing body of knowledge upon which risk management decisions are to be taken. Notably, these remain to be presumptions that are yet to be tested.

There is little protocol that tests the direct impact of moving from tactical purchasing to strategic supply management on a firm's operational integration with their supplier and suppliers' suppliers and on managing the pertinent risks. Such risks include supply chain disruptions due to insufficient inventories at times and having excessive inventories at other times, and to the lack of coordination and information sharing among the supply chain tiers. Strategic supply management practices require taking a holistic view of the supply chain that entails increased cooperation and systems capabilities on the part of firms in the supply chain. Could strategic supply management be the answer to failed risk management and poor performance? The objective of this case study is to examine this presumption.

CASE BACKGROUND

The major issue faced by the buyers at the focal firm, which is Vitalk (pseudonym) in this case, was the late deliveries of the cartons by their supplier. Vitalk, a division of RJR Vision Care headquartered in Jacksonville, FL, revolutionized the vision correction industry in 1988 with the invention of the world's first soft disposable contact lens. North Ocean Cartons supplies finished cartons to Vitalk for the packaging of contact lenses. The late deliveries of cartons forced Vitalk to carry excess carton inventory, resulting in an increase in annual inventory expenditures.

North Ocean Cartons is located in Charlotte, NC, and is recognized as a leading supplier of packaging materials. Pearl Paper Company is the paperboard supplier to North Ocean Cartons. The paperboard supplied by Pearl Paper Company to North Ocean Cartons is utilized in the production of contact lens cartons. Pearl Paper Company is located in St. Mary's, GA, and is a nationally recognized bleached board and craft paper producer. This relationship is shown in Figure 17.1.

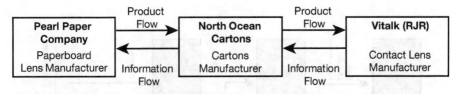

Figure 17.1 Information and product flows.

METHODOLOGY

Case studies in general are suited for What, How, and Why questions. Action Research (AR) is one form of case study that can produce relevant research findings because it deals with real-world organizational and managerial problems (Coughlan and Coghlan 2002). In AR projects, research informs practice and practice informs research synergistically and the goal is to contribute to the practical concerns of an organization and to the goals of science (Gummesson 2000). AR methodology was used in this study, which entailed actively working with the buyers of Vitalk (a multinational firm), their major supplier of cartons (North Ocean Cartons), and North Ocean's paperboard supplier (Pearl Paper Company). Thus, the team involved provided concrete tips and ideas with respect to how to map, analyze, and improve the supply process and manage the risks involved.

AR projects are often characterized as being cyclical in nature—corresponding to the cyclic loop of learning—with phases of planning, action (implementing), observing (evaluating), and overall analysis and reflection as a basis for new planning and action. This study followed a cyclical process with three clear cycles that started with attempts to gain considerable preunderstanding of the context of the case.

The case team did not remain an observer outside the subject of investigation, but became an active participant. In the first cycle, data was collected via interviews at the focal company. The core context of this case study is derived from several supply problems the focal company (Vitalk) experienced. An initial meeting conducted with the Purchasing Director of Vitalk summarized the problems their team was encountering.

One of the major problems facing the supply management team was the surplus inventory for the lens cartons. Disposable lenses are packaged to meet various eye vision strengths and also provide the consumer with a readily identifiable marker to locate the product at various retailers such as Walmart. Regarding the carton purchase process, the director stressed the ineffectiveness of the current demand forecast generating system. There was also a desire on the part of the management to reduce cost throughout the supply chain and not expose the company to excessive risk. Moreover, Vitalk's management was dissatisfied with North Ocean Cartons' supplier delivery performance. Next, brainstorming sessions were conducted with the aid of the research advisors, and probable alternatives to solve the supply chain problems were discussed.

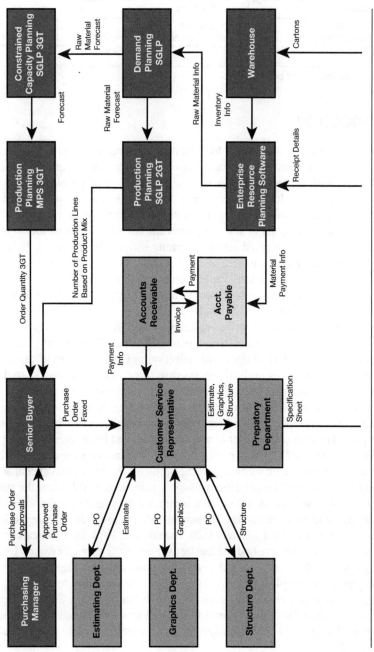

Figure 17.2 The original supply management process.

Continues

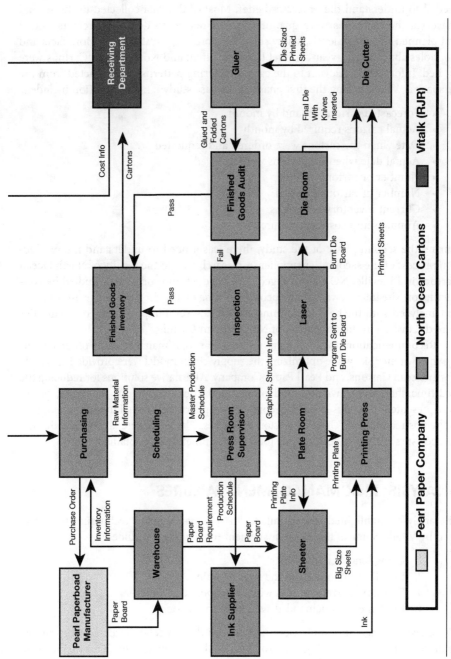

Figure 17.2 (Continued)

The second phase included an analysis of historical (retrospective) information needed to understand the processes better. Most of the data collected in the second phase via the databases were quantitative and related to demand forecasts, actual and planned inventory levels, safety stock, and order quantity levels. More facts and loopholes about the 12-year contract between Vitalk and North Ocean Cartons were studied. Information relevant to the carton-ordering patterns was extracted from the database at Vitalk during the first phase of the case study. The information included:

- Forecasted carton demand by month
- Actual cartons required by month
- Date when the cartons were ordered and requested
- Actual date when the cartons were received
- Number or cartons ordered
- Number of cartons received
- Current inventory of cartons
- Annual setup cost expenditure

During the second phase of the study, there was a need to understand the production process of the second tier supplier. A research visit to the facility of North Ocean Cartons in Pineville, NC was arranged. The production process was studied by conducting on-site interviews with the people working on the shop floor. The information was analyzed with the help of planning software. Several improvement opportunities were discovered in the operations of North Ocean Cartons.

Recommendations to move to a more strategic supply management in order to manage the current risks while optimizing the supply chain model were provided to Vitalk, North Ocean Cartons, and Pearl Paper Company. Alternative solutions for reducing the lead-time, sharing the inventory, and improving the demand forecast generating system were presented to Vitalk's first and second tier suppliers. This constituted the major part of the upstream supply chain for carton purchases. The tasks were arranged with their predecessors and successors and the total project timeline was obtained.

ANALYSIS: RISK MANAGEMENT FAILURES

The analyses highlighted several failures in risk management techniques that were used by Vitalk. Some of the risk management tools utilized included:

1. Using long term contracts
2. Enabling technology in the supply chain
3. Partnering arrangements with key supply chain players
4. Implementing demand-driven inventory system

These risk management tools were not met by the expected success in the supply chain at hand. Fully mapping the processes of the carton supply chain (depicted in Figure 17.2) indicated to the case team that the *absence of strategic supply management* was behind these unmet expectations.

Long Term Contract

Vitalk had a 12-year contract with its major supplier North Ocean Cartons as a means to guard against uncertainties and potential risks in the supply of cartons. However, the interviews revealed that Vitalk management was not satisfied as the relationship with North Ocean Cartons presented certain risks. Various uncertainties were involved in this relationship that made the whole process difficult to accurately map. The major uncertainties in the relationship stemmed from inconsistent supplier delivery times and delivery quantities. The cartons were not shipped in the agreed upon contracted lead time. This resulted in carrying additional safety stock in Vitalk's warehouse to meet the uncertainty in supplier lead-time and guarantee Vitalk's customers 100 percent service levels.

Technology

Vitalk's production planning group used sophisticated MRPII software and an advanced e-SCM platform to generate the demand forecast schedule for the cartons. Once generated, the forecast was then transmitted to the senior buyer on a monthly basis. However, the senior buyer would often determine the order quantity based on his own experience, as the demand forecast produced by the existing system was not trusted. In a way, the demand forecast schedule generation system was ineffective in the decision making process regarding the order quantity of the cartons.

Partnering with Key Players

Vitalk had not attempted to develop closer linkages with its suppliers in the carton area. For example, whenever North Ocean Cartons received an order from Vitalk, they placed a paperboard order to Pearl Paper. However, Pearl Paper Company had a fixed production cycle system for the paperboard manufacturing. The production cycle was run twice a month to produce the paperboard required by North Ocean Cartons. Pearl Paper Company had to maintain this rigid production cycle because they also had to meet the paperboard requirements from other customers.

Using a Demand Driven Inventory System

Vitalk's carton orders were based on the forecasts of their customers' demand. Nonetheless, Vitalk was spending too much on the setup cost for the carton orders because of the inconsistent pattern of the ordering quantities that resulted in a longer lead-time for the entire process. Guaranteeing Vitalk's *no back order* promise to their customers also meant stockpiling inventories. The three tiers of the supply chain relied on different inventory management systems, which made it impossible to standardize the operational flows.

One of the major reasons for increases in the lead-time of the carton procurement process was the inconsistency in the structure of the ordering system between North Ocean Cartons and Pearl Paper Company. North Oceans Cartons placed orders for the paperboard whenever they received the purchase order for cartons from Vitalk. Typically, North Oceans Cartons would have to wait for the paperboard to arrive from Pearl Paper Company before they could start their carton manufacturing process. Also, Pearl Paper Company would begin the manufacturing of the paperboard after receiving the order from North Ocean Cartons. In order to deal with this inconsistency, Vitalk allowed North Ocean Cartons to ship large order quantity variances of cartons. North Ocean Cartons was permitted to ship 10 percent above or below the actual ordered quantity listed on the purchase order. Taking advantage of the window, North Ocean Cartons always shipped 10 percent above the ordered quantity. This behavior resulted in excess inventory for Vitalk.

INTERVENTIONS: *STRATEGIC SUPPLY MANAGEMENT*

The suggested solution required an expanded strategic supply management vision by directly cooperating with the second tier supplier. Figure 17.3 illustrates the new supply chain model for Carton's manufacturing and procurement process. The graph depicts the suggested change in the supply process, moving it to a greater strategic level. A complete supply chain solution for Cartons was designed. We also provide some specific examples of changes in the order process.

Inventory Management Process

One reason for the long lead-times in the order process was the inconsistency in the structure of the ordering system between firms. The new order process was prepared to meet the uncertainty in the demand for the cartons and in the lead-time of the cartons. A mix of the periodic review and the fixed order quantity system for inventory management replaced the previously uncoordinated systems. The new inventory management system was tailored to meet the fluctuations in demand as well as to provide a smooth and constant flow of cartons by reducing the overall inventory carrying and setup cost. Various permutations and combinations with the order quantity and the order time were evaluated to design the new inventory management system. The order quantity was calculated as a product of the weekly demand and the number of weeks of the order time. The safety stock level and reorder level took into account the fluctuations in the demand.

Contract Order Process

The new order process was also tailored to various order constraints put in place by North Ocean Cartons via contract requirements. The first constraint referred to the annual order, which stated that Vitalk had to meet minimum annual order quantities of 10 million for the 2GT cartons and 20 million for the 3GT cartons. The second constraint referred to the minimum order quantity, which stated that there should be at least an order of 1.5 million for the 2GT cartons and order of 2.5 million for the 3GT cartons on every purchase order placed by Vitalk. Failure to meet the above constraints significantly affected the annual setup cost. As part of the order solution, the service level models were built.

A major reason for the failed risk management problems in the order process was the push system between North Ocean Cartons and Pearl Paper Company. In the new process, the forecast for the paperboard is directly transmitted to North Ocean Cartons and Pearl Paper Company via fax or email. The direct transmittal of forecast helped Pearl Paper Company to anticipate the size of paperboard order from North Ocean cartons. The renewed system gave Pearl Paper Company knowledge about the requirements of the paperboard so they could convert the demand for cartons into the demand for paperboard. This simple step made Pearl Paper Company ready with the paperboard whenever they received orders from North Ocean Cartons. This step trimmed the lead-time of the complete carton manufacturing and procurement process by almost two weeks.

Interdepartmental Communication Flows

Another example of a corrected problem was that of inefficient interdepartmental activities at North Ocean Cartons. Previously, the inventory information went to the Scheduling Department from the warehouse via the Purchasing Department. The Scheduling Department had to wait for the raw material availability report before they could prepare the production schedule. In the new process, the interdepartment quick response management system solved this issue by transmitting the inventory information directly from the warehouse to the Scheduling Department. The major impact was to reduce the operational lead-time of the complete supply chain by 18 hours (over two days' reduction).

RESULTS: *IMPROVED RISK MITIGATION AND PERFORMANCE*

Reduced Lead-time of the Complete Process

As a result of the strategic supply management system, interdepartment quick response management system, cancellation of the nonvalue added activities, and process improvement among all the supply chain members, the lead-time of the complete carton manufacturing and procurement process was reduced in half. The lead-time for the complete process averaged 8 weeks in the original system, but the newly implemented system reduced the average lead-time to 4 weeks. The newly implemented system reduced the supply chain lead-time by approximately 320 hours, or 8 weeks at a 40 hour work week.

Defined Reorder Levels

Being able to see the big picture helped purchasing to determine reorder levels to correspond to the service levels set for all the SKUs for the 2GT, 3GT, and 3GT Japanese cartons. The original system had no reorder levels for cartons. But after the study was conducted, the senior buyer at Vitalk established reorder levels for all the SKUs in the newly implemented system.

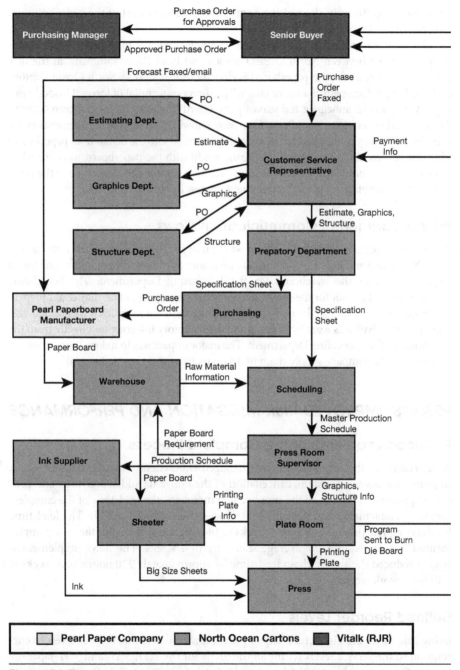

Figure 17.3 The suggested strategic supply management solution.   *Continues*

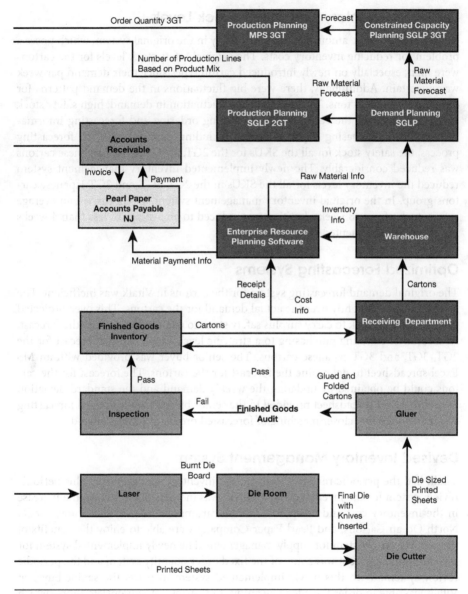

Figure 17.3 (Continued)

Reduced Inventory and Safety Stock Levels

Vitalk carried a large amount of extra inventory in the original system, which poses a problem for reducing inventory costs. The original safety stock levels for the cartons were high, especially on newly introduced carton types since their demand per week was uncertain. Additionally, there were big fluctuations in the demand patterns for different types of cartons. To counteract the fluctuation in demand, high safety stock was maintained for the cartons. Due to sharing ordering and forecasting information with the purchasing department and including purchasing in the forecasting process, the safety stock for all the SKUs for the 2GT, 3GT, and 3GT Japanese cartons was reduced considerably. The newly implemented inventory management system reduced the inventory levels for all the SKUs in the 2GT, 3GT, and 3GT Japanese cartons group. In the original inventory management system, Vitalk carried an average safety stock of over 8 weeks, but that was reduced to an average of less than 4 weeks in the newly implemented system.

Optimized Forecasting Systems

The original demand forecasting system for the cartons in Vitalk was inefficient. The forecast was consistently over the actual demand for the cartons. This over-projected forecast forced Vitalk to carry surplus safety stock to counter the error in the forecast. As a result of elevating purchasing to a strategic level, Vitalk had the forecast for the 2GT, 3GT, and 3GT Japanese cartons. The senior buyer was provided with an MS Excel spreadsheet to determine the forecast for the cartons. The forecast for the cartons could be obtained by updating the weekly demand and the standard deviation in the MS Excel spreadsheet provided to the senior buyer. This optimized forecasting system resulted in a closer matching of forecasted orders to actual demand.

Devised Inventory Management System

Vitalk had the periodic review system for the inventory management. This periodic review system for the inventory management was inefficient and caused the increase in the inventory cost and setup cost for the cartons. Because of this study, Vitalk, North Ocean Cartons, and Pearl Paper Company were able to enjoy the benefits of the new effective system for supply management. The newly implemented system for inventory management was a mix of the fixed order quantity system and the periodic review system. With this newly implemented system in place, the senior buyer at Vitalk was able to order the adequate amount of cartons at appropriate times, which resulted in better inventory management.

Established Information Sharing System

Pearl Paper Company never received the forecast from North Ocean Cartons and Vitalk in the original supply chain system. Broadening supply management's vision of the supply chain resulted in establishing a better information sharing system between

Vitalk, North Ocean Cartons and Pearl Paper Company. In the newly implemented information sharing system, Vitalk faxed forecast for the cartons to Pearl Paper Company and North Ocean Cartons. Because of this newly implemented information sharing system, Pearl Paper Company was always ready with the just-in-time shipment of paperboard as demanded by North Ocean Cartons.

Decreased Setup Cost

Vitalk's annual setup cost expenditure was approximately $22,000 for 2GT and $68,000 for 3GT and 3GT Japanese cartons combined, with a total of $90,000 in the original supply chain system. Subsequent to raising supply management's vision to a strategic level, the ordering process solution was devised to minimize the annual setup cost. In the newly implemented supply chain system, the order pattern was devised to reduce the annual setup cost for the 2GT cartons to $12,000 and zero for 3GT and 3GT Japanese cartons combined. Therefore, the total annual setup cost savings of $78,000 were realized by implementing the new supply chain system.

INCREASED ANNUAL SAVINGS

Not only significant annual savings resulted from the aforementioned reductions in setup costs—inventory carrying costs were also lowered in the newly implemented supply chain system. Vitalk was able to lower annual inventory carrying costs by $52,797 at the 90 percent service level; $48,805 at the 95 percent service level; and $41,470 at the 99 percent service level.

NEW CHALLENGES

This chapter has shown that engaging in strategic supply management practices benefits multiple parties in the chain. The benefits included managing the risks of supply chain disruptions due to not having enough cartons at times and having excessive inventories at other times, and to the lack of coordination and information sharing among the three tiers. Strategic supply management practices require taking a much more holistic view of the supply chain. The focal firm has changed from an unmanaged relationship with their tier 2 supplier to a managed type of relationship. However, doing this requires increased cooperation and systems capabilities on the part of firms in the supply chain. One example of this is the direct transmittal of the focal firms demand forecast to the paperboard supplier, enabling them to anticipate earlier the demand from their customer, the carton manufacturer. Benefits to the supply chain included reduced carton inventory levels, optimized demand forecasting system, better inventory management system, improved information sharing system, decreased annual setup cost, and increased annual savings.

Vitalk was successful in managing supply risks of cartons through coordinating all three supply chain tiers. It now plans to extend the success to other commodities that are plagued by excessive inventories, high costs, or poor forecasts of demand. In the case of cartons, the expanded vision of the supply chain resulted in increased service with lower inventory levels and improved risk mitigation capabilities through the coordination. However, these challenges are significant since cartons were characterized by a fairly structured supply chain. Extension to other areas of spend may reveal a much more fragmented and unstructured supply chain at the tier two level. Vitalk plans to continue addressing these challenges to allow it to become a *lean* supply chain organization with the coordination mechanisms in place to manage risks. In this specific case study the process efficiency was constrained by the practices of the focal firm's tier 2 supplier (i.e., the carton manufacturers tier 1 supplier of paperboard).

REFERENCES

Coughlan, P. and Coghlan, D. 2002. "Developing organizational learning capabilities through interorganizational action learning." M. A. Rahim, R. T. Golembiewski, and K. D. MacKenzie (eds.), *Current Topics in Management*. New Brunswick, NJ: Transaction, 33–46.

Frankel, R., Y. A. Bolumole, R. A. Eltantawy, A. Paulraj, and G. T. Gundlach. 2008. "The domain and scope of SCM's foundational disciplines-Insights and issues to advance research." *Journal of Business Logistics* 29(1):1–30.

Giunipero, L. C., Handfield, R. B., and Eltantawy, R. A. 2006. Supply management's evolution: Key skill sets for the supply manager of the future. *International Journal of Operations & Production Management* 26(7):822–44.

Gummesson, E. 2000. *Qualitative methods in management research*, 2nd ed. Thousand Oaks, CA: Sage.

18

ASSESSING PROJECT RISKS WITHIN THE SUPPLY CHAIN OF SELEX SISTEMI INTEGRATI (FINMECCANICA)

Barbara Gaudenzi

INTRODUCTION

The purpose of this chapter is to describe PRORAM (PROject Risk Assessment Method), an approach for assessing risks in projects, by extending the analysis to the relationships with suppliers and customers. PRORAM was tested in the firm SELEX Sistemi Integrati SpA, a company of the Italian Finmeccanica Group. The company is a world leader in the provision of systems and radar sensors for Homeland Security, air defense, battlefield management, naval warfare, coastal and maritime surveillance, air traffic control and airport solutions. Each year SELEX Sistemi Integrati works on 400 projects, mainly based on orders, which provide complex and technical systems and are characterized by long life cycles.

SELEX Sistemi Integrati develops strong relationships with stakeholders by means of two key strategies:

1. Projects are customized on the specific requirements of individual customers who may affect the effective management of projects and their risks
2. SELEX Sistemi Integrati works with different suppliers in each project and their integration is required to ensure a high level of service and to meet customers' expectations

SELEX Sistemi Integrati is a project-based organization, where an effective risk management strategy requires the ability to protect both individual projects and the entire projects' portfolio in a supply chain-wide perspective.

In developing this research, key managers from SELEX Sistemi Integrati were involved in the identification and evaluation of risks. Particular emphasis was placed on cross-unit collaboration, to address both projects' risks and also supply chain risks. For this reason the team involved in PRORAM was composed of the risk manager, the project manager, the procurement manager, and the key account manager. During the research period, the evidence of PRORAM had been compared with the risk registers provided by the procedures in place in the firm.

PRELIMINARY CONSIDERATIONS ABOUT PROJECT RISK ASSESSMENT WITHIN SUPPLY CHAINS

As mentioned, SELEX Sistemi Integrati has a complex portfolio of about 400 projects with complex risks' correlations. About 70 percent of the portfolio consists of complex and long-term projects characterized by competitive pressure related to costs and timeliness. A project life cycle spans (on average) 3 to 4 years, with over 3000 personnel employed mainly in the design and development of high tech components and integrated systems. A key objective for Finmeccanica is the coordination and implementation of risk management. This is achieved by identifying, assessing and managing risks with the purpose of pursuing the success of the projects, being compliant with the expected results, and catching business opportunities, while preserving the earned value.

The study started by developing PRORAM as a method based on the assessment and evaluation of risk indicators, applicable to projects and at the level of the relationships with suppliers. PRORAM's intent is to provide a framework for evaluating both self-standing project risks and the correlation between supply chain and demand risk, in order to support the organization's management in achieving the strategic objectives of the company.

PRORAM is based on the identification of four drivers for the successful management of projects' risks:

1. Risk assessment should be linked to the objectives that companies assign to the projects under analysis. The assessment of risk indicators should be linked to the projects' objectives and managerial priorities. This means that risks potentially affecting a prior objective should itself be treated as critical. SELEX Sistemi Integrati is focused on the optimization and protection of the Group's overall investment, by setting products, projects and investments. For these reasons, PRORAM was oriented towards the objectives of efficiency and financial equilibrium.

The critical suppliers and the main customers should be involved in the definition of the main objectives because suppliers are often not aware of projects' priorities, and customers do not care about the technical implications of their requirements on delivery times, costs, and performance. This lack of integration can open the door to subsequent stressful negotiations at the stage of a projects' execution. For this reason, it is important to involve supply chain's actors and customers in risk assessment procedures.

2. An integrated team of managers should be involved in the risk assessment. The data collection and all the risk assessment phases should be supported by the involvement of key actors from the different business units. In SELEX Sistemi Integrati, managers were involved throughout multiple anonymous interviews and site visits. The interviews allowed the respondents to evaluate their experiences and express their different perspectives. This was extremely helpful for evaluating the potential impact of events, the cause-effect relationships along the projects' phases, and hence, for addressing an effective risk assessment.

3. The objective of project risk assessment should be defined as soon as possible. Project risk management is a complex process, usually structured in the phases of project classification, risk assessment and recovery. In this context, PRORAM was focused on the phases of *projects classification* and *risk assessment*. In order to evaluate the effectiveness of PRORAM in SELEX Sistemi Integrati, we applied the methodology on a selected type of projects (pilot projects) and extended the analysis to the network relationships.

The objective of the implementation of PRORAM in SELEX Sistemi Integrati was to obtain a set of information which could help managers in the following activities:

a. Evaluating project risk profile
b. Deciding mitigation actions such as prevention (actions seeking to prevent risk occurrence), protection (actions aimed at reducing effects) and/or transfer (actions for elimination of risk by transferring them to insurance, for example)
c. Providing directions for defining *contingencies* as a set of mitigation actions selected for each risk

4. The risk assessment methodology should be linked to the actual company's environment and risk management practices. SELEX Sistemi Integrati classifies projects on the basis of strategic impact and intrinsic risks. Strategic impact is derived from the evaluation of the product complexity and the amount of resources required. Intrinsic risk is derived from evaluating factors like the political stability of the customer's country and the knowledge about the market.

In the PRORAM application, three projects with similar profiles were tested. The selected projects are focused on the design, execution, delivery and installation of Radar Systems. These projects are characterized by long technical experience, but still required large investments in terms of R&D.

PROJECT RISK ASSESSMENT METHOD: PHASES AND PRACTICAL EVIDENCES

PRORAM was implemented within three phases:

1. Identifying project's objectives
2. Building the risk factors panel
3. Drawing directions for risk estimation

Identifying Project's Objectives

During three brainstorming sessions, the managers of the integrated project team (IPT) highlighted the importance of focusing their measures on two objectives: efficiency (i.e., costs and resources related to the projects) and financial equilibrium (equilibrium between customers' payments and project costs cash flows).

PRORAM confirmed that effective procurement management may reduce both the probability of occurrence and the severity of several downside risks, but it requires an integrated supplier risk assessment. In fact, the method showed that supplier (and also customer) relationships are often not fully evaluated within the risk registers for their correlations with project risks. The preliminary estimation of their impact on the project's objectives is essential.

Building the Risk Factors Panel

The managers decided to assess risks in three project life cycle phases (project definition, engineering-execution, and manufacturing) and in two areas of external relationships (relationships with customers and relationships with suppliers). Each area was expected to be subject to different risks, which could influence the SELEX Sistemi Integrati's objectives: efficiency and financial equilibrium (see Figure 18.1).

The most relevant risks, considered risk *barometers* in the different areas, are now briefly described.

Risk factors in the area of supplier relationships:

- *Number of suppliers.* The managers highlighted the need for a reduction in the number of suppliers and the risk of nonintegration and short-term relationships with extemporary collaborations; they also recognized that a cost reduction might reduce the capability to cope with variability and responsiveness.
- *Lack of supplier selection processes.* Supplier selection is often incomplete in terms of evaluation of commercial, financial, technical, and process capability. This implies that stable deliveries may not always be assured.
- *Unclear definition and agreement about the service and support requirements on the supply side.* The suppliers and subcontractors were not always aware and signed off on the conditions.

Objectives Areas	Efficiency	Financial equilibrium
Relationships with suppliers	Risk indicators	Risk indicators ....
Project definition	Risk indicators	Risk indicators ....
Engineering-execution	Risk indicators	Risk indicators ....
Manufacturing	Risk indicators	Risk indicators ....
Relationships with customers	Risk indicators	Risk indicators ....

Figure 18.1 Areas and objectives.

- *High dependence from specific suppliers.* Being reliant on single source suppliers is a risk, especially in case of dependence on foreign suppliers. It could affect lead time and quality.
- *High number of urgent or rapidly changing orders.* These orders to suppliers were likely to be delivered later than standard orders.
- *Delays and errors from suppliers.* In each phase, frequent delays and errors from suppliers (in terms of time and performance) were analyzed as potential *trend of risk.*
- *High number of damaged products and errors in each project phase.* The level of errors or defected inbound may result in potential exposition to the risk of defected deliveries.

Risk factors in the area of project definition:

- *Unclear definition of authority and responsibility.* All the decisions about project organization and management of risk and uncertainty should be identified in a strategic plan in order to avoid errors and omissions.
- *Lack of awareness about the responsibilities.* When the participants were not aware of the interrelation between the phases, there was the risk of noncoordination and noncommunication.
- *Errors and omissions in the identification of risk.* The risks should be measured in all the phases and evaluated globally to evaluate whether the combination of risks is acceptable.
- *Inadequate or ambiguous definition of contract terms.* Contracts should seek to reduce uncertainty, but often substantial ambiguous conditions (performance specifications, payment mechanisms, terms of supervisions and coordination) still were in place and affected the effective management of the project.

- *Ineffective design and dimension of the project.* When appropriately skilled labor resources were not available, because the technology or the design features were new, there was a risk of failure to carry out the activities.

Risk factors in the area of Engineering:

- *Lack of fall-back solutions in place.* When fall-back solutions were not in place there could be a risk of interruption.
- *Dependence on other projects.* When the development was dependent on other projects, there was a need for coordination and all the interfaces needed to be well specified.
- *Novelty of systems, hardware or software.* If new solutions were going to be developed, there was a risk that tools and languages could not be available on time.
- *Lack of support documentation, manuals, and training notes.* The lack of these documents and connected resources could cause errors or delays in the execution of the projects.
- *Lack of internal reviews, control of change, and fixed points in place.* Reviews and controls assured that the specifications for the engineering and execution are well-defined. Quite often problems in the engineering and execution phase were related to weaknesses in earlier phases of the project.

Risk factors in the area of Execution:

- *Lack of capability to meet the customer requirements in terms of performance, reliability, maintainability.* It generally referred to not offering the customers the product and service required.
- *High dependence on purchased technology, components and materials.* Being heavily reliant on specific technology and its suppliers could be a risk.
- *Design and Engineering changes.* These changes, or a lack of change control procedures, could lead to disruption of schedules or technical implications. These could affect cost, time and performance.

Risk factors in the area of Manufacturing:

- *Lack of respect for manufacturing requirements, particularly for quality, reliability, safety, and resilience.* The monitoring and quality controls reduce delays and help to react rapidly against interruptions.
- *Novelty of systems, hardware or software.* If new solutions were to be developed, there was a risk that tools and languages could not be available on time.
- *Dimension of the production capability does not suit the real volumes.* Unpredictable demand and forecasting errors for both positive and negative results could affect costs, time and performance.
- *Lack of test facilities, fault analysis and other test equipment.* These elements could affect costs, time and performance.

Risk factors in the area of relationships with customers:

- *Unclear contract's definition and agreement with the customer.* Problems could occur when parties did not define what to produce, how the client could monitor what the contractor has done, and what the client would pay.
- *Lack of capability to manage client expectations.* When some problems threaten the viability of the target project cost, time or quality, the response should be immediate and drastic, like a change in design.
- *Lack of assessment of specific risks associated with specific customer groups.* These risks could be related to the countries where customers operate, to the contractual power, and to the contract terms.
- *Risks associated with the payment.* All the necessary information, equipment, approvals, sites in supplying should be given. Otherwise, it was likely that the customer will levy penalty charges.
- *Risks associated with the capability of the customers to meet their obligations.* The risk could exist in terms of slow payment or default.
- *Risk of changes in costs, royalties, guarantees, insurance.* All of these risks should be carefully evaluated, also in terms of the risk of fluctuations in currency exchange rates.

Drawing Directions for Risk Estimation

The managers expressed the need to assign to each area a synthetic level of risk in order to address the appropriate risk mitigation actions. For this reason, they measured the dimension of each risk factor and defined potential *cause and effect relationships* among risks and areas. The number of critical risks, which may generate other risks downstream, led managers to define the synthetic level of risk in each area, as shown in Figure 18.2.

PRACTICAL EVIDENCE FROM THE PRORAM APPLICATION

The PRORAM's evidences confirmed the effectiveness and robustness of the traditional projects' risk management procedures in SELEX Sistemi Integrati whose outputs were substantially aligned with PRORAM. The comparison between the results of PRORAM and SELEX Sistemi Integrati's risk assessment shows that there is substantial alignment in the risk analysis in the different project phases. This is due to the fact that a high level of knowledge contributed to an effective, risk-sensitive management in the project phases. For this reason, SELEX Sistemi Integrati's project risk management was confirmed as being a process under continuous improvement, strongly supported by the integrated project team.

What strongly emerged during the PRORAM's application is how critical the areas of customer relationships, especially procurement are. The comparison between

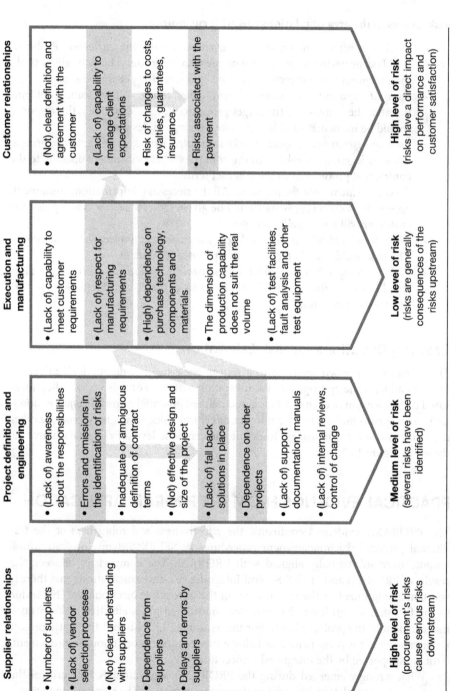

Figure 18.2 The key risk factors in SELEX Sistemi Integrati and their correlations among the areas.

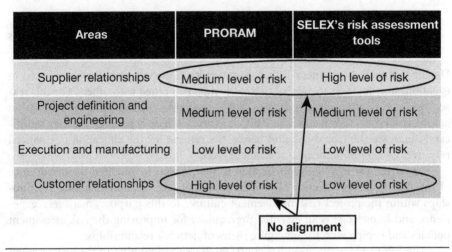

Areas	PRORAM	SELEX's risk assessment tools
Supplier relationships	Medium level of risk	High level of risk
Project definition and engineering	Medium level of risk	Medium level of risk
Execution and manufacturing	Low level of risk	Low level of risk
Customer relationships	High level of risk	Low level of risk

No alignment

Figure 18.3 Evidence from PRORAM and SELEX Sistemi Integrati's risk assessment tools.

PRORAM and SELEX Sistemi Integrati's risk assessment showed that the Finmeccanica company was not used to fully estimate supply chain risks and particularly their impact on the projects. Figure 18.3 shows differences between PRORAM and SELEX Sistemi Integrati's risk assessment at the level of external relationships with suppliers and customers. These results confirmed that project complexity, changes in customers' requests, and shortening of order cycles with suppliers represent crucial elements which can increase the vulnerability of the projects. In this context, the alignment and coordination with suppliers seemed to be crucial. Even though suppliers are treated as partners, the integration is not always effective and their involvement at the early stages of project planning is rare. The importance of suppliers' relationships—which represents more than 50 percent of SELEX Sistemi Integrati's costs—should therefore, be considered a driver for improving projects' performances.

MANAGERIAL IMPLICATIONS

The SELEX Sistemi Integrati's case study confirmed that although projects are inherently risky, the project's risk assessment cannot be limited to the project itself but should be extended to the analysis of external relationships with suppliers and customers, which significantly affect the projects' risk exposure. Particularly, four drivers for managing projects' risks were identified:

- Risk assessment should be linked to the objectives that companies assign to the projects under analysis
- The aim and priorities of project risk assessment should be defined as soon as possible

- An integrated team of managers should be involved in the risk assessment
- The risk assessment methodology should be linked to the actual company's environment and risk management practices

During the analysis, it emerged that several risks (apparently small when viewed in isolation) may increase the global risk level when combined with others. For this reason, while evaluating self-standing risks it is crucial to consider also the correlation among risk types, within and across different areas. These concurrencies may significantly increase the global risk and hence, the criteria for the allocation of financial resources as *self insurance* against all these risks.

Moreover, the PRORAM application to the projects highlighted the importance of integrating the perspective of procurement management and customer relationships within the project risk management culture. To this purpose, managers' experience and knowledge is an essential prerequisite for improving the risk assessment policies and coping with the emerging issues of network relationships.

The PRORAM application has contributed to a redefinition of the procurement policy and to the improvement of the negotiation process with customers to prevent a large part of the previously highlighted network risks. The objective was to review the criteria for allocating financial resources to each area for an effective management of risk.

Note: The author expresses special thanks to Marina Grossi, Chief Executive Officer of SELEX Sistemi Integrati SpA, and to Marco Marinozzi, Roberto Frangella, and Maria Iole Gentile of Risk Management of SELEX Sistemi Integrati SpA, for the collaboration in developing PRORAM.

ESTIMATION OF DISRUPTION RISK EXPOSURE IN SUPPLY CHAINS: THREE CASES

Ulf Paulsson and Arben Mullai

INTRODUCTION

The purpose of this chapter is to present three different cases involving disruption risks, and to introduce a *disruption risk exposure estimation model* for identifying and estimating disruption risks in the supply chain. Furthermore, the purpose is to analyze the three cases with the help of the estimation model presented, and finally to briefly discuss the risk-handling methods presently used in the three cases, and suggest some alternatives.

Each case (Alpha, Beta, and Gamma) is based on a real company that has been rendered anonymous. The cases cover different supply chain risk situations and thus complement each other. They were originally presented in a thesis (Paulsson 2007) but have been enlarged and partly rewritten so that more aspects of each case are included and the principal and most interesting issues stand out more clearly.

CASE ALPHA

Alpha is a large international company operating on a world stage with advanced IT-based products for industrial use. The rate of change in the market is high, which means short life cycles for the products and for many of the components needed to produce them. A range of different products are produced but one is economically dominant and this product, here called product *x*, will be focused upon.

Product

Product *x* consists of a basic module, in five different variants, to which a customized *top hat* is added. About 85 percent of the production costs relate to the basic module and 15 percent to the *top hat*. All copies of product *x* are produced according to customer specifications and thus unique, although one order might include a number of identical versions of the tailor-made product.

Supply side

Input to product *x* comprises about 80 different components, of which 50 are standard and 30 are unique. Most of the latter are advanced, and about half of them are single sourced. Replacement time for standard components is about two weeks and for unique components between two and eight months.

Production

There are several parallel production units (sites) spread over three continents, but more than 90 percent of the total production of product *x* takes place at one of the production sites. At this site, a number of security measures such as fences, guards, checks of all persons entering the building, sprinkler systems, fire alarms, and such have been put in place to protect production.

Ten years ago production was spread over six different sites, each with approximately the same production capacity, but an acute economic crisis in the company led to the decision to concentrate most of the production in just one of the sites and invest heavily in increasing the production capacity at that site. To compensate for the increased risk due to having one main site instead of six, it was decided that it should be constructed as one building complex with two separate production units divided by a firewall. A couple of years later, when demand was extremely high and Alpha had great difficulty delivering, it was decided that the firewall between the two parallel production lines should be knocked down, thus creating one big production line with a somewhat higher total capacity than the two separate lines had previously, together. At the same time, the general security measures protecting the site were upgraded.

The production process can be divided into assembly, which includes seven different steps, downloading of software, and testing. Standard equipment is used for downloading and testing, but assembly requires unique, advanced equipment which, if damaged, can take up to 6 months to replace. In each production process step there are several (up to 15) identical parallel machines. Production time is about 3 weeks. The basic variant is built during the first two weeks, while during the third week the product is tailored to customer specifications and the downloading of software and testing take place. Since fluctuations in demand are high, Alpha has chosen to employ a limited number of workers in the production department and fulfil most of its production labor needs by hiring from external manpower companies.

Alpha normally keeps a 1–2 week buffer stock of standard components and a 3–4 week buffer stock in the case of unique components. No buffer stock of finished products exists due to the fact that each product is tailor-made.

Demand side

There are several other suppliers of products similar to product x but they cannot be adapted, since each producer has a different technical standard, which makes it difficult for a customer to change to another supplier (or change back). So for technical reasons the customer is, at least in the short-term, tied to a certain supplier. In view of this and the fact that product x is quite expensive, it is very important that the customer has confidence in Alpha's ability to deliver.

Certain product assortment links exist, meaning that the effects of a disruption on product x passing through the demand side will be exacerbated, since the demand for other products in Alpha's range (assortment) will also be negatively affected.

CASE BETA

Beta is a large, international company operating in the European market within the chemical-technical sector. It has a number of production units across the continent. Input to the product comprises different types of basic chemicals. The product and the production process are relatively simple. The rate of change is moderate and price competition, sharp. Beta is mainly engaged in the production part of the supply chain but also, to some extent, in the distribution and sale of the product. The market consists of both industrial buyers and private households. Only the part of the company serving the industrial market is considered here.

Product

The product is a mix of different chemicals and product variants created by changing the chemicals and their proportions. Most of the products are standard, where the same product is bought by a number of different customers.

Supply Side

The different chemicals needed for production are always available on the supply market. Beta has deals with its suppliers based on vendor managed inventory (VMI) and full economic compensation for shortages. So in the event of a shortage, Beta will be compensated by the supplier for any negative consequences that this shortage might lead to.

Production

Production means mixing different chemicals according to a certain prescription, tapping the mixture into tanks or cans, and labelling it. The same, or a similar type of, product is produced at several parallel sites and normally on a single shift basis. All sites are about the same size. No unique, advanced machinery or specially designed factory buildings are needed, but some of the chemicals are highly flammable and have to be treated with great care. A fire in one part of a production unit can easily spread to other sections. Despite insurance policies, a fire would cause economic losses. Fire is, thus, a real danger and some production units have their own fire department.

Demand Side

The customers have a high need for the product because they use it in their own production and have limited buffer stocks. However, they could easily change to another supplier. Delivery problems would certainly mean lost sales for Beta, but since it is also easy for customers to change back, sales might rapidly return to normal as soon as the delivery problem is resolved. Problems for Beta to deliver on time in one period would probably not have any big impact on sales in the following periods. The different final products are sold and used, more or less, independently of each other.

CASE GAMMA

Gamma is a medium-sized company producing expensive, high quality electronic consumer products with an advanced design. The company tries to keep the design of a product series more or less unchanged for a number of years by designing in a way that is both bold and futuristic. Design can be said to be the core of the company and the design for a new product series is bought from internationally recognized designers. Production comprises assembly and testing. The market consists of a number of countries primarily in Europe, but also Japan and the United States. The products are sold through specialty shops that only sell Gamma products and have exclusive sales rights within a particular area. Gamma is involved in designing, producing, and marketing its products.

Product

Gamma produces high quality electronic consumer products with an advanced design. The range consists of about 10 different product series based on the type of product and targeted customer segment.

Supply Side

Input can be divided into electronic and design-related components. The electronic components have a high rate of change, while the design components change more slowly. All the electronic components are high-quality standard components and alternative suppliers can be found. Gamma is a small buyer of electronic components. Since the company is prepared to pay well for components, the supply is ensured as long as they are available on the market.

The components related to the design are unique but not particularly difficult to produce. However, they require certain molds and special tools of which there might be only one example. If that is destroyed it can take some time to construct a new one.

Production

Production is concentrated in one big production site operating on a single shift basis which normally has a great deal of spare capacity. Standard assembly and testing equipment is used in the production process, which takes place in the normal factory premises. Most products are built to order, but if a certain component is missing the customer might, in many cases, accept another, better component (upgrading). This is technically possible but Gamma's costs will be somewhat higher. Buffer stocks of standard and design-related components exist. There is almost no buffer stock of finished products.

Demand Side

The products are sold on many markets through a number of retailers. The sales of the different products are more or less independent of each other. The fact that the ordered product is produced according to customer specification makes the customer less willing to cancel the order and buy from another manufacturer in the event of delay. As mentioned earlier, the customer will, in many cases, accept upgrading.

When a new production series is introduced on the market, it has to be so creative and bold that it is easily distinguishable from earlier products and, most especially, from its competitors. However, it must not be too bold because the market reaction might be negative.

THE DISRUPTION RISK EXPOSURE ESTIMATION MODEL

Perspectives

Focal Unit. Here the supply chain is considered from the point of view of an individual unit in the chain. That particular unit is called the *focal unit* and might be a single company, a group of companies, an organization, a group of organizations, a working site, a legal unit, or some other specified unit in the supply chain that the users select as their focal unit. *Focal unit is the individual unit in the supply chain from the perspective of which the supply chain flow risk issues are seen, interpreted and acted upon.*

Continuity in the supply chain flow. The focus here is on continuity in the supply chain product flow, where product is defined as *that for which the focal company gets paid to deliver.* Anything that might threaten to cause a disruption in this flow is regarded as a risk, irrespective of whether it is a fire, machine break-down, late deliveries, financial problems, poor quality, theft, or something else.

A preperiod time perspective. We employ *a preperiod time perspective.* This means that we try to act before something happens, thereby eliminating or affecting the likelihood and/or the negative consequences of the event. When we imagine the negative consequences, we assume that if the event happens, appropriate risk handling actions will be taken to mitigate them. Since we are using a preperiod time perspective, the focus is not on actual disruptions but on disruption risk exposure. This means that the focus is on the *negative business profit impact (BPI) on the focal unit of supply chain disruption risk exposure.*

Pre-event and post-event handling. The focal unit reacts to the risk exposure through risk handling. The potential events lead to pre-event and post-event handling. *Pre-event handling* could mean that actions are taken, like arranging new insurance or building up a buffer stock, to eliminate or mitigate the risk. *Post-event handling* could mean taking actions like working overtime or temporarily buying from another supplier. Both types of risk handling have to be considered in the model.

Estimation model

Disruptions affecting the focal company can originate in each of the three parts of the supply chain: supply side, production, and demand side. We thus have three different disruption risk sources. Regardless of whether the source of the disruption is on the supply side, within production, or on the demand side, it can spread to other parts of the supply chain where it can be eliminated, decreased, or increased depending on the circumstances in that part of the chain. The economic impact of these consequences must also be included when estimating the risk for the individual part.

In this simple model, risk is measured at five different levels: very low, low, medium, high, and very high. Each risk level set should be accompanied by a justification explaining the reasons for the choice of risk level. In many situations these explanations might be even more interesting than the risk level itself.

RISK PATTERNS FOR EACH CASE

Analysis Method

The analysis is based on the structure presented in Figure 19.1. It starts with an analysis of the demand side, followed by production and finally the supply side. For each part (demand side, production, and supply side), the disruption risk factors are discussed, as are those factors that might eliminate, increase or decrease a disruption

Disruption risk* source	Risk level**	Why? (+higher, -lower)
on the supply side		
within focal unit (production)		
on the demand side		

*Risk = Potential negative business profit impact
**Risk levels: very low, low, medium, high, very high

Figure 19.1 Supply chain disruption risk exposure estimation model.

from one of the other two parts. An aggregate judgment of the risks for each of the three parts is then made and one of the five risks levels is chosen.

Case Alpha

Demand side. There is no information indicating any major disruption risks on the demand side, but certain characteristics have an impact on disruptions from production. One is the existence of certain product assortment links, which will increase the economic consequences of failure to deliver. Another is that since, for technical reasons, a customer is tied to the producer and product *x* is quite expensive, it is very important for the customer to have confidence in Alpha's ability to deliver. The risk level can be regarded as *medium*.

Within production. There is a buffer stock of unique components for three to four weeks of production, but there is no buffer stock of finished products. Concentrating most of the production in just one unit with only one fire cell is risky. On the other hand, the security level at the site is very high and, in production, several parallel machines exist for each step. However, part of the unique advanced production equipment has a replacement time of up to six months. Most of the labor for production is hired externally, which might increase some risks, such as workers who are not as skilled and loyal as permanent staff. Considering the fact that basically all production takes place in one fire cell in combination with unique production equipment that has a replacement time of up to half a year, in addition to tied customers and assortment links on the demand side, the risk level is judged to be *very high*.

Supply side. There are about 30 unique components, of which half are single sourced. This becomes especially critical in combination with a replacement time of between two and eight months. The existence of a buffer stock of unique components in production reduces the risk somewhat, but there is no buffer stock of finished products, and the existence of assortment links and locked up customers on the demand side increases risk. Taking all of the above into consideration, the risk level can be judged to be *high*.

Summary. We can conclude that Alpha is exposed to several serious risks especially in relation to supply and production and the aggregated supply chain disruption risk can be regarded as *high*, as shown in Table 19.1.

Case Beta

Demand side. There are no major disruption risks as such on the demand side, but it has certain characteristics that affect disruptions coming from production. The main characteristic is that it is easy for a customer to change to another producer but also to change back again, since the product is a standard one that can be delivered by many different producers. The various final products are sold and used more or less independently of each other. The risk level can be regarded as *very low*.

Within production. Some of the chemicals used in production are highly flammable and constitute a real danger to the individual site. However, there are other

Table 19.1 Estimated disruption risks for Alpha

ALPHA:		
Disruption risk* source:	Risk level**	Why? (+ higher, − lower)
on the supply side	High	+ *about 30 unique components, half of which are single sourced* + *between 2 and 8 months replacement time for unique components* − buffer stock of unique components in production (P) + no buffer stock of finished products (P) + assortment links on demand side (D) + customers tied for technical reasons (D)
within the focal unit (production)	Very high	+ *mainly just one production unit with only one fire cell* + *partly unique production equipment with up to ½ a year replacement time* + *no buffer stock of finished products* + *most production workers are hired* − *buffer stock of unique components* − *high security level* + assortment links (D) + customers tied for technical reasons (D)
on the demand side	Medium	+ *assortment links* + *customers tied for technical reasons*
The aggregated risk	High	

* Risk = Potential negative business profit impact
** Risk levels: very low, low, medium, high, very high

production units within the company with the same or similar products and production equipment that could take over the production. Normally a site runs just a single shift and could therefore increase its capacity comparatively easily and rapidly by adding overtime or extra shifts. Since delivery problems will have little long term effect on the market, the risk level can, despite the considerable fire risk, be regarded as *medium*.

Supply side. The different chemicals needed for production are always available on the supply market and, in addition, Beta has VMI agreements with its suppliers that ensure full economic compensation for shortages. If we also consider the possibility of considerable flexibility in production and the fact that it is easy for a customer to change to another producer and back again, the risk level can be regarded as *very low*.

Summary. We can conclude that the overall impression is a company with low disruption risks in its supply chain and thus a *low* aggregated risk level, as shown in Table 19.2.

Table 19.2 Estimated disruption risks for Beta

BETA:		
Disruption risk* source:	Risk level**	Why? (+ higher, – lower)
on the supply side	Very low	– *basic chemicals that are readily available* – *VMI agreements with suppliers ensuring full compensation for shortages* – several parallel production units (P) – overtime work/additional shifts possible (P) – *easy for a customer to change to another supplier and back again (D)*
within the focal unit (production)	Medium	+ *highly flammable chemicals used in production* – *several parallel production units* – overtime work/additional shifts possible – *easy for a customer to change to another supplier and back again (D)*
on the demand side	Very low	– *easy for a customer to change to another supplier and back again*
The aggregated risk	Low	

* Risk = Potential negative business profit impact
** Risk levels: very low, low, medium, high, very high

Case Gamma

Demand side. There seem to be no major disruption risks on the demand side. Some assortment links do exist, but the customers are willing to accept certain delivery delays. The risk level is regarded as *low*.

Within production. There is just one big production site. It normally operates in a single shift and has a great deal of spare capacity. Standard assembly and testing equipment that can be replaced relatively quickly is used in the production process. Buffer stocks of standard and design-related components exist. There is almost no buffer stock of finished products, since most products are built to customer order. If a certain component is missing, product upgrading is technically possible and often accepted by the customer. The risk level is therefore regarded as *low*.

Supply side. The required components can be divided into electronic and design-related components. All the electronic components used are standard, and alternative suppliers can always be found, especially since Gamma is a small buyer on the market willing to pay a somewhat higher price. On the other hand, the design components are unique, and custom-built moulds and tools are needed to produce them. There is sometimes only one item of them and, if destroyed, it can take some time to construct a new one. However, as production is very flexible and the customer fairly patient, the risk level can be regarded as *low*.

Summary. We can conclude that the risks related to disruptions are low in all three parts of Gamma's supply chain and consequently, the aggregated risk is *low*, as shown in Table 19.3.

Table 19.3 Estimated disruption risks for Gamma

GAMMA:		
Disruption risk* source	Risk level**	Why? (+ higher, – lower)
on the supply side	Low	+ *unique design components* + unique moulds and tools for the design components – *electronic standard components* – *small portion of the total market for electronic components* – flexible production (P) + some assortment links (D) – patient customers (D) – upgrading often accepted by the customer (D)
within the focal unit (production)	Low	+ *just one production site* – *considerable overcapacity* – *standard assembly machinery that can be replaced quickly* – *possible to outsource assembly* – *upgrading technically possible* + some assortment links on demand side (D) – patient customers (D) – upgrading often accepted by the customer (D)
on the demand side	Low	+ *some assortment links* – *patient customers* – *upgrading often accepted by the customer*
The aggregated risk	**Low**	

* Risk = Potential negative business profit impact
** Risk levels: very low, low, medium, high, very high

Gamma is, however, exposed to fairly large risks related to design. Advanced, bold design is the prime competitive advantage of the company and every launch of a new product range based on a novel design concept is critical because Gamma can never be sure of market reaction.

RISK HANDLING METHODS

Case Alpha

Presently used risk-handling methods. At present, Alpha uses dual or multi-sourcing for half of the unique components and also keeps a buffer stock, which would last for three to four weeks. Although the company has several parallel production units, one is totally dominant. A high level of security is maintained at this main production site.

Potential risk-handling methods. Risk could be affected in many different ways. One could be to use less unique and more standard components, another to change to dual or multisourcing for each unique component. Yet another possibility could be to spread production more equally among the different production units. Alpha could also use more standardized assembly machines, which probably have shorter replacement times than the unique, custom-built machines. Moreover, an overcapacity could be created in those custom-built assembly machines that have long replacement times and/or standby copies of those machines could be kept in reserve in a separate, safe building.

The creation of a buffer stock of all potential final product variants is probably not possible but the company could keep a buffer stock of the five different ready-made basic modules, which could then be quickly turned into finished, customized products, as shown in Table 19.4.

Case Beta

Presently used risk-handling methods. Beta has VMI agreements providing full compensation for shortages. It also has its own fire department at several of the production sites. The company has several parallel production units and possibilities to add another shift and/or overtime in each of these units. These facts can also be considered a risk-handling method.

Potential risk-handling methods. Beta can change its product prescriptions and use less flammable chemicals in its products. The company can also install different

Table 19.4 Risk-handling methods for Alpha

Alpha: risk-handling methods	
In use	Suggested
Dual or multisourcing for half of the unique components	Use more standard and less unique components
Buffer stock of unique components	Change to dual or multisourcing for each unique component
Several parallel production units (but one is totally dominant)	Spread production more equally among the different production units
High security level at the main production site	Use more standardized assembly machines to reduce replacement time
	Create an overcapacity in those unique, custom-built assembly machines that have long replacement times
	Keep standby copies of those custom-built assembly machines that have long replacement times in a separate, safe building
	Create a buffer stock of readymade basic modules (five different) that can be quickly turned into finished products

fire cells at production sites so that a fire cannot easily spread to other parts of the site, as shown in Table 19.5.

Case Gamma

Presently used risk-handling methods. Gamma keeps a small buffer stock of design components, and if necessary, is prepared to buy the standard components at a higher than normal price. The company also has an overcapacity in production.

Potential risk-handling methods. Gamma could keep multiple suppliers of design components and/or increase its buffer stock of design components. It could also make copies of its unique, custom-built molds and tools and store them in a safe place. Another method could involve the creation of parallel production units or entering into production backup agreements with other assembly firms. Finally, Gamma could keep a buffer stock of finished products for some of the basic models in each product range, as shown in Table 19.6.

Table 19.5 Risk-handling methods for Beta

BETA: risk-handling methods	
In use	**Suggested**
VMI agreements ensuring full compensation for shortages	Use less flammable chemicals in the products
Own fire department	Install different fire cells at production sites so that a fire cannot easily spread to other parts of the site
Several parallel production units	
Possibilities to add another shift and/ or overtime	

Table 19.6 Risk-handling methods for Gamma

GAMMA: risk-handling methods	
In use	**Suggested**
Small buffer stock of design components	Multiple suppliers of design components
High buying power	Increase the buffer stock of design components
Overcapacity in production	Create copies of unique, custom-built moulds and tools and store them in a safe place
	Parallel production units
	Production backup agreements with other firms with assembly capacity
	Buffer stock of finished products for some of the basic models in each product range

CONCLUSION

The three cases represent three quite different risk situations. Beta is exposed to fairly low disruption risks in its supply chain. Alpha, on the other hand, is a company that is exposed to considerable disruption risks and has to spend a great deal of time and resources on these issues. Finally, Gamma illustrates the fact that, for some companies, it is not the disruption risks in the supply chain that are their biggest problem but instead, risks outside the supply chain.

The cases, although quite short and simple, illustrate the fact that many factors affect the disruption risks in the supply chain, that companies use many different risk-handling methods, and that there are many more potential risk-handling methods— some of which we might not have even considered as a risk handling method. The model presented can be used in a number of different ways, such as part of a regular risk audit or as a *tool* to start discussions on supply chain flow risk issues, which could yield information about perceived risks and ideas of how to handle them. This includes finding a good balance between proactive and reactive risk handling.

REFERENCES

Paulsson, U. 2007. *On Managing Disruption Risks in the Supply Chain*. Lund: Department of Industrial Management and Logistics. Lund University. Doctoral Thesis.

INDEX